key ACCOUNT MANAGEMENT

3rd Edition

a complete action kit

of tools and techniques for achieving profitable key supplier status

peter cheverton

KOGAN PAGE

London and Sterling, VA

First published in Great Britain in 1999 by Kogan Page Limited
Second edition 2001
Third edition published in Great Britain and the United States in 2004

120 Pentonville Road
London N1 9JN
UK
www.kogan-page.co.uk

22883 Quicksilver Drive
Sterling VA 20166–2012
USA

ISBN 0 7494 4169 0

British Library Cataloguing-in-Publication Data

A CIP record for this book is available from the British Library.

Library of Congress Cataloging-in-Publication Data

Cheverton, Peter.
  Key account management : a complete action kit of tools and techniques for achieving profitable key supplier status / Peter Cheverton.-- 3rd ed.
    p. cm.
Includes bibliographical references and index.
  ISBN 0-7494-4169-0
  1. Selling--Key accounts. 2. Marketing--Key accounts. 3. Customer services. I. Title.
HF5438.8.K48C47 2004
658.8'04--dc22

                                        2003024861

Typeset by Saxon Graphics Ltd, Derby
Printed and bound in Great Britain by Cambrian Printers Ltd, Aberystwyth, Wales

Contents

Foreword

Good books on key account management are rare. One of the reasons for this lies in the past, in the way that key account management (KAM) has been defined and described. The past 40 years have been characterized by a view that KAM is mainly a selling task, albeit at a high level, and that the responsibility for its implementation rests almost entirely with the sales team.

Yet all our research at Cranfield School of Management indicates that, above all else, it is this mentality that prevents the forging of mature, trustworthy and profitable relationships. Key account management is not a sales *initiative*, it is not something you do *to* customers, and key account strategies will require the full support of the business.

Key account management is a team effort and, more than that, it is a business-wide effort. Our research has shown repeatedly that major clients want more than a sales–buyer interface and they want more than a traditional salesperson managing the relationship. If suppliers and customers are to forge significant relationships, as businesses, then both sides must look to new ways of managing those relationships.

Relationships are at the very heart of KAM. They provide the source of information and understanding that can be built into added value activities. They also provide the foundations for long-term business based on mutual trust and confidence. If you care about customer retention then you should care about KAM.

So let's escape the trap of the last 40 years – KAM is not something we do *to* customers, it is something we do *with* customers, and perhaps the greatest single motivation for developing key account strategies is that the customer is looking for new ways of working alongside key suppliers.

Purchasing organizations are looking more and more to the techniques of supply chain management as a means of prioritizing and managing relationships with significant suppliers. Those suppliers must respond with customer-sensitive strategies that will touch on everything, from the people involved to the systems and processes used, and even to the structure and organization of the supplier's business.

Key account management provides the strategic base, the processes and the disciplines to handle this situation, alongside those other common challenges – globalization, market maturity and customer power.

The purpose is clear – the pursuit of competitive advantage. The days are long gone when major customers would tolerate average, overpriced products and services. Being a 'pimply me too' just won't work any more. Just stop to consider for a moment – whoever heard of Alexander the Mediocre?

Competitive advantage puts you in a position to succeed, but there is more that you need to do. There is the question of profit. Most companies, if they are honest, are not able to measure the profitability of their key accounts. Many companies, once they determine to measure these things, often find their largest customers to be their least profitable. Very few companies measure the long-term returns of customer retention – annual results are often all that count. Key account management should be seen as the route to *profitable* key supplier status – the challenge of understanding profit must be taken head on. This book will provide the help required.

Peter Cheverton has used the Cranfield research to great effect. I have worked closely with him for many years and have respect and admiration for his work as a trainer and consultant with major clients. The task of implementing key account strategies is far from easy, and Peter brings a combination of clarity, experience, enthusiasm and common sense to the task. This book is an excellent distillation of his experience, building on the Cranfield research and producing the essential guide to global best practice.

Please be assured that reading this book will be a rewarding experience.

Professor Malcolm McDonald

Preface

This book is designed as a practical guide to implementing key account management strategies. Wherever it has been helpful to use real examples of good and bad practice to illustrate important points, this has been done. Many of these examples come from my own experience in working with clients of INSIGHT Marketing and People, an international training and consultancy firm. Wherever possible the companies involved are openly discussed, but, for reasons that I hope are obvious, this is not always the case. In some of the more anonymous cases, details may have been altered slightly, either to aid clarity, or to protect the not so innocent!

I am pleased to be able to say that my training and consulting work brings me in contact with far more examples of good, than bad, practice, but the purpose of this book has not always permitted such a ratio. I hope that my own clients will forgive me for not filling these pages with more stories of their undoubted excellence in this field.

Please regard examples of good practice as merely examples, not role models, and those of bad practice as ways of illustrating the warning signs that line the route towards key account management (KAM).

Preface to the third edition

The preface to the second edition opened with the words – time marches on…, and so it is with the third edition.

It seems that each year that passes a new set of challenges arise, largely for two reasons – customers grow more sophisticated and more demanding, and competitors grow more challenging.

The section on selecting key accounts has been enlarged quite dramatically, as it becomes clear that this is not a simple one hit exercise but something that must be understood and sanctioned right at the top of any supplier organization.

Following on from selection, a whole new chapter on customer distinction has been added. This discusses the need to develop separate sales and service strategies for each group of customers – whether key, key development, maintenance, or opportunistic – and most importantly it recognizes the need for the sales team to free up the energy spent on non key accounts before it can properly turn its attention to the key accounts themselves.

Many of the examples and case studies have been updated to take account of developments – many of them still being 'work in progress'.

The CD ROM has been upgraded, with new tools and models, and an improved software package for the all important key account identification and selection matrix described in Chapter 20.

Acknowledgements

Without doubt the biggest thanks must go to the excellent clients of INSIGHT Marketing and People with whom I have worked as a trainer and consultant on Key Account Management over the last 10 years. I feel sure that I have learnt as much from their experiences as from any other source.

Professor Malcolm McDonald of Cranfield University School of Management has been as generous as ever with his support for this book, providing access to his own researches as well as encouraging me with my own.

My colleagues at INSIGHT have been kind enough to allow me the time to complete this book, and I thank them for their *endless* suggestions and for putting up with mine!

ALSO FROM KOGAN PAGE

Key Marketing Skills

Peter Cheverton

Not just another 'introduction to marketing', Key Marketing Skills contains information, advice and guidance on the marketing issues of the moment, including key account management, customer relationship marketing and the impact on marketing of the e-revolution. Using real-life examples of good and bad marketing practice to provide insights and warnings, this book covers:

- how to conduct a market audit;
- developing a marketing plan;
- writing a marketing plan;
- segmenting your market;
- marketing and the e-revolution;
- strategies in the marketing mix;
- delivering value.

The *If You're So Brilliant...* Series

Series Editor: Peter Cheverton

IYSB: How Come You Can't Identify Your Key Customers?
IYSB: How Come You Don't Have an E-strategy?
IYSB: How Come You Don't Understand Your Accountant?
IYSB: How Come Your Brand Isn't Working Hard Enough?
IYSB: How Come Your Marketing Plans Aren't Working?

A provocative and challenging new series that tackles the major 'blind spots':

- fast but not quick-fix;
- more 'why aren't you?' than 'how to';
- definitely not for the faint-hearted novice, but for all thinking professionals who want a short, sharp boost to their business skills.

The above titles are available from all good bookshops. To obtain further information, please contact the publisher at the address below:

Kogan Page Limited
120 Pentonville Road
London N1 9JN
United Kingdom
Tel: +44 (0) 20 7278 0433
Fax: +44 (0) 20 7837 6348
www.kogan-page.co.uk

And it was all going so very well...

Have you ever found yourself in front of a new customer and, after 10 minutes of conversation, realized that you are speaking to the wrong person?

It could be all sorts of things that are wrong – too junior, too new, too hung up about your price rather than your value.

And worse, you're starting to think you know who the right person is, but try going behind your first contact now and they'll cut you off at the knees.

If nothing like that has ever happened to you then maybe it's because you plan your sales calls well, or maybe you're just lucky. . . unlike Ken Reilly.

Ken Reilly is in the chemical business. The products he sells are far from the cheapest, but he knows they are the best. His customers are mostly manufacturers of high-quality goods, and most of them rate Ken's products highly. Ken is new, and he's learning, but sometimes it's the hard way.

What makes Ken's products so good is the money they save the customer. They make the customer's process faster, they reduce wastage and they reduce harmful emissions. A dream sell, if you know how to go about it – meaning, whom to see and what to say.

Ken is calling on a new customer – a potential key account. He doesn't know the people at all, but he has managed to make an appointment with one of the buying team. He puts that down to his persuasive skills with secretaries and, of course, his natural charm.

He's led into a small office; the walls are bare, the carpet is frayed and the desk has been the site of a hundred spilt coffees – but that is not the real problem. The real problem is the buyer, a nice enough man, but the wrong man.

Ken has been talking for 10 minutes, and he's getting nowhere. The buyer is writing things down but, for all Ken can tell, it might be the man's shopping list, or a letter to his mother.

This is a junior buyer, a *very* junior buyer. He has been with the company for three months, knows next to nothing about the business, still less about manufacturing, and spends most of his time, or so it seems, meeting sales-people who leave him their brochures.

Ken realizes that all this buyer sees is an expensive product – 20 per cent higher than their existing suppliers. He also realizes that he should be talking to someone else – perhaps a more senior buyer who would under-stand the proposition, or maybe someone on the plant who needs his kind of help, but how can he go past his current contact? He can't just ask to see the boss.

The interview is coming to an end, and the buyer makes a suggestion.

'Why don't you look me up again, in six months, once I've got my feet under the table a little bit?'

Six months! He could be out of a job by then.

'Perhaps I could see someone on the plant, someone who might...' but Ken's voice tailed off as the buyer got to his feet.

'Oh no, they're very busy down there, and we can't have reps running about the place. I'll see you in six months.'

And that was final.

Part I

Defining Key Account Management

What is a key account?

Perhaps you have key accounts already. So how have they come by that name?

- Are they just the big ones?
- Are they the ones you mustn't lose?
- Are they the ones that offer future profit?
- Are they the ones you want your staff to focus on – to look after the very best?
- Are they the ones where extra effort will bring extra returns?
- Are they the ones that demand more from you?
- Are they the ones that will take your business where you want it to go?

This is a far from exhaustive list, and calling a customer a 'key account' might be the result of any one or more of these distinctions. Better definitions almost certainly exist, with greater relevance to your own circumstances and aspirations. It is for you to choose the definition, based on the dynamics of your own industry, your own customers and your own business.

So, how much thought do you give to this – or is it just word play?

Given that the definition may determine how your business thinks of, and works with, your customers, then it is certainly more than just word play. We only need look at the potential limitations of each of these seemingly good definitions to see the point (Table 1.1).

Table 1.1 *Key account definitions and their limitations*

The big ones	What about tomorrow's oak trees? Do you always let the sales statistics make your decisions for you?
The ones you mustn't lose	You'll do anything to keep them happy, even if it kills you…
The ones that offer future profit	And where does today's profit come from?
The ones your staff focus on	So, do they ignore the rest?
The ones where extra effort brings extra return	Not bad, but now define return – and how many can you do this for?
The ones demanding more	Every industry has its loud mouths; does that make them important?
The ones that will take your business where you want it to go	Perhaps the best, but are you that certain? Do you know? The future is never clear…

SO, WHAT IS THE RIGHT ANSWER?

Rule number 1: You make the rules

As ever in life, 'it depends' – on your market, your aspirations, your current level of success, your competitor's activities and a lot more besides.

There is only one rule, and that is, you make the rules.

Don't leave it to the sales statistics. Last year's largest customer may not be next's. As they say in the investment adverts, 'past performance should not be taken as a guarantee of future potential'.

My first sales manager took great delight each year in telling the annual sales conference how many of our top-10 customers (by sales), from only five years previously, had dropped out of that list, or even no longer existed as customers at all. This was said neither out of spite nor despair on his part, simply a clear message to our team that times change. More significantly, he would remind us of those customers we had defined as key accounts five years previously and point out that each of them was most definitely still on that list, and growing in importance. In a fast-changing market, as ours was, he saw his job as picking the winners – and he had an excellent record.

This book aims to provide a process for identifying your key accounts on a basis that will save you from a dangerous, business threatening, case of myopia. Of course, just how long-sighted you have to be depends, again, on your own market and business circumstances. For some, a year might be forever, for others, 10-year planning is still quite feasible. Remember, there is only one rule, and that is, you make the rules. Just remember to think about it.

THE KEY ACCOUNT 'INVESTMENT'

Yes, there is a good chance that your largest customers will also be your key accounts, the 80/20 rule applies here as everywhere, but don't let the distinction stop there. Key account management is as much concerned with the future as it is the present and, as such, it must constantly reassess the grounds on which customers are considered key, or otherwise. Perhaps a key account is like an investment in the future, and just as you won't want to rely on past performance as a guide, nor will you want to depend on good fortune to come up with the right answers.

The UK in the 1970s and the 1980s witnessed an enormous growth in the DIY market. If the Englishman's home was his castle, then the moat was dug on Bank Holiday Sunday, and the drawbridge came from B&Q. Throughout these growth years, there were big manufacturers of DIY products, the likes of Dulux and Black & Decker, claiming to have built this DIY boom. But, at the same time, there were big retailers like B&Q, Texas, Homebase and Do It All making just the same claim. There is no question, *after the event*, that these retailers were the key accounts of those big suppliers, but who chose whom, or did it just happen?

Choosing or being chosen – who makes the first move?

The truth of the matter is that many big suppliers rode on the back of a retailing revolution – the growth of the out-of-town DIY superstore. And no shame in that. The key accounts, again with hindsight, were those retail chains driving the revolution and, as a result, growing fast. But it was only some among those manufacturers who really understood why some customers were growing, while others, like the high-street specialists, the department stores or the food supermarkets, were in decline. Indeed, huge energies and vast budgets were applied in trying to prop up some of these declining customers, particularly the supermarkets, because they were big and, more importantly, had recently been the biggest.

With hindsight, we can see that some manufacturers were plain lucky – they backed the right horse. We can also see that some wasted a great deal of time and money backing the losers, and some of those never recovered from their mistake.

The most important question had to be: what was it that made a customer in that market a key account? Understanding that would help any manufacturer to back the right horses. Or, to put it another way, to make the right investment of time, money and resource.

This was the market that I cut my sales teeth on, and of which my first sales manager (he of the sales conferences) proved such a good crystal ball reader. He backed the emerging DIY superstores in preference to the future of our largest customers, despite the fact that those were the very customers with which he had built his own career. His judgement was based on how he saw the dynamics of the retail market changing. He was aware that while department stores and supermarkets were the largest retailers of our products, *for now*, a new style of retailing was emerging, and that was what mattered.

This breadth of analysis also allowed him to listen to the 'subtext' of what the department stores and supermarkets were saying to us, and all their suppliers: 'If you want to keep our custom, we need to buy more cheaply.' Those manufacturers who based their judgements on past and current sales volumes heard only the words themselves. The subtext, unspoken, but quite clear in the broader analysis, was, 'We don't see our future in DIY.' We backed those retailers who did.

Now, there is little doubt that my first sales manager relied to a huge extent on gut feel – an important thing in business for sure, but is it enough? Could you persuade your board that they should invest in key account management based on *your* gut feel? This book aims to provide you with some processes for analysis – use these *as well* as your gut feel.

DOES EVERYBODY KNOW?

Speaking of boards, I was once asked to convince a management board that they should train their key account managers. The reason was that they didn't think they were very good, and I was given thirty minutes to convince them that this would be better than firing them all and starting again with a new team.

So I asked them a few questions, and the first was to write down who they thought their current key accounts were. There were seven directors in the room and guess what – seven different lists. Having seen them fail that one I moved on to question number two – define a key account. There were seven different answers again – the ones that keep the factory running, said the production director, the ones with the most predictable order patterns, said the logistics director, the biggest, said the sales director, but the finance director had the best of them all – the largest and least delinquent debtors....

You make the rules, but make sure that your definitions are agreed at the very top

They began to see why KAM was failing for them, it wasn't down to the key account managers, at least not yet, they weren't even given a chance to perform well. Unless the whole organization agrees on who is, and who isn't a key account, and in particular this needs clarity from the very top, then this journey is likely to become over long, over drawn out, and incredibly frustrating.

WHY KEY 'ACCOUNT'? A JUSTIFICATION

Some people object to the word 'account' – 'Surely it should be key customer', they say. 'Account makes it sound like a bank.'

I justify the word on only one ground, that it represents the customer as an investment made by the supplier in its own future. It is an investment of time and effort, in many cases requiring a short-term sacrifice for prospective long-term gains.

If a key account is an investment, then it implies that you seek a profitable return for your efforts. This is a key feature of key account management (KAM), to be explored further in Chapter 7.

If key accounts are those customers that promise to take you where you wish your business to be, then identifying them is as important as choosing a portfolio of investments – some must give a quick return, some are longer term, while others are speculative, balanced by those that offer more certainty.

Key account management is about managing that investment, it is about managing a very different kind of relationship with the customer and, as importantly, managing the implications of that relationship on the supplier's own business.

Put simply, *key account management is about managing the future.*

2

Managing the future

If KAM is about managing the future, then we had best try to understand how that can be done in a complex business amid the confusion of an ever-changing market environment.

Business strategies, or sales strategies, are instruments for managing the future, and they seek to balance three important elements, as illustrated in Figure 2.1.

The *business objectives* are concerned with where you are trying to get to – what sort of business you want to have in the future.

The *market opportunity* is a consideration of the forces that will help and hinder. Among the latter are, of course, your competitors. Among the former are those customers that will best help you get to where you want to be.

Figure 2.1 *Managing the future*

The *business resources* are those things that will support, or constrain, your progress – your capabilities, production, R&D, logistics, money and, not least, your people.

This is not a static model. As the future gets closer, so it changes, and as opportunities alter, so must your objectives be modified in balance with any new resource requirements. The all-important 'balance' will shift almost continually as the market changes, which, as we know, is now almost a permanent experience.

Managing the future must be a continual process of analysis, reassessment and change.

The closer we get to the future, the more our certainties are challenged

WHERE TO START?

Objectives?

Starting with objectives is of course the easiest, which is why most do in fact start there, but the perils are clear. Too many hockey-stick graphs in business plans project splendid growth after a period of no growth or even decline. When you see such graphs ask two questions – what has changed with the market opportunity, and how are you using your resources differently to take advantage of this? If the answers are nothing and we're not, then ignore the projections for growth – why should they happen just because someone writes it down?

Resources?

Sounds sensible, but here's a thought for you. Your current resources are probably ideal for the opportunity of about two years ago. So why start with what you've got today? This can only restrict your view even before you start your journey.

Market opportunity?

Of course, but it's not so easy. You are already plunged into the market, already responding to today's demands. Stepping back and viewing the future is not easy, but it is vital. More than that, it is one of the purposes and one of the benefits of the KAM approach.

THE IMPORTANCE OF BALANCE

We must stress the importance of balance between these three elements; the objectives must be balanced by the realism of the opportunity and the resources available. All too often, in the real world, we see how resources lag behind the opportunity, while the objectives surge ahead of it.

Such an imbalance can, of course, be damaging in any business circumstance, but particularly so in the arena of KAM. We are dealing here with customers and their perceptions of us as a supplier. It is all too easy to profess objectives that, unmatched by adequate resources, are not met. Where this results in customer discontent or disillusion, the penalties can be severe indeed. Some businesses, particularly in fast-growth, high-tech fields such as biotechnology, have grand objectives, designed for the attention of the city as much as prospective customers. They may 'talk a good talk' for some period of time, convincing customers of good times just around the corner, but if their objectives outstretch their resources, or they misjudge the market opportunity, then their chickens will come home to roost in a startling hurry. It is then that we read of the tumbling share price of some one-time wonder stock. And worse, the damage to customer trust and confidence can be terminal.

Realism is vital in the management of expectations; in enhancing your customer's perceptions and in winning the support of your own colleagues – something, as we shall see, that is fundamental to successful KAM.

Realism is not to be feared as suggesting any lack of vigour or ambition. Wild hopes may seem brave, but they can be the source of stress that pulls you and your business apart at the seams. George Soros, the international financier, said that when he was hopeful he didn't sleep at nights – it was worrying that made him feel secure!

It is only in this context, the balance between these three elements, that you can properly define your key accounts.

Let's say you are a manufacturer of a food product.

Chasing the big guys...

If your business objective is to achieve dominant market share, with a standardized, low-cost product (objectives), then you must find customers that will accept standardization and will provide the volume required (opportunity). If you have the production capacity, and enjoy the economies of scale derived from large orders (resources), then you might find a happy balance in identifying your key accounts as those largest, most straightforward customers – probably the major food supermarket chains.

or...

Chasing the rich guys?

Change just one element and you may need to change your key accounts.

A business with restrictions on its scale of production (resources), cannot take full advantage of the economies that come with large orders. Indeed, they become a burden, and the business may choose to avoid the larger customers. And if economies of scale don't apply, then why restrict yourself to low-value sales to the largest buyers? If there are customers that demand greater added value (opportunity), perhaps you can secure a premium price and greater profits by acting as a quality producer (objectives?). Such a supplier might regard Harrods or Fortnum and Mason as their key accounts.

Looking at another example and taking a different starting point, let's say you are in the biotech industry and you aspire to a reputation for leading-edge technology, gaining competitive advantage from a highly differen-tiated product rather than volume and market share (objectives). Let's also say that there are customers in your market that require complex, high-tech, bespoke solutions to very specific problems (opportunity). If you have an R&D department well placed to work on a wide range of different projects and product applications (resources), then your key accounts need not be huge; they will be defined more by the value of the projects involved, finan-cially, and in how they enhance your reputation.

Of course, should a new technology appear in the market, one that meets your target customer's needs with far less complexity and cost, then your whole strategy, and notion of key accounts, might have to change. Such changes in the market opportunity will often come from outside your own area of influence or control. For good or ill, there are forces that impact on your competitive strength (see Chapter 3).

Objectives and resources rarely lie entirely within your own control; shareholders (for one) demand returns, just as they restrain your ability to invest; but of the three elements it is the market opportunity that is perhaps most fickle, and so requires most study.

GUESSING THE FUTURE – CERTAINTY OR DRIFT?

Like all economists, John Maynard Keynes was in the business of predicting the future, but at least he was honest enough to express his own self-doubts; there were only two certainties, he said: death and taxes.

If KAM is about managing the future, how certain do we need to be about what it holds in store, and how brave should our predictions be? Can we go even further, to suppose that we might even take a part in making the future happen?

Let's just compare two philosophies of 'making it happen', two extremes. We might label them the *'Viking'* and the *'gently does it'*:

The 'Viking' philosophy argues that you should row on to the enemy **Viking...** shore, disembark your troops and burn your boats. That way, making things work is your only option. Success in such circumstances is bold, daring and the stuff of legend. Failure is brutal and unsung.

… or gently does it?

The 'gently does it' philosophy argues that you should hold off shore, viewing the enemy through long-range binoculars, looking for signs of weakness, hoping that they might fall into a hole of their own digging, and then creep ashore to take their place. Success is met by praise of your great wisdom and tactical genius. Failure brands you a coward.

HOW FAST DO WE EXPECT THE FUTURE TO ARRIVE?

Don't expect KAM to be a quick fix. The essence of KAM, as we will see, is in building relationships, and this all takes time. If your sales objectives are short term and call for big volume increases then you might be better placed seeking these from what we might call 'opportunistic customers' (see Chapter 21) rather than key accounts. There is perhaps an essential conflict between, on the one hand, building relationships based on trust and, on the other, pressuring for short-term sales volume.

Sales growth targets are part of the real world, but don't expect to satisfy them solely through KAM, and certainly don't compromise your future security by 'abusing' your KA relationships.

WHAT KAM IS NOT

We have yet to fully define what we mean by key account management, but we can already assert what it is not:

- KAM is not a short-term sales drive. The implementation of a KAM strategy is unlikely to see any beneficial impact on the bottom line in the short term. Remember, KAM is a series of investments.
- More than this, KAM should not be seen as a sales initiative at all. If it is to succeed, it should be viewed as a business-wide management process.

3

Assessing the opportunity

Trying to read the future can be like nailing jelly to a wall, but crazy as it seems we must try. Our own crystal ball techniques include the following:

- The PESTLE analysis.
- Porter's analysis.
- Market chains.
- The 'opportunity snail'.

Each of these tools has one thing in common – the pursuit of long-term competitive advantage.

PESTLE ANALYSIS

The market opportunity is subject to many forces and the acronym PESTLE reminds us to consider some of the larger-scale factors:

P – Political changes.   **T** – Technological changes.
E – Economic changes.   **L** – Legal changes.
S – Social changes.   **E** – Environmental changes.

Nothing is forever, times change; we know all that, but finding a way to assess the changes should be our goal, not hiding behind the platitudes. It is the need to consider these larger-scale factors that starts to place the key account manager's role and responsibilities above those of the traditional salesperson.

PORTER'S ANALYSIS

Understanding the barriers to entry; aiming to raise them, or surmount them

Michael E Porter has provided a model much used to assess the different competitive forces that bear in upon a business and so formulate strategies that aim to raise barriers to those forces, or take advantage of them (Figure 3.1).

Porter shows how a business operates within the ferment and flux of five different competitive forces. As well as some general comments on each, we might look at the position of the UK food supermarkets to illustrate the different forces at work.

Figure 3.1   *Porter's five determinants of industry profitability*
From Porter (1980)

The current competitors

– each 'jockeying' for position through price, quality, or service.

There has been an ever-more heated 'battle of the giants' between the big players in this market – Tesco, Sainsbury's, Asda, Safeway and Somerfield. The fallout has manifested itself in price wars (baked beans for 2p a can, bread for 5p a loaf) and a race to launch new services, from home shopping to ever-more generous loyalty cards. This latter service has taken a particularly heavy toll on supermarket margins over recent years.

The threat of new entrants

– perhaps attracted by the profitability, or growth, of this market.

New forces are continually hovering, spotting gaps in the market left by the ever-repositioning major players. First there was Aldi and Netto promising cut-price shopping and, most recently, the most dynamic grocery chain in the US, Wal*Mart, has threatened to bring its 'category busting' tactics to the UK through its acquisition of Asda. Not all of these new entrants are as successful as their aggressive launch plans promise, but their very presence reshapes the competitive dynamics of the market.

The threat of substitute products or services

– replacing your offer, perhaps through new technology, or a lower-cost alternative, or a 'simpler' solution (see Chapter 6, 'The bad story').

Will it or won't it – will the Internet and home shopping replace the supermarket as we know it?

The bargaining power of customers

– often reducing in numbers through amalgamation, and consequently increasing their buying power, or simply the swings of supply and demand.

Consumer pressure grows daily, fanned by the media, although it still has a long way to go before it matches the organized consumer group lobbying in the United States. Particular impact has been seen in the move towards more detailed product labelling and the provision of organic food alternatives. Of course, the retailers aim to turn such pressures to their own competitive advantage, with high-profile campaigns promising an end to battery-farmed eggs (Marks & Spencer) or a banning of genetically modified food products (Iceland).

The bargaining power of suppliers

– often through the provision of increasingly specialist, high-value, but unique services, or, again, simply the swings of supply and demand.

At the other end of the supply chain, major suppliers can wield enormous power, whether through brand names (who could envisage a major supermarket without Coca-Cola or Cadbury's?) or simply through the scale of their operation – genetically modified food products will be on the shelf simply because of the scale of Monsanto's activities in such a wide range of food areas.

Retention or growth? Key account management can be designed to pursue either

How these forces appear to you will depend on your starting point. A company with a well-established position in the market is somewhere at the centre of the model and will tend to see these forces as threats to its position. Its strategy might be to raise barriers to each one of them.

A company seeking to enter a market will be on the outside of the model – a new entrant – and will tend to see the various forces either as obstacles or opportunities. Their strategy will be to find means to overcome them, or take advantage of them.

We have just summarized two broad, almost generic, sales strategies, each stemming from a relative position in the market. These are further illustrated in Table 3.1.

Table 3.1 *Sales strategies based on market position*

Market Position	Sales Strategy
Established position, perhaps in a mature market	**Retention** through raising barriers to entry against those competitive forces
Potential entrant into a growth market	**Growth** through finding ways to overcome barriers to entry

In both cases, the nub of the matter is the same: one thing is required, either to defend or assault a market position – *competitive advantage*.

And here we come to a central plank of most KAM strategies, indeed a key purpose for KAM:

KAM is a means to gaining **competitive advantage**.

We will talk about competitive advantage on many occasions, principally in Part IV, but for the moment, let's just consider the problem of competitive advantage as a route to a secure future.

A SECURE FUTURE THROUGH COMPETITIVE ADVANTAGE?

Competitive advantage, or customer loyalty, can result from many things: products, services, people, declining competitors, changing circumstances, or just plain good fortune.

All these things, including 'earned luck' (the sort you make for yourself through analysis and planning), are of interest to the key account manager, but as sources of competitive advantage they are often fragile. Competitive advantage, like loyalty, unless continually earned, can be easily lost.

Times change

It hardly seems credible that OTIF (those four little letters that have focused so many suppliers' minds – 'on time in full') should once have been a source of competitive advantage. It is today so much the standard requirement from ever-vigilant customers that we can forget how some suppliers were able to use it as a means of ousting less efficient competition. In some industries and markets it was the supplier and not the customer who introduced the measure, as evidence of competitive superiority. How times change!

Laws that once favoured you turn against you; competitors in decline find new leases of life, superior products become ordinary, the buyer who loved you leaves you. This is particularly true where a supplier has become 'lazy', perhaps having enjoyed for too long a position of power and security. Customer dissatisfaction, pent up over a period of time, can suddenly blow its lid. (Much the same can happen to governments at general election time!)

The decline of IBM and the massive rise of Microsoft, Dell, Compaq and the rest (although there are also many other features to this case) illustrate the power and speed of changing customer preference and loyalty. It is so obvious as to hardly need saying, but loyalty based on monopoly is rarely loyalty at all.

Now, at the other end of the spectrum, we see Microsoft's freedom to market their own product called into question – a situation where loyalty is said, by Microsoft's detractors, to be 'forced', and that Microsoft's competitive advantage has grown unfair. Whatever your view, it is certain that their competitive advantage, fair or unfair, has brought them considerable business security, such that now it seems only the courts and the law might undo them. (We may well need to revisit this example in 5 or 10 years' time... times change...)

Size alone does not bring security

When customers 'snap'

When there is very little competition, and customers have few options for changing their suppliers, customer dissatisfaction has to be quite high before they put in the effort of finding an alternative. There is inertia in the market (Figure 3.2).

Figure 3.2   *When customers 'snap'*

Add competition – new suppliers eager to win new customers – and the picture changes. Now, small lapses in a supplier's performance can result in the loss of the business. Relatively small increases in customers' dissatisfaction can cause them to 'snap'. The market has become fluid.

Where there is no real competition, and perhaps an arrogant incumbent supplier, then you might expect to find customers at their most twitchy, and most ready to 'snap'.

One leak British Gas found hard to fix...	When deregulation began to hit the gas supply industry in the UK, British Gas had a virtual monopoly of industrial customers. Within months of the change, industrial customers were starting to leave, but there were few plans in place to keep them from departing, and still fewer for winning them back. The notion of customers 'snapping' was just too foreign to a supplier that had enjoyed such 'loyalty' (or was it apathy?) for so long. Of course, the loyalty was artificial, and in the end a large number of big players left British Gas behind for alternative suppliers. More recently, with the consumer market now up for grabs, we can see the gas suppliers behaving a lot more aggressively to retain customers, and win new ones.

In assessing the future opportunity, a business seeking to retain its position must heed the lessons. Such a business might expect to go through a series of 'makeovers'; continually reassessing its flexibility in the face of changing competitive pressures. A business seeking to enter a relatively low competition environment might hope to find advantage simply through an open-minded attitude.

The sad tale of the slide rule manufacturer

There was once a hugely successful company making slide rules (for those of you too young to remember, slide rules were calculating 'machines' using logarithmic scales and highly engineered sliding parts, before the days of electronic calculators), and as there were not too many alternative tools for calculation (logarithmic tables and the abacus being about it), they held their customers, effectively, to ransom.

Retailers were obliged to stock this leading brand, schools were obliged to buy them for their pupils who were put through the agonies of learning how to use them, despite the fact that they, like everybody, hankered for something better, something easier to use.

Some customers said as much to the slide rule manufacturer, but the letters and the phone calls never made it down to the R&D department. There, they spent their time working on making even better slide rules, with 'slidier' slidy bits, clearer printing, a smarter case – and steadfastly refused to listen. Who needed to listen to customers when you made the best slide rules in the world?

Change came in the guise of the electronic pocket calculator and customers were only too happy to jump ship – they 'snapped'. Seen any slide rules lately?

Of the competitive forces impacting on the slide rule manufacturer, substitute products might seem the most apparent, but there were other forces at work, forces in the *market chain*. The end-users were a captive audience for a simpler method of portable calculation – I was one of the throngs of schoolchildren eager to break my slide rule into pieces! The market for electronic calculators was warmed up well before we had ever heard of such things.

The successful key account manager, with an eye on a managed future, must learn to understand the significance of their place in such a market chain.

UNDERSTANDING THE MARKET CHAIN AND WHERE YOU SIT

Of course, the market is more than just *your* customers; it is a chain of suppliers and customers stretching down to the end-user. Change can occur at any point of the chain, and where you sit (up or down wind, as it were) will have a lot to do with how the change impacts on you and what sort of influence you might expect to have on that change. It may not be *your* customer that starts the ball rolling, nor even theirs.

Consider the market chain of an agrochemicals supplier, selling pesticides to wheat farmers (Figure 3.3).

Figure 3.3 *Pesticides market chain*

Understanding the market beyond your customer is one of the key goals of the key account manager

In this market, as we have seen when looking at the example to illustrate Porter's five forces, there is a significant driver of change at the supermarket/consumer interface. A combination of consumers demanding 'greener' products, and supermarkets seeking competitive advantage by offering products free of anything that could be construed as 'harmful', has led to the development of what some call 'food passports'.

In order to label their products accurately, the supermarket asks suppliers to indicate the source of their products' component parts and, in this example, how they were grown and treated. The food passport is a detailed history of the product's journey to the supermarket shelf.

The impact of this trend on the agrochemical supplier is as clear as it is on the baker, the grain merchant or the farmer. How should they respond? Perhaps they can help their own customer, the farmer, to cope with the resultant pressures. Perhaps they can develop products with lower dosages or less residue. Perhaps they can influence the consumer's understanding of what 'harmful' means – after all, pesticides help ensure disease-free food. Perhaps they can agree standards with the food industry, including the supermarkets.

A traditional sales approach focusing on the farmer as the customer, with those most supportive of pesticide use seen as the key accounts, might very well end in disaster. The KAM approach would be to look beyond the farmer; understand the dynamics of change in the market; perhaps even consider the supermarkets as a kind of key account.

Suppliers distant from the consumer will do well to recognize a general principle: *the greatest value, and so the greatest impulse for change, is usually to be found closest to the end-user.*

Let us look at another example of a market chain, and this time not simply a linear one. We sell film material that is used in the consumer goods packaging industry. Our direct customer, perhaps our key account, is the 'converter', the company that takes the film, prints it, and manufacturers the final packaging item, whether it be a crisp packet or a 'glossy' box for an upmarket perfume. A summary of the market chain is shown in Figure 3.4.

The film supplier that denies any need to understand the market beyond their immediate customer is in effect denying their full potential to help that

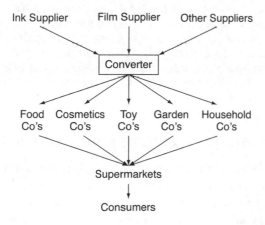

Figure 3.4 *The packaging market chain*

23

customer. More than this, it is handing ownership of the market to that customer, and thus the lion's share of the rewards from the market.

The specific end-users of packaging material each have their own demands: a food company requires high standards of hygiene; a cosmetic manufacturer is concerned principally with image; a toy producer looks for safety; a garden chemicals company will be most concerned about longevity and durability; and the household goods firm will perhaps be most interested in costs.

Knowledge of these differing demands will enable the film supplier to work with their customers more proactively. Of course, some converters might enjoy keeping their suppliers in the dark – they have the knowledge and they take the reward. If that is the case, then not only will such suppliers be unlikely to be regarded as key suppliers, but it will also be difficult for them to regard the converter as a true partner, or perhaps even a key account.

It is not only down the chain towards the consumer that you need to be looking. The other suppliers could have an impact on your business. For example, an ink supplier approaches a cosmetics firm with a new ink that will make their product 'glow' from the shelf, but it requires a different kind of film. And guess what? It's not yours. Is that ink supplier a competitor? No, but their actions determine your future. The key account manager must look at all of these influences and forces to manage and safeguard the company's investment.

In the market chain, the real customer is not always the one who pays the bills

An interesting twist on the market chain, showing that it does not always proceed in a straight line from supplier to customer, and thence to the customer's customer, is seen in the business of Hays Crate Services. HCS supply reusable plastic crates for the delivery of products to supermarkets, therefore doing away with cardboard boxes and providing an environmentally friendly service. They save everyone involved in the supply chain a small fortune into the bargain. They regard their customers as the supermarket chains, yet they receive no payment from them. If the supermarket accepts their proposal then they will instruct their own suppliers to make use of these crates, and it is these suppliers that make payments to HCS. The success of HCS is dependent on convincing the end-user that their service is of value and not just the people who pay the bills.

Why chains matter – *getting your just reward*

If you don't understand the customer's position in the chain and so the challenges they face, then it is very likely that you will not fully understand the value that you bring. That is not to say that you don't make good value propositions, you still may, often out of luck as much as anything else, but you will almost certainly not properly understand just how valuable you are being – and that's a problem.

It's fairly easy to have clever ideas, and to come up with novel solutions to problems, easy that is when compared to getting the proper reward for your brilliance. Consider the plight of a manufacturer of cardboard cartons.

Fresh out of value

The carton supplier was approached by a soup manufacturer looking for an alternative packaging solution to the standard tin – they wanted a cardboard tub.

The packaging supplier knew little of their client's challenges, and worse, rather than making enquiries proceeded to make some assumptions on their behalf. Cartons were not as good as tins or bottles – they were less durable, more likely to be damaged in transit, liable to leak, and would have a markedly shorter shelf life. The client could only be looking for a low cost solution and so the carton supplier cut its costs and its margins to oblige.

It won the contract and celebrated, only to find what an opportunity they had missed. In the supermarket, where a tin of soup might sell for £0.60, a carton might sell for four times as much at £2.40. Why? Because soup in a carton is fresh soup, up-market soup, added value soup, gourmet soup, and it is the packaging that communicates this positioning. Soup in a carton would *have* to be fresh!

The supplier underrated its own importance and value because it didn't understand what the customer was really looking for. In this case they could see their error because it appeared on a very public supermarket shelf. How often have you committed this sin and never been any the wiser?

Opportunity networks

Market chains, or as we might call them, opportunity chains or maps, don't just work in straight lines, indeed it is far more normal for them to be networks of influencers rather than straight supply chains. Understanding these networks can be the secret to finding genuine solutions rather than simply selling products along a supply chain, and for many businesses it is this desire to sell solutions that is one of the most important reasons for embarking on the KAM journey in the first place.

Selling solutions – understand your value and get your reward

Take the case of a paint supplier, it supplies the kind of paint that is used to repair damaged cars, often called Refinish Paint. Its traditional view of the market chain and its opportunity is shown in Figure 3.5.

The paint is sold through distributors to three kinds of body shop, and it is fairly clear who the key accounts will be – the all-powerful distributors. The result of this apparent clarity is that they too often just sell products, and it is the distributors who manage to come up with the value added solutions. This was before they started to analyse the chain more deeply.

Figure 3.5 *The traditional market for refinish paint*

Figure 3.6 shows the addition of a key group of people, the end users, motorists like ourselves, car hire firms, and the like.

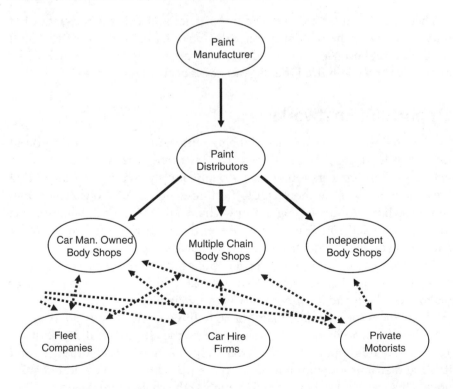

Figure 3.6 *Adding the end users to the chain*

Now consider what you do, if you crash your car and need to get it repaired. Your first port of call isn't even on this map, it's the insurance company.

The paint supplier now begins to realize that there is an external entity that in effect determines its future. If the insurance company sends the motorist to a body shop stocking the supplier's products then fine, but if not....? Their answer has been a sales approach that aims to have the widest possible distribution and so hopes to win more often than it loses. Such blanket coverage sales approaches can be expensive.

By considering the insurance company however a new gleam begins to appear in the supplier's eye – couldn't they begin to influence where motorists were sent?

Before leaping to any conclusion however there is at least one more player to add to the map, the motor car manufacturer. We all know that car makers no longer make money selling cars, they look increasingly for their profits from the repair of cars, servicing, spare parts and etc. For the likes of Ford it is vital that when we crash our car we actually take it to one of their body shops. Warranties have been the traditional mechanism for ensuring this, but could there be another solution?

How about if the paint supplier took a grip of this complex map and provided a solution, as shown in Figure 3.7.

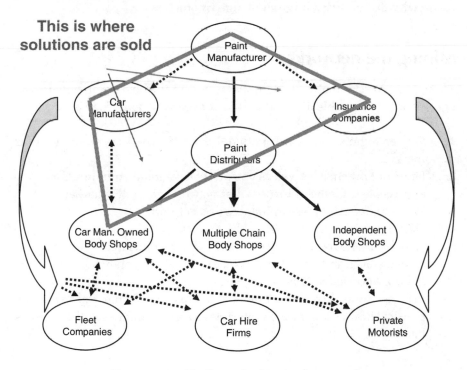

Figure 3.7 *Finding solutions in the network*

They approach the motor manufacturer – in return for stocking our product in all your controlled body shops we have a means of bringing customers to you…

They approach the insurance company – in return for sending your clients to the body shops we recommend, you will get a commission, paid by the motor manufacturer…

They approach the distributor – please keep delivering the product, they say…

Managing complex networks – the route to competitive advantage

So who is the key account now? Is it any one entity, or is it in fact the network. Perhaps in such a case we should be referring to key network management and the task of the key network manager.

This is in fact how many suppliers are beginning to view the wider task, a task that leaves simple selling well behind. A pharmaceutical supplier faces a market map even more complex than the one described here, with a myriad of influencers from doctors to nurses, GPs, hospitals, formulary committees, pharmacists, Primary Care Trusts and many more. Perhaps the key to genuine long term competitive advantage for such pharmaceutical companies is in finding the way to manage these markets as active networks. Easy to say, but given the huge inertia that comes from existing sales approaches to these markets, large field sales teams each targeting its own narrowly focused group of customers, it is equally easy to see why this is such a huge challenge in practice.

Mining the networks

There is an exercise that you might like to consider at this point, not an easy one, but a very valuable one, and I lay it out below in some logical steps:

1. Gather together a cross-functional team, focused on one particular market.
2. Draw out the chain as well as you know it, keeping your minds as open as possible to all the influences that play on and in this market.
3. Try to understand these influences as a network.
4. Take the chain right through to the end user.
5. Note by a series of ticks and crosses at which points in the network you have contacts and knowledge (ticks!) and where you have no contacts or poor knowledge (crosses!).
6. Having done this, draw lines on to this 'map' that represent the physical flow of orders and materials – what we might call the logistics lines.

7. Then draw the lines of influence – these are more complex, are certainly 'messier' and will take some thought (Figure 3.8 shows the sort of thing – logistics in bold, influence by dotted lines).
8. Now comes the hard part – you will have identified the strengths and weaknesses of your current contacts, and you will have identified the lines of influence – do you have a problem, or do you have an opportunity?
9. Now an even harder part – how will you go about improving contacts and knowledge where it is weak, and what reward do you expect to get for this effort?

If you can do all nine steps of this exercise then you will have made an enormous leap forward in your preparation for KAM.

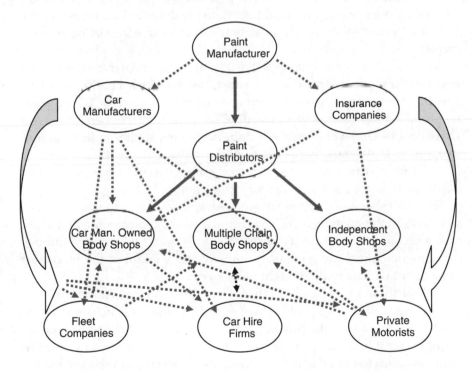

Figure 3.8 *Mining the opportunity network*

THE 'OPPORTUNITY SNAIL'

Just as key account managers must seek opportunities by looking beyond the customers with whom they deal and trade, so there are opportunities to be found within the immediate customer but beyond the people that they are used to seeing.

It is no great surprise that, without an active plan to do otherwise, customer contacts tend to settle down to a few regular meetings with the same faces. Most commonly these are faces within the purchasing department. The feeling of comfort and stability that this can bring is dangerously illusory: when the face changes so can your fortune. Genuine security is usually the result of deep relationships with as broad a range of contacts as possible.

Even while the face remains the same, the supplier is in danger of missing out on the real opportunities. Working in the realm of the gatekeeper (the role of many a commercial buyer) can be a very limiting experience.

If we consider the way that ideas and decisions are generated in the customer's organization, we might begin to see the way to uncovering real opportunities, whether for new business or to add value to existing arrangements.

Let us consider as an example the way that a particular customer goes about deciding to launch a new product, one to which you hope to be a supplier. The customer is a fast moving consumer goods (FMCG) company, the manufacturer of a number of leading food and confectionery brands – a company like Unilever, Nestlé or Cadbury's. Our supplier in this example supplies food flavours, high-specification products of significant value to the customer. The supplier's principal contact is with the purchasing department, but is this where the real opportunities lie?

Figure 3.9 shows an example of what we will call the 'opportunity snail', as it exists in this customer. The snail represents the typical route that a new idea takes as it develops on its journey from 'wouldn't it be great?' through to a product launch. In our fmcg company, the initiator is the marketing department with a hundred bright ideas a year.

Each of these ideas proceeds through a series of checks and developments, often called 'stagegates'. These include: market research, to see if the market is interested in the product; R&D, to see if it can be made; manufacturing, to see if full-scale production is viable; purchasing, to source the raw materials; back to manufacturing to make the materials; and then on to sales and distribution to get it into the market. This snail is something of a simplification, as in reality there would be a complex series of loops, and loops within loops, but it clearly illustrates the problem of making contact with the customer only at the outer edge.

Figure 3.9 *The 'opportunity snail'*

What will the buyer be interested in? Price. Is this the area the supplier has most to offer? Probably not. Worse, the chances are that the real decisions on suppliers have already been made. Specifications are already set and there is little you can do as a supplier to improve your chances other than talking money. The only good news is that you are talking about a real purchase requirement – an order is imminent – but is this really such good news?

Contact with the R&D department could bring a significant advantage. Here you would be talking technical capability, and perhaps this is your real strength? And better still, you are now involved with potential products where decisions are not yet made and there is much to influence in the decision. Possibly this 'idea' might not see the light of day but this simply highlights the skill required in managing a key account – where to invest your time and energy.

Penetrating the snail – in search of the real opportunity and the real value

Of course, the buyer might not allow you immediate access to the R&D people; it may take some time and skill to penetrate the customer's decision-making process. The techniques for such a penetration are discussed in Part V. At the moment, we are concerned with why it is a good idea.

Should we penetrate further into the snail, right back to the marketing department? There are pros and cons to doing this.

Reasons in favour of penetrating to the centre:

● You can discover the real hopes and ambitions of the customer.

- Your skill in working on new product development programmes can help the customer improve their success rate from 2 to 4 per cent of ideas seeing the light of day (not untypical for a fmcg company) to about 4 to 8 per cent – surely the route to being considered a key supplier?
- Early contact allows you to set the criteria so that you are the only viable choice, and price is a very minor issue once the buyer becomes involved.

Reasons against penetrating to the centre:

- What does the buyer or R&D people make of you talking to marketing? For some this would be tantamount to dealing with the enemy!
- If only 2 to 4 per cent of new ideas see the light of day, couldn't this close involvement lead you horribly astray, perhaps even pull your organization apart at the seams?

The need for a Key Account Team

Can you do this alone?
Are you really sure?
Let me just ask you this again...

The more complex the snail, the more it involves people in specialist functions, the less likely that a sales professional can do this on their own. Even if they can, perhaps it is still best that they don't try to go it alone.

- Penetrating beyond the buyer is never easy, but if it is someone other than the salesperson doing the penetrating that can sometimes ease the way.
- Can the sales professional really be credible in so many different guises?
- Why should these specialists see a salesperson in any case – wouldn't they prefer to speak with someone who speaks their language?
- You'll be amazed at what a real expert can uncover when speaking with their opposite number.
- Where were you going to find the time to do all this penetrating?

Putting chains and snails together

What do we conclude from these thoughts?

We can conclude that to succeed at the centre of the snail we must understand the customer's business as well as they do. One hugely successful key account manager I have had the privilege of working with summed it up succinctly as 'the need for a degree in horse racing – you had to know which opportunities to back'.

Any business with a decision snail as drawn out as this could benefit from a supplier who was able to help the company speed up its progress. This is a delicate task to perform, but success will be well rewarded.

Each snail is unique, with its own challenges, its own driving force at the centre – sometimes marketing, sometimes R&D, often 'the boss'. Time taken to understand your customer's snail will be time well spent.

The advantages of penetration are substantial but the potential pitfalls are serious. The answer is to manage the penetration so as to avoid the pitfalls, and here we come to the heart of what KAM involves and calls for. Relationships must be managed so that they develop to your advantage and not to your detriment. As they develop, so must your understanding of the customer's business and market, ensuring that you can take advantage of the information the relationship brings without suffering the pains of an 'anything the customer says is right' innocent. One way to avoid such pains is to remember the reason for wishing to penetrate the customer's opportunity snail – the pursuit of a long-term competitive advantage.

The section on supply chain management in Chapter 8 looks at how the purchasing revolution has modified the nature of the opportunity snail, and whether this is to the advantage or the detriment of the supplier seeking to penetrate beyond the commercial buyer.

Chapter 26 shows how the concept of value chain analysis provides some further clues as to how best to penetrate the snail.

LONG-TERM COMPETITIVE ADVANTAGE?

Is this the Holy Grail of KAM? Undoubtedly, one focus of KAM has to be on securing something sustainable, something that will last (if looked after) through all the vicissitudes of the market. And here we come to another central plank of many KAM strategies, indeed, another potential key purpose:

KAM is a means to key supplier status.

This is so easy to say, yet such an important idea, I will say it again, only this time, louder:

KAM is a means to key supplier status.

What does this mean? What is a key supplier? How can you achieve key supplier status?

Competitive advantage brings key supplier status, which brings competitive advantage...

We will attempt to answer these questions, from the customer's perspective, in Part II. Suffice it to say, for the moment, that key supplier status is rarely the result of products, technologies or service alone – however superior they might be. It will involve developing relationships, building trust, building customer knowledge, using that knowledge to deliver value and, very importantly, jointly managing the future to avoid surprises.

First, we should continue where we have just started, by looking at the future – identifying the purpose of KAM – the objectives part of managing the future.

Key account management – its purpose

WHY KAM?

Chapter 4 may seem rather late to be asking such a fundamental question, but before a supplier has developed some understanding of what KAM is and what it might involve it is surprisingly hard to be clear about what it will do for you. Choosing an objective before considering the opportunities is an all too common mistake which we should be aiming to avoid.

There are plenty of good reasons to practice KAM, and then there are the reasons that have driven most businesses in this direction. What do I mean by this? The truth of the matter is that most businesses that have developed KAM strategies have done so because they had little choice, and that's a rather sad state of affairs.

Do you need 'good' reasons, or will 'bad' reasons work just as well?

Lets just list eight very common reasons that have been behind the development of perhaps the majority of recent KAM approaches:

- Customer consolidation.
- Global customers demanding a uniform approach and service.
- New purchasing practices.
- The supplier's own complexity – multiple business units selling to the same customer unit.
- The growth opportunity requires the prioritisation of resources.

- Your products alone no longer provide a source of competitive advantage – relationships matter.
- The desire to sell solutions, not products.
- The desire to make a positive impact on the customer's business strategy through value propositions.

If you were an FMCG supplier in the early nineteen-eighties it didn't take a genius to see that the number of supermarket chains was falling fast, and that concentrating more resources on to those who were growing fastest was a good idea – and so KAM was born.

If your customer tells you that from now on you must deliver the same products at the same prices with the same services wherever they operate around the globe, then you will probably start to coordinate your different sales teams around the world to ensure that this happens – and so KAM is born.

If the buyers you meet are using new sources of information to make your life difficult, and are demanding such things as open book trading, then perhaps some new responses are required, using your own internal expertise – and so KAM is born.

If the buyer tells you that starting next month they will no longer entertain four different sales representatives with four different stories from the one supplier, then you may start thinking about which one can best represent all the interests – and so KAM is born.

Defensive...?

And very often that's it – KAM is the result of pressures from outside, the supplier is made to do it. There is good and bad news in this. The good news is that this pressure makes things happen. The bad news is that nobody really wants to do it!

...or offensive?

The final four motivations listed above are of a different nature – KAM because it will do something for us, give us an edge, give us competitive advantage. Surely these sound the better reasons, but sadly they are not very often sufficient to make the supplier take on the challenge of the changes required.

Here is one of the ironies of the story – KAM often get implemented the fastest for the least good reasons, and sometimes not at all even though the best of reasons are there to be seen.

Be very clear what you want from all this effort.

Before you proceed any great distance with your own KAM journey please be sure that you know very clearly what you wish it do to for you. If your reasons *are* defensive, then be pleased that at least you will have a lot of pressure from outside to make things happen, but there will be plenty of resistance from those who don't yet understand the need. If your reasons are offensive, then well done, but don't expect the organisation to change overnight just because you think it's a great opportunity.

THREE SIMPLE PURPOSES

The previous chapters have raised three very clear purposes:

- KAM is a process for attempting to _manage the future_;
- KAM is a means to _competitive advantage_;
- KAM is a means, if possible, to _key supplier status_.

And we should now add an extra requirement: that it should do all this profitably. Perhaps this was already clear to you? It certainly isn't to all…

A client interested in KAM training for their team once told me, with some pride, that they had 72 key accounts. My interest was suddenly raised – 72 key accounts; they must have an enormous sales force – and I saw the number of events running into the distant future. It turned out that there were four key account managers, so that was 18 key accounts each.

I asked a few questions:

- How does the label 'key account' help in allocating resource, time and money?
- How do you behave differently with those 72 customers compared to all the others?
- How do those 72 customers see their own business enhanced as a result of this label?

The answers, after some pressing, were: 'It doesn't, we don't and they probably don't.'

In addition to the reasons cited above, the purpose of KAM is to ensure that you have _positive_ answers to these sort of questions.

I might have asked further, or with different emphasis:

- How does the label 'key account' help to manage the investment in your customers?
- How does it help you to manage the relationship between the two businesses – supplier and customer?
- How does it help you to manage the future?
- How does it help you to balance sales objectives with resources and with the opportunity?
- How does it help you to identify activities that would give competitive advantage?
- How does it help you to secure key supplier status?

Does it mean anything?

The purpose of KAM is to have positive answers to all of these questions.

KAM is, in short, a *means* to achieving your objectives – not an objective or an end in itself. There is too much effort involved in establishing and maintaining a KAM strategy for there to have been no better purpose than being able to say that you did it.

SALES AND BUSINESS OBJECTIVES

In the last chapter we discussed two broad sales objectives – retention and growth. We have seen already that there is plenty more that KAM might do for your business.

Let's consider just six possible objectives:

1. Retention of customers in a competitive environment – *Building barriers to entry.*
2. Growth through entry into new customers – *Overcoming barriers to entry.*
3. Growth with existing customers – *Finding new opportunities.*
4. Managing customers with a cross territory perspective – *Global Account Management.*
5. Managing customers serviced by a multi business unit supplier – *Uniform Service.*
6. Going beyond product and benefit selling – *Selling Solutions.*

Remember, from Chapter 2, that KAM is a means of managing the future, and that requires a balance of **Objectives**, **Resources**, and **Opportunity**. We should consider these objectives then in the light of those other two elements. I like to think of this as a series of 'sanity checks'.

SANITY CHECKS

Does the *market opportunity* exist to achieve these objectives?

1. *Building barriers to entry* – Do you have a Sustainable Competitive Advantage? Can you secure Key Supplier Status? With which customers?
2. *Overcoming barriers to entry* – Do you have a unique value proposition? Which customers would consider it? Are your competitors failing anywhere?
3. *Finding new opportunities* – Are you at full capacity with this customer? Are they creating new needs?

4. *Global Account Management* – Do such customers exist? Are they organized to operate 'globally' (as opposed to just being in lots of places)? Do they want global service?
5. *Uniform Service* – You might crave uniformity, but do the customers? Which ones?
6. *Selling Solutions* – Do you understand their challenges? Can you help them, and be rewarded?

(This last question is a big one, and we will return to the notion of the needs of Key Account's driving and directing a supplier's wider business activities in Chapters 19 and 20.)

Do you have the right **Resources**, and deployed in the right way, to achieve these objectives?

1. *Building barriers to entry* - Do you have the right team? Is it deployed correctly?
2. *Overcoming barriers to entry* – Is the team sufficient to seize the opportunity, and is it deployed correctly? (This is not just a matter of size of the team, the approach is of far greater importance)
3. *Finding new opportunities* – Is your team still looking, or have you grown complacent? Do you penetrate their snails?
4. *Global Account Management* – Is your business globally orientated – physically, or psychologically? Will teams work to such objectives?
5. *Uniform Service* – Will different units collaborate?
6. *Selling Solutions* – Can the business cope with the diversity of solutions? Are all functions organised to be responsive?

The following table summarizes only these thoughts, against these six objectives. A similar table should be completed for your own circumstances.

Table 4.1 *Sanity check summary*

Objectives	Market Opportunity	Resources
Building barriers to entry	Do you have a Sustainable Competitive Advantage? Can you secure Key Supplier Status? With which customers?	Do you have the right team? Is it deployed correctly?
Overcoming barriers to entry	Do you have a unique value proposition? Which customers would consider it? Are your competitors failing anywhere?	Is the team sufficient? Is it deployed correctly?

continued overleaf

Table 4.1 *Sanity check summary*

Objectives	Market Opportunity	Resources
Finding new opportunities	Are you at full capacity with this customer? Are they creating new needs?	Is the team still looking? Do you penetrate their 'snails'?
Global Account Management	Do such customers exist? Are they organized to operate 'globally'? Do they want global service?	Is your business globally orientated – physically, or psychologically? Will teams work to such objectives?
Uniform Service	Do customers really want it? Which ones?	Will different units collaborate?
Selling Solutions	Do you understand their challenges? Can you help them, and be rewarded?	Can the business cope with the diversity of solutions? Are all functions organized to be responsive?

IMPLICATIONS OF KAM

Some issues will doubtless be starting to arise by this point in our assessment of KAM. However far you intend to take KAM in your business, the following implications will almost certainly have occurred to you by now:

1. How many key accounts can you have?

Most businesses have too many key accounts

Everything we have said so far would tend to suggest that it is a relatively small number – if you are to prioritize your resource on these customers, if you are to behave differently, if you are to allow their needs to drive your business processes, etc.

Part IV will look in detail at the question of identifying your key accounts, looking at the link between market segmentation and KAM and providing a process for making your selections. Leaving it till Part IV may appear rather late in the day, but it is important to understand what KAM actually involves before making these decisions.

2. How should you use your team?

KAM is not for loners

This is really the heart of KAM in practice and Parts III and V will look at this in some detail – asking who is in your team, how should they be used and what help will they require?

3. How will KAM impact on the running of the business?

Depending on how far you wish to take it, KAM might be anything from a sales initiative (rarely successful!) through to a revolution in how you run your business. Chapter 14 will look at some of the obstacles that stand in the way of implementing KAM in your business and will help you to conclude on a key question: just how far do you wish KAM to change the way you operate?

KAM is not just a sales initiative…

SO, WHAT WILL KAM 'FEEL' LIKE?

How will you know that you are doing anything different from before? If we summarize some of the varied purposes of KAM, we might be able to draw some simple conclusions.

First, I hope I have demonstrated that the title 'Key Account Manager' is not a badge of status, on a par with the key to the executive washroom. Nor is it a response to the too simplistic notion that the biggest customers must have our 'best' sales people – whatever that means. Nor is it an internal process about selecting, labelling and pigeonholing customers.

So what is it? There are several possible purposes and objectives of KAM, which are to :

- manage the future;
- identify customers that will help us achieve our objectives;
- retain and grow customers against competitive forces;
- gain entry to new customers;
- develop intimacy with customers' needs and values;
- gain competitive advantage;
- increase long-term customer loyalty;
- secure key supplier status;
- balance business objectives, market opportunity and business resources;
- allocate and deploy resources, particularly people;
- identify customer-focused activities, and commit to them;
- direct and drive the business, particularly support functions;
- secure a profitable future.

Being single minded is OK too!

We have one client who uses KAM for a very singular purpose. Their business relies on continual technical innovation, which is expensive and often the benefits are short lived.

If they are not careful, these two factors can act as internal brakes – the choice to do nothing can be strangely tempting, with disastrous results in the longer term.

They have chosen to identify key accounts as those customers that will not only force them to innovate, but will support them in their efforts. In practice this usually means customers who will promise to take their innovations on board, before they are actually begun!

It is always a good idea to innovate alongside customers, but this approach has an added benefit, the customer can be used as a kind of battering ram to break down internal inertia and complacency.

GOOD PRACTICE?

The following elements of KAM practice continually appear in the most successful applications. By 'successful' I mean that the supplier achieved its aims, and on those grounds I feel justified in calling them elements of good practice.

- Relationships with the customer go further than the purchasing department.
- Multiple contacts are maintained by a key account team composed of commercially aware functional experts.
- The key account manager is of sufficient stature (and perhaps seniority) to win credibility with the team and with the customer.
- The supplier understands the customer's business and market as well as the customer, and perhaps even better.
- The supplier regards KAM as a cross-business process, not just a sales initiative, and this is supported from the top.
- The supplier is prepared to invest in KAM and measures performance over the long term. To paraphrase a comment of Professor Malcolm McDonald's: *'Pulling up the plant every five minutes to see if it's grown any roots yet is hardly likely to encourage healthy growth.'*
- Key accounts are identified on a rational basis that takes into account both your customer's view of your capabilities and your view of their attractiveness.
- Only as many key accounts are selected as the business can manage. There must be a balance between objectives, opportunities and resources (see Chapter 2).

And the conclusions? In all likelihood there will be two features of KAM that stand out above all others – we might even call these the defining features:

- **developing the nature of the customer relationship in order to enhance understanding;**
- **aligning the business to act on that knowledge in order to secure competitive advantage.**

The first of these two features is the subject of the next chapter. We will return to the second in Part IV.

All in all this will be quite a journey. This is something beyond 'selling' in the traditional sense. Some people would say that KAM isn't about *selling* at all, rather it is about *relationship marketing* (see Chapter 20) ie forging partnerships with customers that are designed for mutual benefit. Perhaps that is how you define 'selling' already? If so, then you have less of a journey to make.

IS THERE A KAM PROCESS?

In the next chapter we will identify five stages through which a customer relationship might develop as a result of KAM. We will describe the kind of activities that might apply at each stage, although this is not a prescriptive process.

The activities described are in response to the nature of the relationship and in turn help to define the nature of that relationship – a virtuous circle when it goes well. One thing is clear: by the time the relationship reaches what we will be calling the 'partnership stage', you will have long left behind any simple linear process of 'do this, then that, and then, *bingo*, the sale'.

If there was any such linear process at the outset of the relationship then it soon becomes a question of everything happening at once. Not only that, but as the relationship develops, so the intensity of the activities in this process will increase. In an attempt to bring some order and structure to what could soon become an overwhelming situation, we might try to identify a process or series of activities, even if this does not represent a purely chronological sequence. This process is shown in Figure 4.1 but care should be taken not to oversimplify this into a series of separate steps; rather it is a collection of activities that proceeds sometimes in sequence and sometimes in parallel.

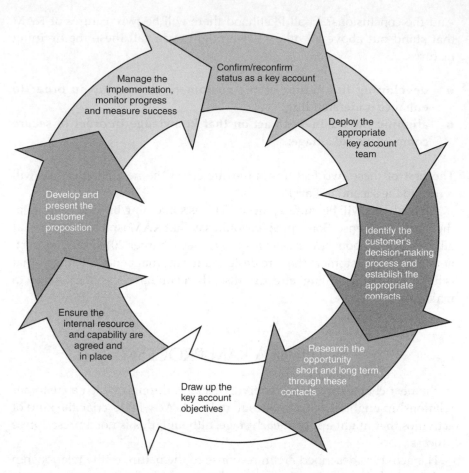

Figure 4.1 *The KAM process*

5

Developing the relationship

What constitutes the *best* relationship depends very much on the circumstances. If your ambitions are high with a particular customer, and they in turn think well of you, then perhaps anything short of a deep relationship might be a missed opportunity. If, on the other hand, the customer does not deserve much attention and asks only for the briefest of contacts with you, then the deep relationship you have envisaged could be inappropriate.

Before turning to a model that will help us to discuss the different kinds of relationship we might encounter (for example, what *is* a deep relationship and how does it differ from a shallow one?), let us consider three different sales approaches and the kinds of relationship they engender. We will call these sales approaches the *milk round*, the *hunter*, and the *farmer*.

THE MILK ROUND

This is (or rather, was) the classic sales scenario in an established market with little prospect of change: a team of sales representatives armed with weekly journey plans – clover leaf or whatever – seeking an ever more efficient way to service a group of customers where all customers are equal.

When customers were not only always right, but were also equal…

When looking for an example we find most of them in the past, as this was after all the sales methodology of the 1960s and 1970s with massive sales forces managed by multiple layers of sales managers – area, regional and national. Sales and merchandising teams of 200 or 300 were not uncommon in servicing the retail industry, particularly for big brand foods or DIY products, such as Heinz or Dulux. While the market was dominated by independent outlets, and even once the supermarket and superstore chains began to appear but still took local buying decisions, such an approach was both appropriate and successful.

However, it is a rather self-fulfilling approach to selling; if all customers are regarded as equal then the clues that might distinguish greater potential in one over another can easily be missed. This aspect of the milk round approach has led to its rapid decline throughout the 1980s and 1990s, with sales teams shrinking from the hundreds down to the teens.

Technology has also hastened the reduction in numbers. The mark of a good milk round sales force is its efficiency, and salespeople have been replaced by the more 'efficient' methods of telesales and e-commerce.

Milk rounds still exist – perhaps the pharmaceutical company's field sales teams targeted on GPs represent the single largest example of the approach. Performance measurement is by coverage and the efficiency of that coverage.

Perhaps it is still right to sell in this way, in this market, although many are beginning to question the returns for such huge expense (pharmaceuticals representatives are not poorly paid!). The problem is how to change – large field sales forces carry an awful lot of inertia (see below under 'watching the elephants dance').

THE HUNTER

The hunter approach to selling is most commonly found in fast-growing markets and is typically practised by new entrants. An aggressive sales force, usually young and driven by a well-designed commission package, is out to win clients, often from an incumbent competitor, in a short-term blitz. It can be very effective in the short term, and if there is a sudden growth opportunity in the market it may be the best option.

Chasing the sale in a growth market

When the laws regulating the provision of telephone services started to be relaxed across Europe in the late 20th century, companies like Mercury and MCI Worldcom made rapid inroads into the territory of established giants such as British Telecom and Belgacom. Customers were hunted with a ruthless energy that left the incumbents standing – and some big commissions were earned. (The success of the hunters was an excellent example of how customers can *snap* away from an existing but essentially monopolistic supplier, as described in Chapter 3.)

The downside of the hunter mode is seen in the poor level of customer retention, which is not very serious while business is booming but of grave concern when the market opportunity reaches a more mature stage. In the early years of the 21st century, the giants are fighting back – 'thousands of customers coming back every week' read the adverts – an intriguing mixture of candour and boastfulness.

There are all sorts of problems with the hunting mode, particularly if you are seeking to develop a key account strategy:

- It lives for the moment. Investment is of little consequence to a sales-person who is focused on this month's commission and may not plan to be on the team next year.
- It does not discriminate – a kill is a kill. Think of a real hunter, a lioness on the Serengeti Plain surveying the ever-moving herd of wildebeest. Does this lioness pick out the healthiest-looking specimen, the one with the most meat and the longest eating potential, or does it prey on the sick and the weak?
- It is fun – at least the successful hunter will regard it as such, and when compared to the plod and the slog of the farmer, who would want to change?

THE FARMER

This is the sales approach that seeks to develop the customer's potential over time. Investment is the name of the game – investing time and effort for a pay-off next year or beyond. Customer retention is paramount and this long-term view encourages, indeed necessitates, broad and deep contacts with the customer, nurtured in anticipation of a future beyond today's sale. We are describing KAM of course, but it is not as easy to operate as it might first appear. A number of things can work against the farmer's approach:

- short-term targets imposed from above;
- inappropriate commission or reward packages based on volume today;
- sales management that favours efficiency over effectiveness;
- the insistence that all customers are equal – you can't farm them all.

FROM HUNTER TO FARMER

The very nature of a sales force makes change difficult, mainly because it is made up of people who have emotions and are unpredictable. A big issue is the time taken to bring about change whether it is through training, new processes, or replacing those people. By the time the shift is completed, the circumstances that gave rise to the change will probably be quite different.

Watching the elephants dance

The pharmaceutical industry experiences this problem more than many – exacerbated by the scale of its sales teams, still in the hundreds – but it has found a solution. The use of outsourced sales teams provided by companies such as Quintiles has allowed the pharma companies to stay fast on their feet despite their size. Teams of hunters, perfect for the launch phase of a new drug, can be switched on almost overnight, and switched off when the campaign is over. Milk rounds can be managed with maximum efficiency and minimal effort, and even farmers can be trained and developed to take over from hunters, though this is perhaps the hardest challenge in an outsourced sales team.

If the farmer mode is the essence of KAM and this is what you seek but your current sales effort is either predominantly milk round or hunter, then you have a challenging journey ahead of you. The relationship model described in this chapter will serve as your route map.

The new journey plan

Most sales people, at some stage in their career, have had to draw up journey plans – where will you be on Thursday at 10 am? Have you got your regulation six calls in the day? Did you drive the most efficient route?

KAM is about managing a journey, but a very different kind of journey plan is required. This is a journey that proceeds from the first 1:1 contact through to a complex relationship based on trust and mutual interest. Perhaps the principal task of the key account manager is to plan this journey and manage the developing relationship.

As with any journey, knowing where you start from is always a good idea. Where you are going comes next. Add to this some good landmarks and milestones along the way and you have the basis for a successful trip. This is the aim of the KAM model – a means of charting your course, as illustrated in Figure 5.1.

Figure 5.1 *Key account relationship development model*
Adapted from a model developed by Millman, A F and Wilson, K J (1994)

THE KEY ACCOUNT RELATIONSHIP DEVELOPMENT MODEL

This model, first developed by Professor Tony Millman and Dr Kevin Wilson in 1994, was further researched and developed at Cranfield University School of Management by Professor Malcolm McDonald, Tony Millman and Beth Rogers. Their findings were published in a research report, *Key Account Management: Learning from supplier and customer perspectives* (1996).

The model describes the developing relationship between supplier and customer, from pre-KAM, through early and mid-KAM, on to partnership KAM and then synergistic KAM.

The following pages trace this development as both seller and buyer increase their 'strategic intent' for the relationship; that is to say, as each side sees more value gained from putting greater effort into the relationship. As it develops, that 'effort' can be detailed by two main factors. First, there are increasing points of contact between supplier and customer, from a simple 1:1 through to a more complex matrix or series of teams. Second, the nature of the relationship builds from one based on short-term 'transactions' – doing deals – to one of genuine 'collaboration' – working together towards joint objectives and aspirations.

Several points should be made clear about this model:

More contacts and greater collaboration

- Progress doesn't happen of its own accord – it needs management.
- Progress takes time – more likely years rather than months.
- Progress requires mutual intent from supplier and customer – this is not something that can be forced on customers (see Chapter 6, 'The ugly story').
- You don't have to proceed beyond the point that satisfies your, and the customer's, intentions – partnership KAM is only *better* than early KAM if the circumstances demand it and there is mutual gain.

Charting the course

Each stage sees the relationship marked by its own 'typical' characteristics. Begin by defining the nature of your current relationship, by identifying its characteristics, then target how you wish the relationship to develop, noting the characteristics that will have to change.

Each stage has its own strengths and weaknesses, for both supplier and customer, with attendant opportunities and warnings. Progress from stage to stage may require changing skills and capabilities. The key account manager must develop their own skills and those of their team as the relationship develops.

It may not be possible to proceed all the way along the line – the customer may call a halt at any point. Setting realistic targets will save you a lot of frustration and help you form more appropriate, and so stronger, links with your customer, at whatever level you reach.

The key account manager is charting a course and the rules of navigation are clear: have goals, look out for helpful signposts, take comfort in milestones passed and keep good track of your progress. This way, not only do you know where you are headed, but you will also recognize the scenery when you get there.

The following pages describe some of those signposts and milestones (Figures 5.2–5.6). At each stage, the characteristics described are likely, but by no means universal. They are described to help you establish the status of your current relationship.

A note on the diagrams

The labels used to denote functions and departments are of course just examples, there is no rule that says these are the people who should be involved. Nor is there any rule that says how many people should be involved. Diamond teams (see Figure 5.5) can have anywhere between three and thirty members.

Possible characteristics of the pre-KAM stage (Figure 5.2)

- Simple, one-to-one contact.
- Supplier presentations focus on their own issues and concerns.
- Response to customer enquiries is yes or no, based on assumed customer needs and supplier's current capabilities.
- The seller will be assessing volume potential.
- The customer will be seeking evidence of competence and competitiveness.
- The customer will judge competitiveness on price.
- The customer may require trials, perhaps at the supplier's cost.
- The buyer may act as 'gatekeeper', denying access to other contacts.

Keeping your eyes and ears open...

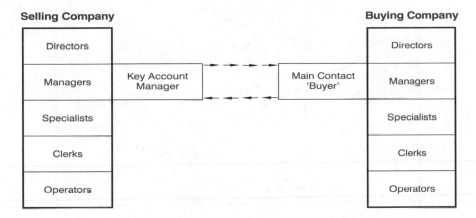

Figure 5.2 *Pre-KAM stage*
Adapted from McDonald, Millman and Rogers (1996)

Possible characteristics of the early KAM stage (Figure 5.3)

Control, but learn to let go...

- Principal contact between two people – salesperson and buyer.
- The relationship may be competitive, each seeking to gain advantage.
- At worst, the relationship may be confrontational.
- The buyer may see any attempt to gain access to other contacts as a threat to their position and power.
- Price discussions dominate – the buyer focuses on costs.
- The supplier focuses on increased volume.
- Suppliers are judged on unspecified performance criteria.
- The customer is still assessing alternative suppliers.
- Disputes can lead to long-term breaks in supply.

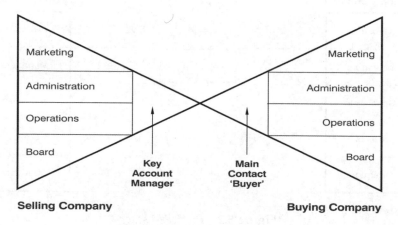

Figure 5.3 *Early KAM stage*
Adapted from McDonald, Millman and Rogers (1996)

Possible characteristics of the mid-KAM stage (Figure 5.4)

- Principal contacts start to facilitate other contacts through mutual desire to increase understanding of customer's processes and markets.
- Increase in time spent in meetings.
- Focus on reporting those meetings, action minutes, etc.
- Increased trust and openness developing.
- Links are informal and are still facilitated through the salesperson and buyer.
- It is perhaps at this stage that the greatest chance for 'mishaps' occurs – expect setbacks.
- This is a lot of work for both seller and buyer!

Hard work... but worth the effort in the long run

Figure 5.4 *Mid-KAM stage*
Adapted from McDonald, Millman and Rogers (1996)

Possible characteristics of the partnership KAM stage (Figure 5.5)

Enjoying the benefits of KAM

- Key supplier status is awarded.
- Relationships are based on trust.
- Information is shared.
- Access to people is facilitated.
- Pricing is stable.
- Customer gets new ideas first.
- Continuous improvement is expected.
- Clear 'vendor ratings' and 'performance measures'.
- Possible contractual arrangements.
- Value is sought through integrated business processes (see Part VI).
- Value is sought through focus on the customer's markets (see Part VI).
- 'Step-outs' are permitted.
- The key account manager's role is one of coordination and orchestration.
- The supplier's main contact, while perhaps still the commercial buyer, is now focused on developing the supplier's capabilities rather than challenging them.
- The supplier's total organization is focused on customer satisfaction through 'supply chain management'.

Figure 5.5 *Partnership KAM stage*
Adapted from McDonald, Millman and Rogers (1996)

Possible characteristics of the synergistic KAM stage (Figure 5.6)

- Joint R&D.
- Transparent costings and margins.
- Focus on innovation.
- Collaborative approach to customer's markets and end-users – actively working to develop those markets.
- Joint business plans.
- Joint marketing plans.
- Shared communications network.
- Shared training.
- Shared resources – including people.
- Exit barriers in place.
- Focus teams involve members of both companies, led by either supplier or customer.

Working as one... rare but not impossible

Figure 5.6 *Synergistic KAM stage*
Adapted from McDonald, Millman and Rogers (1996)

SOME PROS AND CONS OF EACH STAGE

Each stage has its own attractions and attendant challenges for both supplier and customer. It is important to understand these pros and cons if you are to progress successfully from one stage to the next.

Each new stage brings greater effort, greater commitment and increasing potential for mishap. To take your whole organization with you on this journey (and it is no use getting there on your own if the rest of your team is still standing at the station), you must be able to sell the benefits of moving forward, while assessing the obstacles and making plans to overcome them.

Pre-KAM

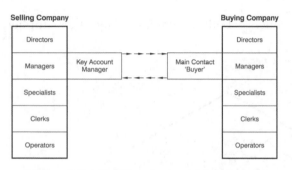

Figure 5.7 *Pre-Key Account Management*

Not many positives for this stage, but a good supplier will be on a voyage of exploration and discovery, asking questions and uncovering customer needs. Done well, with the focus on customer needs and not on satisfying their own requirements, this exploration can show the supplier in a very good light.

Reconnaissance is about listening – not telling

The downsides of exploration are only too obvious – the great unknown: sudden barriers to entry, surprising competitor strengths, obscure customer requirements and, hardest of all at first, unclear customer style and culture. Making the 'big presentation' too early, if it hits the wrong nerves, can spell the end before you really get started. Descending on the customer with a coachload of senior managers, samples, brochures and a 'flash' presentation can be the very last thing to do at this stage. Many businesses feel it necessary to do this at the early stages of their life – to get out there and spread the word about themselves. Resist the temptation; it rarely works.

Effort will be much better spent in researching the customer – seeking for clues as to what makes them tick, what they might need and what they might value. Of course, we are in classic 'chicken and egg' territory here. Without knowledge of the customer, how is it possible to assess their potential as a key account? If you cannot define them as a potential key account, then how do you justify the time and effort for research? To escape from this vicious circle you will need to recognize that, as well as research, there is a need for perseverance, gut feel and faith – not a bad definition of the start of many success stories, but be prepared for the ones that don't come off.

And be prepared for one more problem – the customer may regard the sales person as only a messenger, and the sales person's own colleagues may regard them as an irresponsible 'champion'! Nobody in their right mind will want to hang around at this stage too long!

Early KAM

This is probably the most typical sales relationship, the classic 'bow-tie', and it is a dangerous stage. It is all too easy, and apparently attractive, just to stay here. The salesperson is in full control with no distractions from badly informed colleagues – and gets all the praise for success! This is the stage that promises 'a place in the limelight' at the next

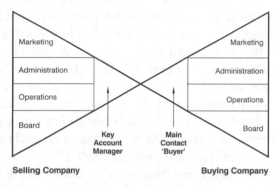

Figure 5.8 *Early Key Account Management*

sales conference. The buyer may also be happy with this state of affairs – they are secure, know all that goes on with the supplier and can keep their carefully guarded secrets.

The buyer as gatekeeper, matched with the salesperson as superstar, make for a relationship with a built-in resistance to change, but the downside of staying here includes:

Sure, this kind of relationship can be effective, but it can also be suboptimal

- Expertise on both sides is seriously underutilized.
- Seller and buyer are expected to be all-round experts – an unlikely scenario.
- Information flow is restricted as buyer and seller jockey for negotiating position.
- When information does flow, it is littered with 'Chinese whispers' as it is translated along the chain – expert to non-expert, to non-expert, to expert… and back.
- Projects and activities are held up by the sales/purchasing bottleneck.
- There is over-reliance on one relationship and if it breaks (buyers retire, sales people get promoted) the whole thing must start again – the future is permanently at risk.
- Sales people become 'kingpins' who cannot be moved on for fear of losing the business (rewrite that last point's comment – sales people retire, buyers get promoted…).

A major limitation of this kind of relationship is the way that it denies the supplier full access to the customer's internal processes and also to their market. A salesperson might have very little knowledge of what happens to their product once it is bought, still less how the customer operates in their own market. These are serious gaps if the supplier is to understand how it may best help the customer (Part V goes into much greater detail on this issue).

Sometimes denial of access will be deliberate. In the retail industry buyers often limit a supplier's access to contacts, and to valuable information. It is a matter of power and ownership of the market. In the past, major brands often dominated relationships through consumer knowledge and huge advertising budgets. Increasingly, the retailer's enhanced knowledge of consumer behaviour, through, for example, electronic point of sale and loyalty cards, is shifting the balance. Knowledge is undeniably power, and why should it be shared? (Purchasing organizations are becoming increasingly concerned with the leaking of valuable information to suppliers, with no tangible return – see Chapter 8.)

There are advantages to this kind of relationship – it is simple, relatively low cost and controllable – and if it gets what you want there may be no need to go beyond it. But take care: be sure your certainty is not just complacency.

Mid-KAM

This is the transition stage between the classic 'bow-tie' and the 'diamond' of the partnership KAM stage. It is a stage full of sensitivity and, if the supplier is wise, slow, measured steps forward.

Noting that the buyer may feel threatened by any increase in contacts

Figure 5.9 *Mid-Key Account Management*

'beyond his or her own control', the key account manager must ensure that new contacts are cleared with the buyer and will almost certainly have to be involved in putting the contacts together, attending the first meetings and perhaps further. Ideally, the buyer will also be involved in these meetings, but if not, their outcome must be reported to the buyer in full.

Hard work – but well worth the effort

Add to this a briefing-and-coaching role and we can see a potential overload of activities for the key account manager. Realizing the work involved, we should look again at the model of managing the future, introduced in Chapter 2, and consider the resources required. How many key accounts can an individual manager have responsibility for at this stage? Add to this the fact that the mid-KAM stage can go on for many months, perhaps even years, and we must think seriously about how many customers can be classified as KAs.

As the benefits of moving towards partnership KAM are unlikely to flow immediately, this mid-KAM stage could be seen by some as not worth the effort. The temptation to go back to the relative comforts of the 'bow-tie' is strong. Resist!

I cannot resist quoting a customer who was struggling to get past this stage.

They had plenty of their people working alongside the customer, but not in any coordinated way. The biggest frustration was that people with contacts were reluctant to go any further than achieving their own narrow objectives – they were not part of a team with bigger ambitions.

The key account manager told me that most of these people were scared to go further. One of them said, *'when I visit the customer I get in and out as quickly as possible, what if I was to meet someone important and they asked me something difficult?'*

Easy to laugh, or to be cynical about the capabilities of non sales professionals, but if you are to get to true diamond teams such fears must be thoroughly overcome

'But we might meet someone important...'

Partnership KAM

This is where the benefits should start to flow. With the proper deployment of expertise on both sides, with the more open and honest transfer of information and with the resultant improvement in cus-tomer understanding, the supplier has the potential to move tow-ards significant competitive advantage. By taking the right actions they may even secure key supplier status, with its attendant increase in long-term security.

If a major downside to the 'bow-tie' of early KAM was the denial of access to customers' internal processes and to their market, the main advantage of the 'diamond' relationship is in seeing those conduits of understanding opening up.

But watch out. As contacts proliferate, so does the speed of activity – and the risk of saying and doing the wrong things. People without experience of 'sales' will be put in front of customers, and might panic at the prospect. The key account manager's role changed through the mid-KAM stage from 'super salesperson' to 'super coach'. It must now move on to 'super coordinator'.

For many, this stage will be the ultimate goal, but arriving here is no cause for complacency...

Figure 5.10 *Partnership Key Account Management*

If it doesn't, then the potential for losing control is great, resulting in well-meaning, but misdirected, individuals charting their own quite separate courses. Without clarity of objectives and shared understanding of what the customer values, you could just be about to race down some blind alleys. Your very enthusiastic IT expert, working with their equally keen customer counterpart, might see this new metalled road as an opportunity to try some unaccustomed speed. Without a *Highway Code*, accidents can happen…

The tale of the CEO

The CEO of a multinational manufacturer was visiting one of their business unit's distributors – a key account customer. The business unit sold clear plastic sheeting, used, among other things, to build all-round-viewing squash courts. The distributor suggested that having such a squash court on their premises would be a great sales aid, much better than the sales brochures. The CEO readily agreed – a free 'sample' would be installed. It was certainly an aid, but unfortunately the CEO had not been aware of two facts.

First, he didn't know that the cost ran into tens of thousands of pounds. Second, and in a sense worse, he didn't know that the distributor had been asking that selfsame question for years, and had been given the selfsame answer – 'Sure, when you pay your bills on time, and stock our new ranges, and employ two new sales reps, and…'.

So, whose fault was this? Well of course the CEO should have known better, but the key account manager is equally, if not more, responsible. They should have briefed the CEO. Key account managers are responsible for all communications, transactions and activities between supplier and customer. Sure, it's not easy briefing the boss, but nobody said KAM was easy!

The three golden rules of partnering

Achieving this partnership stage will perhaps be the hardest part of the whole journey. Plenty of things stand in your way but the benefits are so significant that it deserves all the effort. There are three golden rules, which when remembered and observed at all times will speed your way towards genuine partnership:

- work with a long-term perspective;
- seek out the 'win–win' solutions;
- recognize that trust is more important than money.

None of these rules is easy to adhere to if short-term gains are there to tempt you. Only you can take the decision as to which is most important: that short-term gain or the long-term security and prosperity; or perhaps it is the realistic achievement versus the jam tomorrow dream?

Consider the supplier that found a solution to one of its key accounts' bigger problems – a technical problem in its manufacturing process. This wasn't the cause for celebration that you might imagine because the solution didn't involve the customer buying the supplier's product, it was a tweak that the customer could make in its own manufacturing process and then carry on using a competitor's material. The problem for the supplier was that it was trying to displace the competitor, not lock them in further.

So what does the supplier do: tell them or withhold the answer? The former suggests an intention to partner, but is it foolhardy? Not telling leaves the awful prospect of being found out ('you knew but you didn't tell us'), but also leaves a door open to the sale. The decision can only be made with reference to timescale: will today's loss result in tomorrow's gain?

Heads you win, tails I lose?

Don't sales people 'sell' any more then?

Many companies have made hugely successful use of the diamond model, transforming the role of their sales professionals from lone hunters to business managers and team leaders.

There are of course degrees of application between these two positions, and Figure 5.11 illustrates a very typical mid point where the key account manager continues fully with their previous role as the prime sales contact, but now in a very different environment.

Of course, the diamond model of whatever variation doesn't propose that the sales person ceases to have a significant level of customer contact – or 'touch time' as many like to call it – and neither do they stop selling. What changes is the fact that they play their selling role in new circumstances, as a part of a team sell. The demands on them are enormous. On the one hand they must promote their colleagues, and avoid stealing the limelight. On the other hand their own personal selling skills must be raised to new heights – they must now become an example of sales excellence for the rest.

Figure 5.11 *Partnership Key Account Management – a variation on a theme*
Adapted by Peter Chiu of Huntsman Taiwan, from McDonald, Millman and Rogers (1996)

Must Diamond Teams always be multi-functional?

This particular diamond example suggests a multi function approach, but it is also possible that a diamond team might be made up of sales people, perhaps representing different regions or territories, or perhaps different business units, or responsible for different product lines.

In the pharmaceutical industry it is likely that more benefit will be gained from forming Diamond Teams of different sales professionals, each responsible for different therapy areas, and directing them against specific customers, such as a hospital, than would be gained by a classic multi-functional approach as shown here.

As ever, these tools and models are used to stimulate thought, not to impose a straightjacket – remember rule number one – you make the rules.

Synergistic KAM

The experience gained at the partnership stage – coordinating the team-sell, coaching the team on their customer interface roles and learning to work within the customers' values and culture – will stand you in good stead for moving to synergistic KAM. But take care. The potential problem at this stage lies in trying to get there too quickly. It can be tempting to force the pace, before either side is ready for the atypical requirements of working in this way. The result could be the breakdown of a relationship, through confusion, and, after all the effort and good work of the partnership KAM stage, that would be a tragedy.

Figure 5.12 *Synergistic Key Account Management*

Herein lies another problem: if it is managed well, the partnership stage will be seen as successful for both supplier and customer. It will have been a novel experience for most, and the idea of changing to something even *more* unusual will raise many barriers. 'If it ain't broke, don't fix it.' You will hear this, and similar, a hundred times as you try to move both sides of the relationship on, but it will be worth the perseverance. The benefits are enormous – a truly symbiotic relationship where values are shared and so needs are more easily identified and met. The security of this relationship is enormous; a competitor will find it very difficult to break into this account.

On the other side, the supplier's commitment will be almost total by this stage, so be certain that this really is an account worth the effort – withdrawal will be difficult, embarrassing and, perhaps, terminal.

One possible characteristic of this stage is the collaborative focus on developing the customer's markets. The supplier will need to ensure that they have the necessary expertise to play their part in this activity, or it will soon be seen to be a hollow offer.

This stage requires strong but subtle management, particularly in setting up the teams. These self-managing focus teams must not be allowed to develop into island activities, divorced from each other and heading in ever-divergent directions. But the solution is not heavy-handed supervision, which would defeat the whole purpose of devolving control and empowering the team. The way forward must be through a commitment by all members, supplier and customer, to the joint goals, roles, objectives and expectations of the relationship.

It is usually best that the focus teams are not functionally based – that would encourage the island or 'silo' mentality that you have taken so long to escape from on this journey. They should be based around projects, each of which has clear customer value goals and performance measures. They must exist for their goals, not for themselves. The measure of success for many will be their winding up on completion of their task – harder than it sounds. Resist the temptation to keep a good thing going beyond its useful life.

There is space for at least one team not based on a finite project: a 'long-term vision' team, a strategy team, whatever it might be called, a team focused on managing the future.

True synergy will often take on a formal or legal nature ...

An excellent example of such a relationship involves a supplier to the photographic film industry. They supplied materials that always had a residue after use, and this residue was hard to dispose of cleanly and safely. This was a problem to both sides. The answer, after many years of true partnering, was the setting up of a new entity, a joint venture between supplier and customer, devoted to finding positive uses for this residue material. It was only the joint effort that had the necessary energy, resource and will to uncover positive applications, rather than merely following safe waste-disposal procedures. An excellent example, because not only was the new venture a success, but it also represented something greater than the two halves – true synergy.

One feature of a synergistic relationship will be the openness of both organizations to each other. This may go as far as allowing the customer access to your own operational processes – letting them interrogate your inventory, letting them place orders directly with production, and other such terrifying ideas... If these thoughts are indeed terrifying, then it suggests you are probably not ready for synergistic relationships.

SOME THINGS TO WATCH OUT FOR

This is a journey and, with the right customer for your companion, it is one worth making. But remember, it is a journey of exploration and discovery; expect the unexpected.

All truly worthwhile activities are accompanied by difficulties, which must be pursued and overcome with patience and resolve. The risks may be high, but not desperate, the obstacles large, but not insurmountable. The possible disasters seen at the outset seem many, but they are not certain and, by thoughtful planning, the majority can be prevented. And, if the journey is made for good reason, you can expect the support of your team, your management *and* your customer.

The hardest part of the journey will almost certainly be the transition from 'bow-tie' to 'diamond'. Working through the transitional mid-KAM stage can be very hard work indeed. At times, it will seem more effort than it is worth, to both sides. This will call for all the patience, understanding and resolve you can muster. It will call on every skill and tool within your grasp, and some that are beyond your reach. At this point, you will need friends and allies. This, let it be understood very clearly, is not a task for loners, so:

- Don't expect your journey to be one way; there will be 'U' turns and side alleys.
- Remember that the strategic intent must be mutual and, even then, don't expect the customer to make it easy for you. You will have to lead a lot of the way, and while stamina and persistence will be two valuable assets, so will subtlety and finesse. You will know when you are getting there, when the customer starts to pull.
- Remember, the buyer has a lot of power when they are the only point of contact. Your efforts to develop broader contacts might be for the good of their company, but they might not see it as good for them! You are about to threaten their control.
- To sell, or not to sell? If the customer sees your 'selling' activity as a pushy concern for satisfying your own needs, don't be surprised if you come up against obstacles. If they perceive it as seeking solutions to their problems, the doors will start to open.
- Some customers will demand that the key account manager should not be a 'sales person' at all, but a business manager and a relationship manager.
- Some customers might not like being called 'accounts' – so this is a word for internal use, not your business card (in the end, you can call them whatever makes them feel good!).
- Don't let your organization loose on theirs with no direction and no control – chaos can be the only outcome, quickly followed by a rapid raising of the customer's drawbridge.
- Don't allow the commercially 'innocent' members of your team to be taken for a ride by the customer – brief them first and, above all, train them. This goes for everyone, including the boss (actually, especially the boss).
- Don't describe this journey, internally, as an initiative – many companies have had 'initiative overload' and your own team will steer clear of this latest 'seven-day wonder'.
- One sure 'killer' of progress, from early to mid- to partnership KAM, is the unrealistic tightening of travel budgets – strong relationships require personal contact.
- Be careful how you present your intentions to the customer: being told that you wish to be more 'intimate' may concern them, confuse them, or worse!
- Take care if you are the first to use the word 'partnership'. Try to hear it on the customer's lips first.
- Perhaps your customer will use 'partnership' as a trap. 'Let's work in partnership,' they say, meaning, 'You tell us your cost breakdowns, then we'll take you to the cleaners.'

The tale of the pig and the chicken

Is this last point unduly cynical? Perhaps you should be a little wary until you are sure?

I am reminded of the story of the pig and the chicken that decide to go into partnership together – it was the chicken's idea. They decide to go into the catering business, specializing in traditional English breakfasts. At their first business meeting, the chicken explains its ideas.

'Tell you what,' it clucks, 'why don't I supply the eggs and you supply the bacon ...'

The moral of the tale? If you don't mean it, and they don't mean it, then stick to old-fashioned selling – the early KAM model is fine for relationships that don't aim to progress beyond the transactional.

Making diamond teams work

This challenge will be discussed at various points throughout the rest of this book – it is after all perhaps the biggest of them all.

For now, there are two things that I can suggest as almost mandatory actions to ensure that diamond teams work well and avoid the pitfalls that are just waiting out there for the unwary – a Contact Matrix and clear GROWs.

The Contact Matrix is discussed in full in Chapter 24. It is not a complicated tool, simply a chart that lays out all the points of contact between supplier and customer – who is responsible for seeing who.

GROWs, also described in Chapter 24, are a little more involved. GROW is an acronym:

- G – Goal
- R – Role
- O – Obligation
- W – Work Plan

Each point of contact in the matrix should have a set of GROWs to express its purpose.

These two simple tools (and keep them simple, please!) will help you to direct and monitor and control the activities of the key account team.

The diamond team – *core and full*

How big should a diamond team be? The answer depends of course on the specific circumstances, but there is also a more general answer. A team of anything more than six people is going to start hitting problems of getting together, communication, and all the rest. Yet there may be more than six people involved with the customer – so what to do?

A good solution is to identify what we might call the _core team_, the few people, probably three or four, who meet and discuss the customer very frequently, and are responsible for the key interactions. They are rather like a steering team. Around them is the full team, as many as required, and a changing group as projects come and go.

The core team should aim to meet regularly, and should be copied on all significant developments. The full team might only meet once or twice a year, and might be copied on developments on a 'need to know' basis.

AVOIDING FRUSTRATION

It cannot be said too often that a developing relationship requires mutual intent. The result of any imbalance in that intent will be frustration, sometimes minor but sometimes resulting in the termination of the relationship. The relationship zones are depicted in Figure 5.13.

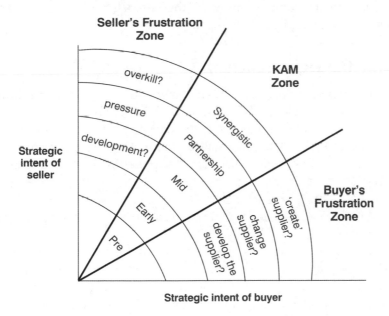

Figure 5.13 _Buyer–seller relationship zones_
Adapted from a model developed by Millman, A F and Wilson, K J (1994)

Seller's frustration zone

If the supplier's intent outpaces the buyer's then the attempt to involve the KA team in front of the customer is not likely to result in any change in the nature of the relationship – it does not progress from transactional to collaborative and the contacts are rejected.

At best, the supplier is frustrated. Worse, the supplier is wasting the customer's time. Worse still, the key account manager is wasting their own company's resources, and this is hugely damaging to the profitability of that customer. Worst of all, the supplier's frustration may lead to undue pressure on the customer, with serious, potentially terminal, consequences.

If the supplier *is* ahead of the customer in their strategic intent (and this, of course, will very often be the case) then develop a KA team by all means, but don't foist it on the customer – prepare the ground so that when strategic intents *do* match, the team is ready.

Buyer's frustration zone

If the supplier's intent lags behind the buyer's then the customer may have to take steps to develop the supplier. If they still lag behind, they will soon be seeking a new supplier.

Getting the right match

It would be easy to suppose that the customer will be most demanding at the early stages of the relationship, a sort of 'show us what you're made of' phase. Easy but quite wrong! While the deeper relationship found in the partnership or synergistic stage will be more stable, it will also be more demanding. The expectations placed on a supplier increase with each stage of the relationship:

- At the *early* KAM stage, the main expectation is that the supplier should be proficient.
- Entry into the *mid*-KAM stage suggests that the customer is looking for more; they now expect the supplier to be a problem solver.
- By the time the *partnership* KAM stage has emerged, the customer's expectations of the supplier will have risen to just that – a genuine business partner.

Viewed in this light, it becomes clear that a supplier should understand where the customer sees the relationship. Misunderstandings can lead to more than just frustrations, they can be terminal. I have heard a customer say that a supplier was fired because the supplier thought that being proficient was enough. The customer was looking for something beyond the *early* KAM stage and the supplier didn't read the signs or recognize the frustrations. I have also heard a customer say that a supplier was fired because they had ideas well beyond their station. We might even go so far as to say that a mismatch of perceptions about where the relationship lies is more damaging, even when the relationship is quite advanced, than a relationship that bumbles along at an elementary level but both sides can see it for what it is. It is well worth monitoring the joint perception of the relationship to ensure that these damaging mismatches don't occur.

AN UPDATE TO THE KAM PROCESS

Chapter 4 suggested a KAM process: a series of activities, not necessarily linear, shown in Figure 4.1.

At each stage of the relationship described in this chapter, these activities will be pursued, each in more depth and with greater accuracy, efficiency and success as the relationship develops. The process builds on itself and thus the relationship advances. Rather than a flat circular process, it can now be seen as a spiral working upwards, with the activities being carried out at ever higher planes.

Of course, sometimes the spiral will work downwards and steps previously covered, that might appear rather mundane from your until-recently high vantage point, will have to be repeated. There is little place for false pride in KAM.

6

The good, the bad, the sad and the ugly

This chapter shares five examples of real experience: two good, one bad, one sad and one ugly. They are all genuine cases, but for reasons that I hope are obvious some details have been changed.

It is usually easier to come up with bad, sad and ugly stories than it is to come up with good stories. This is not because there are more failures than successes, but because we can usually learn more from the failures. Good stories can sometimes suffer the problem of their context – it worked, but only in *those* circumstances people will say. Anyway, I have gone for a total of two positive stories and three negative.

The good are very good, and will be kept till last. The other examples are here as warnings of the potential downsides of KAM at its various stages.

The bad is bad because KAM was abandoned on a wave of 'we've got the best product, so who needs customer intimacy?' It demonstrates the limitations of early KAM, even when your story seems good.

The sad is sad because partnership KAM was in place and the supplier was trying hard to work with, and through, its customer. Yet, still things can go wrong.

The ugly is worse than the bad and the sad put together – it is about KAM gone wrong through misapplication, and it nearly pulled the business apart.

THE BAD STORY

A while back, the international community came together to ban a particularly damaging product, which had been identified as being a major contributor to global warming – CFCs.

Surprisingly, this was particularly good news to one manufacturer of that product, or perhaps not so surprisingly – they had been looking ahead and had developed an alternative product, one that didn't have the same bad effects. Not only that but, for now at least, they were just about the only one with such an alternative.

The old product had been used in a range of applications, from refrigerators to air conditioning and aerosol sprays. The manufacturer had simple, but good, relationships with their customers in these diverse markets – the 'bow-tie' of early KAM was the norm.

Based on their current sales of the old, soon to be banned product, plus a margin of growth for their technical brilliance and for their new competitive advantage, the supplier made plans for manufacture of the new 'wonder' product – the company built a large, brand new plant.

What they didn't do, at least no more than usual, was talk to their customers. Why should they? After all, the old product was banned, the company had a replacement and customers would surely beat a path to their door. All the suppliers needed to do was to ask their existing contacts, the buyers, how much of the old they bought, theirs and their competitors', and use this as a forecast for the new – simple.

Unfortunately, it wasn't and, instead of beating a path to the manufacturer's door, the customers 'snapped'. They resented the 'arrogance' of the supplier and they resented the new prices that were to be charged. They actively sought alternatives. Not alternative suppliers of the new product, there were none, but alternative solutions altogether. The supplier had forgotten Michael Porter's model (see Chapter 3).

The aerosol market accounted for half of the manufacturer's sales projections. How many aerosols with clever propellant gases, banned or otherwise, do you see nowadays? It's all roll-ons or pump-action sprays. Admittedly, they are often inferior in performance to the old aerosols, with a tendency to dribble down the elbow, but they *are* the choice of the market.

Moral of the story? A product, no matter how good, will risk failure if the supplier does not talk and act *with* the channels to market. This manufacturer chose to go it alone, forcing something into the chain that some parts did not want, and blocked successfully. They had no access to the customers' customers and the changes going on there – a typical limitation of early KAM. KAM means working with, *and through*, your customers, understanding *their* aspirations, in *their* markets, not presenting them with a *fait accompli*.

What happens when you ignore 'snails' and 'chains'…

Chapter 2 argued the need, when managing the future, for a balance between objectives, opportunity and resources. This story is an example of imbalance and its consequences. The objectives (at least in terms of scale) were not in line with the opportunity – seen as carved in stone. But why? Wasn't this a company that looked ahead? Sure, but over-confidence in technology acted as a blind to enquiry in the market. Little or no attempt was made to speak with those customers whose job was to consider even bigger change.

THE SAD STORY

Partnership is great, but it should never lead to complacency

A very capable supplier of ink had an excellent partnership KAM relationship with its number one customer, a manufacturer of computer printers. So good was the relationship that the supplier was happy for the customer to set their own research and development targets and timetable. The two R&D functions would meet, discuss the customer's needs and a project would spring into action. On this occasion, the project was the search for 'dry fastness' – something in the ink that would make it dry faster on the page. If they succeeded, the supplier would gain significant competitive advantage.

The project proceeded on target, and time, money and energy was poured in. After 18 months' work, the project was nearly complete. Then the customer rang to say it was all off. To the supplier's great distress, it transpired that a paper manufacturer had approached the customer with a new type of paper, one that would help ordinary ink to dry faster.

The story gets worse, and sadder. Not only was the project a waste, but if ordinary ink was OK then so was anyone's. Worse still, this particular paper was good with much cheaper inks, inks that had been regarded as third-rate products up until then. So, not only did the project fold, but also the supplier saw their existing business decline. And the customer was working on a mechanical (printer) solution to the same problem…

Moral of the story? Asking the customer is great. Doing what they tell you is great. Managing successful projects is great. But, if you are really to help the customer, you have to understand the dynamics of the market in which they operate. As we have seen, KAM must go beyond the 'buyer/seller' interface; it must extend into an understanding of the customer's market and, indeed, their total business – and that includes their other suppliers.

There is another lesson to be learnt here. Having good 1:1 relationships between functions is not the end of the story. These relationships have to be coordinated as a whole; they mustn't become individual 'bow-ties' of their own. In this story, the R&D 'bow-tie' drove the business.

Of course, what the printer manufacturer *really* wanted when they asked for 'dry fastness' was smudgeless printing. They chose to describe this as one particular product feature in the ink and their racehorse of a supplier (blinkers applied) went at the challenge. They very nearly finished the course, only to discover, nearing the winning post, that the race had changed.

With copious quantities of 20/20 hindsight, remember the first rule of selling: people buy benefits, not features. Everyone in sales knows that, but a whole KA team managed to miss the point on this occasion. R&D became locked into a race for a particular feature; its own problem. KA teams must focus on the customers' problems, not their own. Whichever the route to smudgeless printing – paper, printer or ink – a broader consideration of solutions would have improved the ink supplier's chances of working on the appropriate ink.

After the event, it became clear that there had been some important points of contact with the customer missing. There were strong R&D links with the customer's ink development people, as we have seen, but none with the customer's sales and marketing departments and not enough with their broader new product development team. Links there might just have highlighted the alternative routes to meeting the customer's aspirations – smudgeless printing.

THE UGLY STORY

The ugly story, and the worst by my reckoning, is about the supplier that nearly destroyed themselves through excessive KAM zeal.

As a manufacturer of a fast-selling consumer product, in a very mature market, the company saw their escape from future decline in KAM through seeking competitive advantage in the intimacy of the relationship with their retail customers. An admirable enough objective, but one that was about to turn the business's resources upside down.

Nine key account managers were appointed, for 15 KAs, and were given new authority to act. Their first act was to gather about them key account teams, or KATs, representing the company's functions. *Everyone* was represented. There were teams for each of the company's 15 KAs. So large were these teams, and so many the meetings, that a wing of the head office was refurbished as a suite of 'KAT rooms'. This was to be a high-profile 'initiative'.

Overkill and oversight – two sins to avoid

Now the fun began. Teams met, and met, and met. Interminable meetings, badly run, with key account managers imposing their views on team members from functions they but poorly understood.

The more ambitious teams went out to meet the customer at the earliest opportunity and seasoned buyers were pleased of the chance to lecture new faces on past failures. The teams came back eager to get to work on a huge range of corrective projects.

But this was KAM out of control, and sin was committed after sin:

- Teams did not need representatives from *every* function. Many were confused and then frustrated by the whole affair. The functions began to resent the whole idea.
- Service actually suffered as people met, rather than served.
- Keen, but commercially naive people were put in front of customers who saw them coming and got commitments to all sorts of promises, most of which could not be kept.
- In many cases the customers did not even want this kind of attention. Soon, tired of so many visits, meetings and wordy reports, the supplier was banned from further contacts, even those that might have been to mutual advantage.
- Like the Chinese Cultural Revolution, a thousand flowers were encouraged to bloom. Most were badly conceived projects with little or no real customer commitment, doomed to expensive failure.
- Dominant egos were allowed to run riot and excess followed excess.
- Before long, the words 'key account' brought a bad taste to the mouth and those things that *should* have been done were ignored under an excuse of world-weary cynicism.

In the end, KAMs were seen to fail. They retreated back into a shell of 1:1 contacts, the whole edifice came tumbling down and the KAT rooms were turned over to other use.

Moral of the story? KAM is not a 'sales initiative', nor a reckless revolution. It is a serious, cross-functional management process with disciplined management from the top. It takes planning, with clear objectives and outcomes, and a proper balance of resources against the market opportunity.

More than this, advancing beyond the 'bow-tie' of early KAM is not a one-sided exercise. The customer must wish to make the journey as well. Often, an over-enthusiastic supplier will try to force the pace and, rather than finding the relationship developing as planned, they find themselves in the frustration zone referred to in Chapter 5 and illustrated again in Figure 6.1.

The frustration may start as the supplier's own frustration, but when it is transformed into inappropriate pressure it soon becomes the customer's, with all the ensuing problems – an ugly story indeed.

THE GOOD STORY

Diamond Teams and foresight …

When telling stories such as the sad bad and ugly ones, it can seem that this is all about hindsight. This might blind us to one of the essential strengths of diamond teams – they give us foresight. Diamond teams, worked properly,

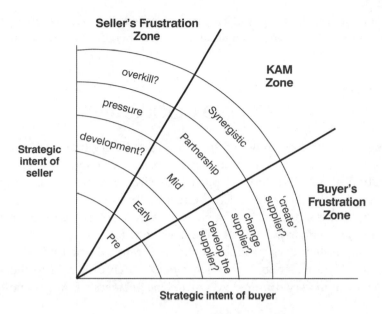

Figure 6.1 *Buyer–seller relationship zones*
Adapted from a model developed by Millman, A F and Wilson, K J (1994)

provide intelligence and so a greater ability to read the future. The bad and the sad stories were about the lack of such foresight and so the apparent paucity of choices.

Lots of choice can be a problem, of course – what to do? But which would you rather – working in the dark?

A customer decided to ask its supplier for consignment stock as it had grown tired of depending on that suppliers less than scintillating OTIF (on time in full) performance. It actually wanted better OTIF and consignment stock to the buyer to be the easiest way to get it.

That could have been it, and in a bow tie relationship almost certainly would have been, but this supplier had a Diamond relationship and those wider contacts began to alert the team to some pending problems. First of all, there was no physical room for such a consignment stock. Then it became clear that the client was shifting its production from a small number of standard lines to a far more bespoke offer that would require a wider range of raw materials often in small or hard to forecast quantities. Added to this, there was a long term plan to spin off much of the manufacturing activity to satellites.

Here then was the future prospect of saying yes – three or four separate consignment stocks of hard to forecast and infrequently used materials.

With that in mind the supplier suggested an alternative. Why not use our contacts with manufacturing and logistics and sales and marketing to help you make better planning and forecasting schedules? The result was the improved OTIF the buyer wanted, and a raft of benefits for the supplier in terms of knowledge.

THE SECOND GOOD STORY

Most investments depend on a little luck. KAM is about making your own luck

We should end these examples with a second good story, one of success. This is not put forward as a role model, or template for action. This particular application of KAM suited the particular circumstances. It is simply a demonstration that disciplined KAM effort can pay dividends.

The supplier is in the packaging business and supplies the food industry. Being a large company, they are organized into four business units, each specializing in their own product: corrugated card, plastic film, glass, and metal cans. Here was one of their problems – each unit sold to the same customers, but in very different volumes. One business's KA was another's nuisance!

The customers saw them as four different businesses, with no strengths carried over from one to another. The result was a patchwork quilt of relationships and customers frustrated by having to deal with so many different people and standards of service.

The example in this story was one of the early successes, at the early stages of a KAM implementation strategy, which helped raise the supplier to a new level of competitive advantage.

One major customer bought cans from the supplier, but nothing else. They were delighted with their supplier, but thought nothing of the other products on offer from the company. Glass, card and film were purchased from competitors.

The customer had a problem, not with the supplier, but with their packing line in general. Hundreds of thousands of cans and bottles were filled each day and yet the whole line could come to a halt, when it came to packing, for shortage of boxes or film at moments of peak volume. It was a matter of forecasting, space on the line for materials and lead times with suppliers.

The key account manager for the can supplier saw the problem, quite by chance when visiting the line, and a solution occurred to her. The manufacturer was privy to the best forecasts available from the customer – as a key supplier this was quite normal. If they could use that information with their sister businesses, perhaps a better flow of materials (bottles, card and film, as well as cans) might ensue.

Moreover, if they could make coordinated deliveries of *all* materials, the customer's goods inward bays would be saved the chaos of peak periods and the materials would find their way to the line more speedily.

At the end of a long story, all of this was achieved – shared forecasts and coordinated deliveries from all four businesses. Deliveries were made in 'just in time' returnable 'pods' that contained the right mix of all four materials. The crowning glory of the idea was the redesign of the customer's packaging area, using these 'pods' as the basic building blocks.

The result was the attainment of key supplier status for *all* packaging materials, plus a significant increase in total business.

Great stuff, but how did it happen? Well, first of all, not in anything like the time this description might have suggested. This was a three-year project.

The toughest challenge was getting the four supplying businesses to work in unison, or even think of working in unison. The breakthrough, one year into the project, was getting an agreement that this was a key account for each of the businesses, despite the very different histories of supply. It took support from the top, it took the appointment of a cross-business account manager, and it took a lot of communicating and educating.

This got the project to the halfway point, a semi-committed supplier with the semblance of a solution. Now came the task of engaging the customer. The supplier, it should be remembered, was only seen as a supplier of cans; the can buyer had no responsibility for other materials and no great interest in the workings of their own production line. Their job was to get cans, and they did it well, within those narrow confines.

Contacts had to be established with those that used the product, the people on the line, but slowly – the buyer was a conservative type and didn't take kindly to people going behind his back. Then came a piece of luck for the supplier – the line was stopped for half a day due to shortages of the right materials. People were suddenly open to suggestions and the gates began to open. Six months of patient meetings finally paid off and supply from all four units began on a coordinated basis. Nearly another year had to pass before the supplier was trusted to get involved in redesigning the packaging area; after all, they were a supplier, not an expert in manufacturing operations – but they were finally involved.

Moral of the story? It was all down to a lucky break? Not at all. The supplier made their own luck – they were ready for this lucky break – and were able to turn an opportunity to their advantage. Perhaps only one or two years previously, it would not even have been seen as an opportunity, but times had changed and, from a senior level down, the notion of KAM was being disseminated.

Slowly but surely the company's resources were realigned to meet an opportunity. Once the objective of company-wide KAM was accepted, it was only a matter of time before the successes began to roll.

The intentions were clear, but how was it actually carried out? How do such objectives get translated, in practice, at the operational level? Parts IV and V of this book will look at this in greater depth.

7

KAM profitability

In Chapter 4, we considered some 'sanity checks'. These were questions asked to make sure that our objectives were in line with the real world – the market opportunity and our business resources.

It is time that we added one last, most important, 'sanity check': will KAM be profitable? Is it reasonable to expect that KAM will be more profitable than traditional selling? We are on potentially dangerous ground here, for two reasons.

First, we might be considering a KAM strategy as a means to survival. To compare levels of profitability with 'what used to be' may be very misleading. What was is gone, and KAM is now a necessity. Without it, we die.

Second, we might consider that KAM offers a more efficient use of resources (and it almost certainly does), but does this inevitably lead to increased profits? Consider an analogy.

THE TALE OF THE NATIONAL HEALTH SERVICE

In the UK in the 1940s, the creation of the NHS was heralded not only as a mark of a new height of civilization, but also as a route to greater efficiency. The planners sincerely believed that the NHS would result in steadily decreasing costs of healthcare. Why? Because the NHS would improve the health of the nation – the populace would therefore require less healthcare.

We know how things turned out in practice – people expected ever-more sophisticated treatments for an apparently ever-growing range of ailments. It was almost as if the NHS invented a whole new range of diseases!

What is the analogy with KAM? It is possible that the diamond relationship, while improving the efficiency of relationships, will in itself uncover a whole new range of needs and actions required. This is almost certainly 'a good thing' in as far as it cements the relationship between supplier and customer; just as the NHS _did_ improve the health of the nation. But does it increase costs and reduce profitability?

WILL KAM BE PROFITABLE?

KAM can, of course be profitable, provided that the following points are kept in mind:

- The costs of KAM _must_ be understood and measured.
- Individual customer profitability _must_ be measured, based on the above.
- Throwing resources at the customer inappropriate to the buyer's strategic intent (see Chapter 6, The ugly story) is a sure way to reduce customer profitability.

We need to consider this in the context of four 'almost truths' (that is to say, they are very nearly always so):

Four 'almost truths' of customer profitability

1. The cost of winning new customers, even in a high-growth environment, is almost always higher than you think – retaining customers is often a more profitable activity.
2. A business's largest customers, by volume, are not necessarily its most profitable.
3. In the context of many purchasing functions' 'supplier reduction programmes', the value of retaining existing customers is higher than ever.
4. Growth with retained customers offers increased profits over time.

What all this implies is the relative value of retaining customers, smaller as well as larger, over time. KAM is as much about this as it is about the more 'macho' drive to win big new customers.

It might be helpful to start considering what we might call the 'lifetime value' of customers – a concept that, unfortunately, rarely extends to the way in which sales people are measured. In a KAM environment, perhaps it should.

The 'diamond relationship' or 'partnership KAM' almost certainly represents an increase in resources committed to the customer but, most importantly, it almost certainly increases your chances of retaining that customer.

Even where the objectives of KAM are to secure growth through new entry, the importance of customer retention remains. The alternative to this notion is permanently to chase new customers in order to replace those lost – an expensive activity even in a growth environment and, in a mature market, an almost suicidal approach.

Why customer retention?

Which is worth more to you – the customer kept...

Finding competitive advantage, or gaining key supplier status, is about security in a world where there is less security almost by the hour. A number of trends conspire to make the seller's life ever-more fraught:

- The strengthening of buying power resulting from customer amalgamation.
- The strengthening of competitors through supplier amalgamation.
- The stated aim of many purchasers to reduce their numbers of suppliers.

Reducing the number of suppliers, sometimes referred to as *supply base rationalization*, has become something of a fad. In pursuit of greater efficiencies, reduced transactional costs, smaller inventories, more control, true alliances and extra leverage on suppliers, many purchasing organizations have stated targets for reducing supplier numbers.

For whatever reasons it is practised – sometimes in pursuit of genuine efficiencies, sometimes as a cynical game of setting supplier against supplier – supply base rationalization means that *customer retention* has become a vital sales objective. In a mature market it becomes vital to existence and even in growth markets it can be every bit as important as winning new customers – particularly on the bottom line.

It is often argued that retaining a customer is more valuable, or at least more profitable, than winning a new one. Certainly it is less costly in time and effort. But profit? How can this be?

The cost of winning new customers

The first point to recognize is that there are costs involved when winning new customers.

There are the more obvious costs – the initial discounts given for trial and first orders and the customer-imposed 'start-up costs'. In some markets, suppliers have to 'buy their way in'. This is particularly true, for instance, in selling to the retail industry in the United States, where suppliers are very often obliged not only to offer excellent terms, but also to purchase their space on the shop floor and to purchase any stock of the supplier they may be replacing. Some US suppliers refer to this, rather euphemistically, as *selling a customer*. Perhaps a more honest phrase would be *buying a customer*.

The story does not end here. Perhaps when a company changes its supplier, it bears a cost in down time or new specifications and processes. Suppliers of pigments and dyes to the printing industry, or suppliers of paint to the automotive industry, will be well aware of such costs to customers – and will often expect to bear some or all of them. Sometimes such costs are 'hidden' from view, expressed as prices guaranteed for a long period, or as extended credit, but they remain very real costs to be taken into account.

... or the customer won?

PPG sells paint for repairing damaged cars and needs to offer the ability to match any colour, anywhere, any time – a massive undertaking requiring great skills of colour matching and reproducibility. Any supplier to PPG wishing to replace, let's say, an existing supplier of a particular pigment has to be aware that their product will be used in perhaps thousands of recipes for individual colours – recipes that have been got 'just right' with the current supplier. The tasks of testing and changing formulations can be enormous, perhaps too big for the customer to even contemplate, at least without significant help from the new supplier. All of this will cost time and money, borne by both customer and supplier.

There is more. When you win a new customer, do you factor in the costs of people's time, the extra travel, the cost of presentations, meetings and entertainment? An advertising agency can sometimes spend its first year's anticipated profits in pitching to a new client. In addition, if you are a manufacturer, you must keep higher stock levels to service new customers, and there will be an increase in debtors, especially if you offer extended credit as a carrot.

Do you also factor in the not so obvious cost of devoting *less* time to your other concerns? What if, while directing your best people to the new pursuit, you took your eye off the ball and lost an existing customer? Then there are the costs of new systems and processes to cope with the new customer, perhaps there are training needs, perhaps new operating procedures, changes to databases and promotional materials... the story goes on.

The costs of large customers

There is plenty of evidence to show that, in many industries, the largest customers are significantly less profitable for suppliers than the middle-ranking ones, despite their larger volumes. Not only were they costly to win but also, in an industry where economies of scale are slight and perhaps margins are low, discounts for volume can be very damaging to profits. Such discounts can even result in a loss with some very large customers.

So why keep them? Often because their volume is what keeps your operation turning. This is OK provided everyone recognizes not only the reasons why but also the different value of other, more profitable customers.

Big isn't always beautiful, but it can be very useful!

Big customers become aware of the prices offered to their competitors and they expect to see a differential for their greater size – a proposal hard to reject, but one that is often based less on logic than on ego. For a supplier making a gross profit margin of 20 per cent, a discount in price of 5 per cent will require an extra 33 per cent volume *just to stand still* in profit terms. If the profit margin was less, say, 15 per cent, the volume to make up for the same 5 per cent discount would be 50 per cent.

Table 7.1 illustrates this relationship between margin, discounts and volume. The figures in the central boxes are the percentage increases in volume required for profits to stand still, if a discount is given as shown in the left-hand column, while the current profit margin is as shown along the top row.

Table 7.1 *Percentage volume increases required to maintain profit over percentage discounts given*

		Current % Profit Margin						
		10	15	20	25	30	35	40	50
	2	25	15	11	9	7	6	5	4
	3	43	25	18	14	11	9	8	6
	4	67	36	25	19	15	13	11	9
% Discount Given	5	100	50	33	25	20	17	14	11
	7.5	300	100	60	43	33	27	23	18
	10		200	100	67	50	40	33	25
	15			300	150	100	60	43	33
	20				400	300	133	100	66

Let's look at an example: a 43 per cent volume increase is required, to stand still in profit terms, if a business making a 25 per cent profit margin reduces its price by 7.5 per cent. (This calculation doesn't take account of any resulting economies of scale, nor of the notion of marginal pricing and 'contribution to overheads', but even so, the figures are rather arresting.)

And remember, this only refers to the cost of discounts – all the other extra costs of winning and servicing a major customer build on top of this. The largest customers expect the most attention, the best services, the best people, the most senior management time and the greatest number of concessions, *as well as* the best prices.

You need to ask yourself some serious questions. For instance, do you know how much profit you get from your largest customers? Are you able to measure profit, after these sorts of costs, by customer?

KAM, as a process of prioritizing effort, resources and commitments, requires that the answers to these questions be yes. The results of such measurement will often reveal much about the right candidates for KA status.

Know your margins

There are two main reasons that people with customer responsibility don't know how much money they make from the customer: (1) their business systems are not able to measure with accuracy down to customer level; (2) the measurements are made, but they are not trusted with the information for fear that they will tell the customer.

Whichever, it is clear by now that genuine KAM is not possible in such a circumstance.

The tale of the marmalader

The most common problem is the way that businesses *marmalade* their overhead costs across customers. They do the same when looking at product profitability, even at different business units – a *laziness* equally damaging to decision making. Take the following example, shown in Table 7.2, of a company that talked itself out of business because of such marmalading.

Table 7.2 *Perils of marmalading*

	Customer A	Customer B	Customer C	Customer D	Company Total
Gross Profit	100	80	60	50	290
Overheads	60	60	60	60	240
Nett Profit	40	20	0	–10	50

The company has four customers and a profit in total, but the marmalading of overheads indicates a loss-making customer – customer D. The decision is taken to cease doing business with that customer. Unfortunately, overheads do not reduce immediately by the 60 units that had been allocated to customer D. But they do go down by 30 and people give themselves a slap on the back for a smart decision. The situation is now as shown in Table 7.3.

Being able to measure individual customer profitability is one of the most important requirements for a successful KAM strategy

Table 7.3 *Perils of marmalading*

	Customer A	Customer B	Customer C	Customer D	Company Total
Gross Profit	100	80	60	xxxx	240
Overheads	70	70	70	xxxx	210
Nett Profit	30	10	−10	xxxx	30

The company is still in profit, but customer C is now a loss-making customer and the troubled board meets to decide action. 'Concentrate on profitable customers,' they say, and customer C is quietly dropped. But, unfortunately, the overheads do not reduce in line, as demonstrated in Table 7.4.

Table 7.4 *Perils of marmalading*

	Customer A	Customer B	Customer C	Customer D	Company Total
Gross Profit	100	80	xxxx	xxxx	180
Overheads	90	90	xxxx	xxxx	180
Nett Profit	10	−10	xxxx	xxxx	0

I think you can guess what happens next.

The moral of the story is that decisions about customers cannot be taken without proper knowledge of their relative profitability. Perhaps customer D was a profitable customer and it was customer A that was the problem (by sucking in resources). Perhaps if they had understood the principle of contribution… but perhaps is not enough.

The answer lies in some form of activity-based costing, where the costs of activities, people, overheads, etc are allocated more precisely to individual customers. Management consultants, advertising agencies, lawyers – these are all examples of businesses that will do this to some degree. What they sell is their time, so that time must be monitored and charged. The outcome is a business that knows where its profits come from and so a business better able to make decisions concerning key accounts.

Cost to serve models

If you were able to measure profitability in the way I have been urging you to do, then you would be able to construct what we will call a 'cost to serve' model. An example is shown at Figure 7.1.

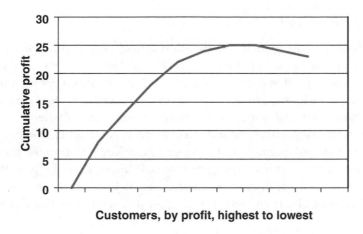

Figure 7.1 *The Cost To Serve Model*

This shows each customer along the horizontal axis, from the most profitable through to the least, with the graph line measuring the cumulative profit. It is very likely that your business will fit the 80:20 rule in this regard – a small number of customers that account for the lions share of the profit. It is also possible that you have some customers where you make a loss.

As ever with such a tool, the importance is what you do with it. Again there are choices.

I have one client who has been toying with the idea of telling his staff that should they receive an order from a customer at the right hand extremity of the graph, where they lose money, they should send the customer a cheque for $500 and a note saying *'this is what it would have cost us to service your order, but having saved ourselves the bother here is the money instead.'* Needless to say he hasn't done it yet, but it's a thought…

Cutting your losses…?

What if the loss maker is a big customer, and they very often are. How dependent is your business on their volume – does it keep the factory running? Even if it does, is that a good excuse for losing money? Armed with the data you are in a better position to consider the need for changing their terms, and calculating the impact on total profits.

A client of mine decided to increase prices in such a case, knowing that they would lose half the business, but the remaining half made real profit. Having shifted that customer leftwards on the cost to serve model they discovered that it suddenly became more attractive to chase this customer on new projects whereas before they may have seen such energy as throwing good money after bad – a happy ending was in sight.

Creating the model

The process of creating such a model is no simple task, and will involve the support and enthusiasm of Finance and IT staff. Most importantly they will want to know why it is worth all the effort. Equally, those people that you start asking to keep some form of record on time spent or costs incurred with specific customers will want to know why – be sure you tell them.

Some businesses will want and need to do this for all customers, some only for the largest, some only for those called Key – you make the rules. One option is to select a sample group of customers, knowingly with very different profiles of scale and demands, and at least create the model on those. If nothing else it will tell you whether it is worth the effort to ask yet more questions.

The benefits of customer retention

Weighted against the costs of winning new customers, and maintaining the big ones, are the benefits of retaining customers over time. Many studies have shown that the longer the customer is retained, the more profitable they become. The reasons depend, of course, on the industry, but might include:

- gradual increases in volume, not matched by discounts;
- reduced operating costs as the supplier grows more experienced in servicing the customer;
- better forecasts, which bring efficiencies for production and distribution;
- better relationships, which result in better customer intelligence;
- learning from this customer is of benefit in dealing with others;
- the customer brings new business through referrals, or the evidence of their own success.

Lifetime value

If key accounts are investments, then their performance should be measured over the long term

It is what we might call the 'lifetime value' of the customers that is the true measure of their worth. Accepting that they were costly to win, we would like to see the paybacks increase with each year of retention. The higher the retention rate you achieve, the bigger the lifetime value and, moreover, the costs of winning new customers reduce as you spend less time and effort fighting to get back into accounts lost in previous years. Winning new customers should be about *genuinely* new customers, not chasing up last year's defectors.

It is simple to see how halving your rate of customer defections would, in effect, double the lifetime value of your retained customers. Table 7.5 illustrates this point.

Table 7.5 *'Lifetime value'*

Defection Rate (per year)	Average Life of Retained Customer	Profit Value (nominal)	'Lifetime Value'
20%	5 years	1,000	5,000
10%	10 years	1,000	10,000

This is, of course, a simplification. Perhaps your defecting customers were the least profitable – maybe that's why you let them go. Perhaps they are in any case the most promiscuous, but the principle is worth remembering: it is the lifetime value of a customer that counts, not just this year's results.

Do you measure sales performance on lifetime value or this year's results? What is so special about 'this year'? (I hear the answers but, quite frankly, is that what it's all about?)

Again we see KAM as a process that takes the long view – managing the future – a state of mind that can be difficult for those brought up in an environment of annual targets and budgets. But there is gain even in the short term. F A Reichheld, quoted in *Relationship Marketing For Competitive Advantage* (ed Payne, Christopher, Clark and Peck), gives estimates of how much profits might improve if a business was to improve its retention rate by only 5 per cent. Industrial distribution companies might see a 45 per cent improvement, while car insurance firms might expect 84 per cent, with advertising agencies seeing the best impact at 95 per cent.

Old or new, big or growing?

None of this is intended to dissuade you from winning new customers.

If you are in a young, growth-orientated business then this is, of course, vital. In such a circumstance, it could be that any 'advice' to be concerned about reducing the 'acquisition costs' of winning new customers would be misplaced, or at least misinterpreted. I can hear the cries from the sales people: 'Spoiling the ship for a ha'pence of tar...'

Rather, these comments on KAM profitability are intended to show that the costs and the benefits of KAM need to be viewed over the long term. Short-termism, where the 'high octane, supercharged atmosphere' of winning new accounts is allowed to dominate to the point that it chokes the nurturing, supportive kind of environment required for customer retention, can be a very expensive mistake.

Remember the idea of KAM as an investment in the future? Then think of KAM as a means of balancing that investment portfolio, with the right balance of old and new, big and growing. Chapter 21 will look at this idea of a balanced portfolio in greater depth.

Relationships, loyalty and customer retention

There has been plenty of research into why customers change suppliers – why loyalty breaks down. The results show a common picture and, at first sight, a surprising one.

Loyal customers don't 'snap' just because an alternative supplier arrives on the scene, even if they bring lower prices or better products. True loyalty, built over time through a breadth and depth in the relationship, can withstand such competition for a surprising amount of time.

Customers 'snap' when the *relationship* breaks down; the result of arrogance, dishonesty or just plain indifference. Long-term customer retention relies on loyalty, which depends on strong, well-managed relationships – something beyond just winning the sale.

KAM is a process for managing those relationships. Before we do business with a customer, they are simply a *suspect* – a customer to be investigated. After some investigation, which proves their worth, the customer advances to being a *prospect* and we set off with the pre-KAM relationship.

As we advance from pre-KAM to early KAM, the picture of the customer changes; they move from being a *prospect* to a *customer*. Then, as the relationship develops through mid- and partnership KAM, the picture of the customer changes again, to *client*, *supporter*, *advocate* and on to *partner*.

We are describing the theory of the 'relationship ladder', the idea that as the relationship grows, so does customer loyalty and, hence, customer retention. Not only that, but we also reap the benefits of a customer that begins to act as a champion of our interests, even an advocate on our behalf.

My own business, INSIGHT Marketing and People, has a promotional spend that barely registers on the annual P&L – for us, growth comes through recommendations. We enjoy the benefits of customers that recommend us to others, because of the depth of relationship we have built with them. We practise KAM and it is through the management of this 'relationship ladder' that KAM provides our prime means to long-term profitability.

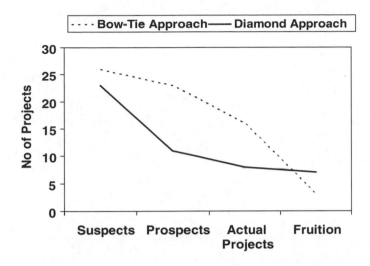

Figure 7.2 *The potential cost savings from diamond teams*

The financial benefits of diamond relationship

Sure there are costs, but there are also cost reductions. Figure 7.2 shows how this might come about.

Let's just consider one circumstance, a supplier who's business calls on them to trial a lot of potential new products with customers, only some of which come to fruition.

In a sales approach based on a series of bow-tie relationships with all customers, where it is difficult to distinguish between the likelihood or the value of one customer/project and another, there is a tendency to chase them all – throwing a lot of mud at the wall and hoping some of it sticks. The costs of this are high, particularly at the early stages.

If the approach made more use of Diamond relationships with key customers, and those relationships gave you the ability to judge a good customer/project from a bad one (based on value and likelihood of fruition) then you might actually undertake far fewer projects, at much lower cost.

Add to this the fact that by taking on fewer projects you will almost certainly do them better, you begin to see the prospect of sharply declining costs and rising profits.

Part II

The Customer's Perspective

8

Purchasing professionals

HOLD ON A MINUTE, WHY SHOULD THEY LET YOU IN?

Why should any customer allow the supplier the sort of access implied by mid, partnership and synergistic KAM? Why should they wish to see the relationship develop beyond early KAM in the way suggested by the key account model?

Well, it won't be simply because you are a long-established supplier, or a big supplier, or the cheapest supplier. It will be because they see some benefit to them in granting this kind of access.

Increasingly, purchasing professionals will use terms like *preferred supplier*, *key supplier* and *strategic supplier* as descriptions of the kind of suppliers that should be granted more access, because it is of benefit to themselves. Customers using such terminology probably also speak of things such as *supply side management* and *supply base rationalization*, terms that imply an increasing professionalism in the purchasing function.

THE PURCHASING 'REVOLUTION'

Purchasing has rarely been seen as the 'sexy' function within a business. Within the commercial functions, young people aspiring to the top have usually preferred to forge their careers in sales or marketing. One only has

There is a danger that, for suppliers, advances in purchasing strategy and tactics are outpacing those in selling to look at the huge range of books, magazines and professional bodies devoted to sales and marketing, compared to the slender range devoted to purchasing, and you can see the relative histories of these functions quite plainly.

But purchasing is making a strong drive, in some cases almost staging a revolution, in order to fulfil its full role in the business supply chain:

- In a mature business, improved purchasing can often provide the most significant opportunity for enhanced profit – greater than chasing new customers or launching new products.
- In a high-growth, high-tech business, improved purchasing practice can provide a key to faster new product development.
- The technology is now available for purchasing functions to behave differently. Information technology allows more sophisticated measurement of suppliers' performance and an array of new systems facilitates revolutionary ways of doing business – 'electronic commerce'.

The shifting balance of power

This purchasing revolution has shifted the balance of power after what had been a long period of equality between buyer and seller to a period of inequality in the buyer's favour – a situation that is rarely good in the long term for either side.

Demands for cost break downs used to go unheeded – what could they do if you didn't tell them? – whereas now a demand for open book trading is hard to resist – it always seems there's some supplier somewhere who will break ranks and go this route. In fact, it isn't the greater number of competitors that makes this sort of thing happen, most buyers are reducing the numbers of suppliers they speak with, rather, it is the buyer's greater power and greater sophistication.

For many, the practice of KAM is seen as a means of redressing this balance, as shown in figure 8.1.

There has been a tendency on the part of some sellers to downgrade the ability or importance of buyers, even their intelligence has been known to be questioned – gatekeepers, 'people who know the price of everything and the value of nothing'…

This is an unwise frame of mind with which to tackle the purchasing revolution.

Underestimate the modern buyer at your peril

Someone who had been both buyer and seller at junior and senior levels said to me recently that the buyer's task was by far the harder, and required a much higher level of skill. They said that they always slept soundly while they were selling, but buying gave them many a sleepless night – there was so much more damage they could cause by a wrong decision! This has

Figure 8.1 *The changing balance of power*

become even more so in recent years, and the calibre of people going into purchasing roles has risen dramatically as a result of this realization.

Supplier Selection

One of the most significant developments (at least for suppliers) is the move towards greater sophistication in choosing suppliers. Most businesses are seeking fewer suppliers and they wish those that remain to take on more and more responsibility for what in the past might have been seen as the buyer's job.

One purchasing director, asked how many people he had in his department, answered, 'I have over 150, but only 30 of them are on my books.' Suppliers' personnel, many of whom actually had office space on the customer's premises, made up the difference. This has become very much the norm in some industries. Back in the 1980s, companies like Nissan were taking the lead in this respect, seeing one of the ways of achieving their 'just in time' objectives being to bring the suppliers closer to the point of action.

If this is the intention of some companies then it is not surprising that they should wish to select their suppliers well. Those that are selected as 'key' will be granted the sort of access that having an office on the customer's premises implies. Those that are not selected as 'key' can expect to experience significant restrictions to access. (All sales people will recognize the most typical restriction on access; it's traditionally called the buyer, or, in more classy environments, the buyer's secretary.)

Of course, there is nothing new in customers choosing suppliers. For some reason, marketing people in particular often live under the misapprehension that they, the suppliers, choose their customers. In fact, as any 'real world' salesperson knows, it is far more likely to be the other way around, the customer that chooses its suppliers. All the more surprising then that suppliers have only recently become interested (that is, *really* interested) in how customers make those choices.

A great deal of buying has been removed from the tactical 'shenanigans' that form many sales people's experiences. Buying isn't just about 'getting stuff' any more. As it is seen in the wider context of supply chain management and business strategy, 'getting the right stuff, in the right way' is more the focus. More and more businesses have *purchasing strategies*. Even the title 'buyer' is on the way out, replaced by ones such as *supply side manager*.

Do these new titles mean anything? Sometimes, no more than the sales people who choose to stroke their own egos and award themselves the title key account manager. Other times, the change is as significant as this book argues it should be for true key account managers.

If we hope to achieve the goals of KAM, one of which might be to gain the increased security of key supplier status (where it is possible), then we had best understand the new concepts, tools and techniques of these supply side managers, or whatever title taken by the purchasing professionals we deal with. We need, in fact, to understand a series of concepts:

- supply chain management;
- supply side management;
- spend intelligence;
- purchasing strategy;
- supplier positioning and key supplier status;
- supply base optimization and rationalization.

This will be something of a 'lightning tour', designed to help see things from the customer's perspective.

SUPPLY CHAIN MANAGEMENT

Supply chain management is one of those things, like the game of draughts, or checkers, that is very simple in concept, but takes a great deal of expertise to master. It certainly keeps plenty of people, consultants among them, gainfully employed.

The concept is no more than to focus the whole chain of activities in a company; from design through to the market, or from purchasing through to sales and distribution, on to the final customer and their needs. It even goes beyond that chain – concerning itself with the suppliers to your suppliers at one end and the customers of your customers at the other. Figure 8.2 illustrates this concept.

The purpose will include any or all of the following, and more:

- To focus all activities on satisfying customer needs.

Figure 8.2 *Supply chain management*

- To ensure smooth and flawless execution, particularly across the links in the chain.
- To ensure appropriate standards of operational excellence in each function and activity.
- To ensure appropriate performance measures for each activity.
- To bring efficiencies to planning, forecasting, data exchange, etc.
- To allow costs to be measured across the operation, cost benefit analysis to be done business-wide and appropriate cost reduction programmes to be put in place.
- To assess the value added by all parts of the chain.
- To engage suppliers in key processes.
- To match customers' key processes.

Any customer seriously engaged in supply chain management will be looking at its suppliers in a new light. How do they fit within this chain? Do their processes dovetail with ours? Are they easy to do business with? Do they represent value to us across the *whole* chain?

These questions will impact significantly on suppliers and those hoping to be regarded as key suppliers had best make sure that the answers are positive. The attempt to measure the value added by suppliers, to the whole business, and select accordingly is of paramount importance and will be discussed in more detail in Chapter 10.

The supply chain and the snail

In general it can be observed that purchasing departments have given more attention to supply chain management than have sales departments. The reasons are straightforward enough. For one, the buyer is more able to see

Buyers are seeking to escape the limitations of the 'snail'

the impact of their decisions on the chain in front of them than the seller can looking back into the chain. More than this, the buyer is usually better placed to measure the costs removed from, or the value added to, the chain by their activities. Most significantly of all, the buyer can greatly enhance the value of their role when they are involved beyond the narrow confines of a transactional function. We are going back here to the idea of the '*opportunity snail*' discussed in Chapter 3.

As described in Chapter 3, the opportunity snail shows the buyer on the periphery of the decision-making process, an administrative rubber stamp once the real decisions have been taken. The purchasing revolution has seen buyers move away from this limited role, taking them closer to the centre of the snail. It is their interest in supply chain management that has been the main motive force behind this change. We see, for example, an increase in such phenomena as '*sourcing teams*', comprised of purchasing, marketing, R&D and others, which are designed to speed the process of new product development, aiming to avoid the bottlenecks of a purely linear stage-gate process.

Is this to the supplier's advantage or their detriment? For the supplier that sees an advantage in penetrating the opportunity snail beyond the purchasing function, this development can be seen as an advantage: it helps to take them inside the snail, escorted there by their purchasing contacts. For the supplier that prefers to hide from such complexity and win on price alone, this might be regarded as a threat. This is not the only example of how the purchasing revolution tends to work in favour of the value-added supplier; one of the intentions of the buyer engaged in this new style of buying is the pursuit of value.

Partnering for 'lean supply'

The purchaser's interest in the supply chain is often described as the pursuit of 'lean supply' ie the removal of non-value-added activities. This can have several benefits for the good supplier prepared to work in partnership towards the same goal.

First, if the customer cannot remove non-value-added activities altogether then they may choose to outsource responsibility for them, often to a supplier. The supplier can regard this as an additional burden, or as an opportunity to bind themselves more closely to the customer (the principle of 'lock-in' is discussed in Chapter 26).

Second, many customers are prepared to share with suppliers the costs of improving the efficiency of the supply chain. Examples of this include joint investment in an EDI capability in order to practice electronic purchasing. Such partnerings can bind supplier and customer very closely indeed.

Third, and perhaps of greatest significance to the supplier in pursuit of a partnership relationship, buyers are prepared to share information with suppliers if this leads to greater supply chain efficiency. The famous 'beer game' is a much-used training simulation that replicates the flow of information along a 'manufacturer to distributor to retailer to consumer' supply chain. It demonstrates admirably how something as simple as the sharing of forecasts up and down the chain, rather than simply placing orders on the next in line, can lead to significant improvements in supply, and dramatic reductions in costs such as working capital.

SUPPLY SIDE MANAGEMENT

Purchasing is an integral part of supply chain management and, to stress this, many companies are using the new title, supply side manager, for their purchasing staff.

It implies that the purchasing function is viewed as something more than an administrative one and that its role is more than the management of transactions. Purchasing is not an island function; its activities have great significance to the whole business.

Some comparisons between the buyer of the past and the supply side manager of the present might help us to understand the changes taking place (with apologies to buyers of the past for some gross simplification and stereotyping!).

Involvement – past and present

In the late 1990's many manufacturing companies looked long and hard at their purchasing practices. This was usually a response to hard times, but also the realization that purchasing was a place where value could be created and managed.

Perhaps the most important discovery in such studies (a very typical one was carried out by ICI) was that when they were developing new products, as much as 80 per cent of the spend with suppliers was committed *before* anyone from purchasing became involved. The buyer was called in once the contracts were prepared, the suppliers nominated, even the terms agreed, and asked to get a 5 per cent discount! It was supposed that a buyer would not be able to contribute any more than that in the complex world of new product development.

This was the world when the 'buying office' was situated in a building set apart from the other commercial functions, quite possibly in a portakabin, and equipped with furniture no longer required by sales and marketing.

The second hand rose...

99

Buyers were not expected to know what happened to the items they bought, beyond their arrival in the company's warehouse.

The supply side manager will be expected to be involved from the outset of any significant new product development. Their office is more likely to be within the heart of the business, and their responsibility for their products extends well down the chain of use, often right to the end customer. (They don't always get the best furniture, even now, and in any case they like to project an air of poverty with which they can taunt their rich suppliers …)

Performance measures – past and present

A typical buyer was measured on their ability to win discounts and their efficiency in handling transactions. The lower the prices they paid and the more transactions they handled, the greater their abilities.

Supply side managers are more likely to be judged on the selection of suppliers, the reduction of supplier numbers, the reduction of transactions and the value that they add to the total business. They are still concerned with reducing costs, but not just through lower purchase prices. Costs, for a supply side manager, are the *total costs in use* of the products and services bought.

It used to be said (mainly by sales people!) that the definition of a buyer was someone who 'knows the price of everything, and the value of nothing'. Such sales people should be pleased at the new responsibilities of supply side managers – value is now the measure. Anyone who has bought a cheap pair of shoes in a sale, only to find a hole in the sole after just a few weeks' wear (usually just when the wet weather sets in), knows the difference between price and value.

Knowledge – past and present

Legends abound of buyers who knew everything there was to know about the products they bought – the world's leading authorities on soup spoons, corrugated card or xanthum gum. Many of the tales were true and buyers are still very often more expert in the products they deal in than the sellers.

It's not what you know, but what you can find out

Yet, when it came to matters of expenditure, in the past, many purchasing departments did not know, with any precision, exactly what they spent by category of product or service. This was sometimes due to a lack of systems to monitor and report; sometimes because plenty of other people in the business made purchases without their knowledge (the salesperson's prey); sometimes because they didn't feel they needed to know.

It is ironic that the supplier would know in great detail exactly what they sold, yet the purchaser, who could potentially have a far greater impact on the outcome, would often have much the poorer information. It is still not unusual for buyers to ask their suppliers for summaries of what they have bought – convenient perhaps, but not very professional.

Now, the systems exist for supply side managers to monitor purchases and report expenditure by category, site, business, process and so on. Supply side managers are keen to talk of 'governance', their desire to control what is bought, from whom and by whom. Woe betide any salesperson that tries to subvert the purchasing systems by going direct to an end-user! (An exception to this is the trend towards the use of company credit cards, held by end-users, for the purchase of minor or low-significance items – stationery, travel, personal expenses, etc.)

Now, the supply side manager is very keen to know about expenditure by category, using this data as a basis for supply base optimization and rationalization. The supply side manager is far more likely to sit behind a computer and talk of 'spend maps' (see 'Spend intelligence', later in this chapter) than swap tales of excruciating technical precision.

Vendor ratings – past and present

In the past, a buyer might have a list of measures that they used to evaluate suppliers, but they wouldn't tell the suppliers. That would upset the balance of power in the negotiation. The seller's job was to find them out, usually by hard experience – failing to match up would bring a rare glimpse of what was required.

The supply side manager might take a very different approach. They might look to their better suppliers to set the standards and then to monitor their own performance against those standards. This would take trust of course, but that is one mark of a key supplier – they can be trusted.

Hewlett Packard is very open in discussing vendor ratings with their more significant suppliers: it is made clear what is required, regular reviews are held, suppliers are expected to manage their own performance improvement and supplier *rankings* are raised and discussed.

There is something very important to note here. Suppliers to companies that, like Hewlett Packard, use such rankings are often surprised by purchasing decisions that go against them. They might have sat in the number one slot for months, but that is not to say that they are automatically guaranteed all or any new business. Purchasing groups use such rankings as a means of managing suppliers, not making their decisions for them. To win the business, a high ranking is important, but never forget all the other aspects of winning business – the deal, the relationship, the timing and so on.

Being the number 1 supplier doesn't mean you always get the business...

Gatekeepers or facilitators – past and present

In the past, buyers were seen as gatekeepers by sales reps and as petty bureaucrats by their own R&D or marketing people – always ready with a reason to slow down the process. No wonder they were brought in only at the last moment. Poor suppliers could get away with murder, provided they got on with the buyer and kept their prices 'sharp' – never mind that their products were the bane of the production people's lives. Good suppliers, ones that might help the production process run smoothly, might never get a look in. This was not an issue of 'undue influence' or corruption, more likely that the buyer just didn't know – not their department.

Now, the supply side manager has a duty to be involved in the whole business chain, involving the right suppliers with the right people in their organization and helping the R&D and marketing departments to speed their new products to market. Their role is to 'add value through the supplier interface', a quote I saw posted behind a supply side manager's desk and, while the language may be grating, the sentiments are spot on. The right supplier is far more likely to win through – though it is still not guaranteed!

Figure 8.3 shows the changing role, from 'buyer' to 'supply side manager'.

Buyer or supply side manager – which would you prefer?

The broader view of the supply side manager – the focus on value rather than price and the desire to involve suppliers in their processes – all of this is potentially threatening to poor suppliers, but welcome news to good ones. The supply side manager's approach will often make the task of the key account manager easier, provided (and here's the rub) they respond to the new demands, provided they are considered a key supplier.

SPEND INTELLIGENCE

A key feature of supply side management is the analysis of purchasing data. It must all begin with some basics – what is bought and from where? Armed with such information, the supply side manager can look for opportunities to make an impact on what they increasingly call the 'supply base' – the list of suppliers, current, listed and potential.

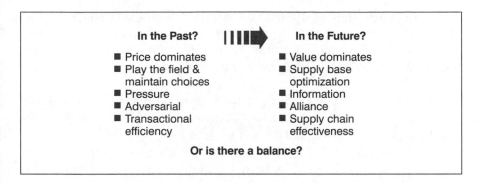

Figure 8.3 *The changing role, from buyer to supply side manager*

This might involve reducing the supply base in the pursuit of more leverage on those that remain, or greater efficiencies through fewer transactions. It might involve seeking greater security by expanding the supply base. Whatever the choice, the decisions can only be made based on good intelligence. Some purchasers might refer to 'spend maps', which at their simplest are really just lists of suppliers, for specific products, presented as bar charts, as seen in Figure 8.4.

Armed with the information shown in Figure 8.4, what would you do if you were the buyer? Assuming that there were no great differences between the suppliers other than scale, a rationalization programme might be your first step. Remove the smaller suppliers (E through to I) and give their business to which one of A to D?

Stage one in the spend-mapper's 'game'...

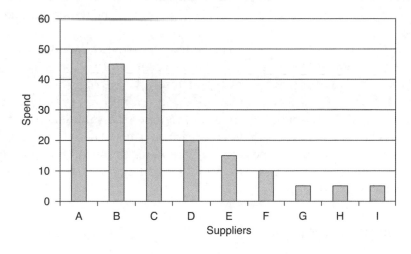

Figure 8.4 *Spend map for product X*

Giving the majority to D and perhaps a little to B and C would serve two purposes. First, a much more significant discount. Supplier D might experience a doubling of their business – surely worth a substantial discount. Second, the suppliers have been evened up, making way for stage two of the buyer's plan.

Stage two is the open tender, asking four equal players to fight it out among themselves, with one loser. The loser's business is divided up equally, again for a substantial discount.

Stage three might be to reintroduce one of the smaller suppliers on the grounds that the three incumbents are growing fat and lazy. Of course, this resurrected supplier will offer very attractive prices, terms, services – sufficient to put the larger players to shame – and offer yet more discounts.

And so the 'game' might go on, but it can only be played by buyers with good and accurate information, otherwise it is a very dangerous game indeed.

The surprising thing, at least to sales people armed with every conceivable breakdown of sales, is that many purchasing operations have difficulty with compiling this sort of information.

Consider their problem. They might buy a similar product from you and five other suppliers, but each supplier gives the product its own name, references, specification, pack size and so on. Is this the same product? A particular difficulty in compiling spend maps is the question of classification. Does a supermarket buy chocolate bars, or milk and plain, branded and own label, or. . . ? The list goes on. Add to this the complexity of a multi-site, multinational business and you can appreciate the difficulty.

Yet it is very important to get right. Big savings can be gained through rationalizing a supply base, but it can be disastrous if the wrong supplier is rationalized out!

Information that you give your customer on what they buy from you will be welcomed. Don't regard any request for information as a threat; see it as an opportunity to work more closely. Get it right and you will earn respect, but this means presenting it in a format that means something to *them*. Until quite recently it was common for suppliers of beer to UK grocery stores to report their sales in barrels. The barrel was the brewery's chosen internal measure but, of course, the store bought bottles or cans – the barrel was not a helpful denomination for anyone's spend mapping exercise!

The leaky buyer?

There is another side to this coin. The more information the purchasing group is able to amass on its suppliers, the more power they are building for their negotiating stance. Some purchasing groups are now becoming aware that they have information of significant value to suppliers and that they should be using it in a proper way. I recently heard the vice-president of purchasing for one of the UK's largest companies say with some force that his purchasing team 'leaked like a sieve' and that they had better start realizing the value of information and managing its use with suppliers in a professional manner.

What this comment makes very clear is that suppliers should not expect buyers to become soft touches just because they have shifted away from some of the more aggressive stances of the past. A supply side manager chasing value from low-value suppliers will be every bit as challenging and demanding, only using new tactics – the power of 'psychological pressure tactics' replaced by the power of information.

PURCHASING STRATEGY

The purchasing function might always have had a strategy, but, in the past, perhaps it was one of an 'island function', with a relatively short-term focus. Supply chain management demands that their strategy becomes part of the whole. They will tend to be longer term, focused as much on the customer as the supplier and seeking 'value', not just lower prices.

At its simplest, purchasing strategy seeks to manage the future, in just the same way as we discussed the purpose of KAM strategy in Chapter 2. And there is just the same need to find a balance between business objectives, market opportunity and business resources (Figure 8.5).

Figure 8.5 *Purchasing strategy*

In the purchasing context, the market opportunity combines two ideas:

- The supply base – who is out there and who can help us meet our objectives? Supply chain managers will talk of supply base optimization.
- What impact can, and will, purchasing activities have on the total supply chain – from suppliers' suppliers through to customer and beyond – and what value can it add?

Some common themes will emerge in most purchasing strategies:

- *Supplier positioning* – spending the right time, in the right way, with the right suppliers and identifying key suppliers.
- *Adding value* – throughout the supply chain.
- *Supply base optimization* – managing the right types and number of suppliers.
- *Integration with business strategy* – ensuring a match of values.

These themes are dealt with in the rest of Part II.

9

Supplier positioning – becoming a key supplier

So often, the challenges facing the buyer and the seller are simply the two sides of the same coin. They have far more in common with each other than their traditional adversarial stance might suggest. A good example is how they use their time.

In a pre-KAM environment, the salesperson might have a 'milk round' approach that views all customers as equal, thus justifying the same amount of time and attention.

In what we might call a pre-KSS (before the notion of key supplier status) environment, the buying office might be inundated by a constant stream of representatives, each needing attention, and an equally constant stream of invoices, each needing handling.

SUPPLIER POSITIONING MODELS

If one purpose of KAM is to determine a better use of time and effort then the purchasing function is seeking the same through the use of supplier positioning models.

It is not unusual for a purchasing organization to find that some 80 per cent of its time and effort is spent on suppliers who constitute only 20 per cent of the total spend – yes, even buyers are subject to the 80/20 principal. ICI certainly found this to be the case when they reviewed their purchasing activities in the late 1990s, leading them to look very seriously at a number of supplier positioning models.

The supplier positioning model is an attempt to redress this imbalance – it has four principal aims:

- determining where to spend the purchasing function's time and effort;
- determining what sort of relationship should be established with different suppliers;
- determining what sort of activities should be worked on with different suppliers;
- identifying the 'key suppliers'.

Any KAMs wanting to develop their relationship and expand on the range of activities with the customer must clearly know how they are themselves regarded in this light.

These next three chapters will look at three different supplier positioning models: (1) the risk/significance/spend model (this chapter); (2) the risk/significance/value model (Chapter 10); (3) the risk/significance/trust model (Chapter 11). First, there are a few preliminary comments to note.

Your customer might use any of these models, or they might use none. They might use them formally, perhaps even sharing them with you, or they might be locked away in the buyer's head. It might be that the models represent not a formal structure, but more of an indication of the buyer's 'gut feel'. Whichever it is, one of the key account manager's jobs is to understand to what extent such models are used, discussed, or considered by their customer. Your customer might not use the words used in this chapter, but they might have similar thoughts with different terminology – from this point forward, use *their* words.

None of these models is easy for the customer to prepare in practice, using hard data. The information required, particularly in large organizations, is hard to compile and much of it remains subjective, but purchasing departments are trying harder and harder – they recognize the value of such modelling exercises.

THE RISK/SIGNIFICANCE/SPEND MODEL

The purchaser uses this matrix (Figure 9.1) to 'position' suppliers, and categories, or groups, of suppliers, for the purpose of determining time spent, type of relationship required, activities undertaken and so on. We will start

Figure 9.1 *The risk/significance/spend model*

by understanding the two axes and then examine the significance of the 'box' labels.

Defining the axes

This model considers two broad issues:

- Risk/significance – how dependent are you on these suppliers, or groups of suppliers?
- Relative spend – how much do you spend compared to other suppliers, or groups of suppliers?

Why these labels?

The two axes can be seen to reflect the balance of power between supplier and customer – significance reflects supplier power, with spend as a marker of potential buyer power. Some purchasing departments might even prefer those labels – supplier power and buyer power, reflecting a fairly hard-nosed, real world approach to determining potential partners.

Risk/significance

This measure is common to all three models. In its broadest sense, it is a measure of how dependent the customer is on the suppliers.

Suppose there is only one supplier for a particular product, or even category of product – perhaps because of a unique technology, or maybe it is a monopoly holder. The significance of that supplier is clearly high, so the level of risk for the purchaser is also high. Life without that supplier would be very difficult, perhaps inconceivable. Where there are many alternatives, the risk involved in losing a supplier is that much lower, so the significance of individual suppliers is also lower.

This is rather a simplistic scenario; in real life there are a number of factors to consider when defining risk or significance. This is the challenge of the risk/significance axis and the value to the purchasing organization – defining the factors for consideration. Enormous value will be had from analysing the factors, prioritizing them and assessing suppliers against them – light will often dawn.

The following is no more than a general list of the sort of factors that might apply. The supply side manager's job is to identify the relevant ones, the KAM's job is to understand their selection:

- number of suppliers;
- geographic location;
- technology;
- patents;
- brand names;
- suppliers are also competitors;
- suppliers supply the customer's competitors;
- criticality of product to own product/process;
- no alternative technologies – no substitutes;
- time required to switch suppliers;
- supplier's financial security;
- politics – (the MD's favourite!).

Relative spend

This is a simpler measure, provided that the purchasing organization has the data. In a typical manufacturing company, viewed on the large scale, you might expect to find raw materials suppliers right of the line and stationery suppliers left of the line. In an insurance company, the positions might be reversed.

Using the model

Buyers are seeking to manage suppliers just as much as sellers have ever wanted to manage customers. And they have an advantage – they're buyers!

A quick reminder of why the purchasing organization might go to all this bother:

- Determining where to spend the purchasing function's time and effort.
- Determining what sort of relationship should be established with different suppliers.
- Determining what sort of activities should be worked on with different suppliers.
- Identifying the key suppliers.

In other words, the purchaser will expect to behave differently with suppliers in different boxes. Just consider your own buying practices for a moment. Would you go about buying the following – a tin of baked beans, a second-hand car, a life insurance policy and a TV licence – in the same way?

Of course not. For most of us, the positioning of these four supply types would probably be as illustrated in Figure 9.2 and our purchasing behaviour would be appropriate to the positioning.

You will want to spend more time with the life insurance salesperson than you will scanning the supermarket shelves for beans. You don't mind putting a bit of effort into haggling over that second-hand car, but you won't haggle over the TV licence. You might go in for a scheme that pays for the TV licence by a regular standing order, to be sure of having it, but beans you will buy when you see them.

Of course, nothing is rigid in this model. For instance, there are differences of opinion or attitude among buyers. For someone, the particular brand of beans, or make of car, might be so significant as to raise its positioning up the matrix. Or, seeing the tin of beans as a single product will place it in the bottom-left box. However, if you were to group together all similar purchases, you might find it heading towards the bottom-right box and you might then be considering doing deals for bulk purchase.

On what level?

On what level would the customer use this model? At a high level, it is used to position categories of suppliers: for instance, all stationery suppliers compared to all raw material suppliers. On a lower level, the matrix might encompass all suppliers from a particular category of supply, say stationery, and then compare the individual suppliers against each other. In practice, the model is *best* suited to the higher-level analysis.

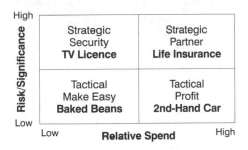

Figure 9.2 *Supplier positioning*

Time and effort

The 80/20 rule applies to buyers just as much as sellers

At its simplest, the most time should be spent with suppliers in the top-right quadrant, the strategic partners – this is where you spend a lot of money and they are important to you. What many purchasing functions are finding, however, is that they are spending a disproportionate amount of time in the bottom-left quadrant. The vast number of suppliers in this area all need handling, vetting, policing, their invoices have to be processed and their deliveries received and checked. Often as much as 80 per cent of purchasing time is spent on simple transactional activities, with suppliers that account for as little as 20 per cent of the spend. That has to be wrong.

The model (Figure 9.3) helps supply side managers to reorientate their efforts on to suppliers away from the lower-left quadrant, the 'tactical make easy'. The label expresses the aims for this box: make things easy – and one way might be fewer suppliers.

How will this manifest itself to the suppliers? If you are placed top right, you might expect the customer to draw you in further – the 'diamond' of partnership KAM will be offered to you, even forced on you. If you are bottom left, then you might expect a tough set of standards to determine whether you should be a supplier at all and, if you do survive, the demands will be for easier ways of doing business – electronic commerce, for one (see Chapter 27).

For the supplier being assessed in this way, one implication is clear (and there is little point fighting it): to some extent you are being pigeonholed and to some extent you will have to behave accordingly.

WHAT RELATIONSHIPS, WHAT ACTIVITIES?

Once the supply side manager has determined where to spend their time and effort, the sort of relationship they wish to develop will follow. Each

Figure 9.3 *Shift of time and effort*

quadrant of the matrix suggests a different relationship and a different focus of activities. Some purchasing groups are so aware of the need for this difference that they will even assign different types of buyer to the suppliers in the different quadrants.

Looking at each quadrant in turn, we will identify the different purchasing objectives and the different purchasing styles that might ensue. If you can identify how you are 'positioned' by your customer then you can assess the appropriateness of your current approach. More than that, such an understanding will enable you to judge the extent of their strategic intent towards you and so help you to maintain a mutuality of intent (see Chapter 5).

Strategic security – top left

This is where there is perhaps a relatively small choice of suppliers, or where they provide some significant product or service and where the total spend is relatively small. An example might be a unique raw material that makes up only 1 per cent of a manufactured product, or a branded item that forms part of your own product.

If you are a clothing manufacturer and choose to stamp 'contains Lycra' on your product then they *must* contain Lycra – and that makes the supplier of Lycra (DuPont) very significant. DuPont is expert at elevating their significance to customers through the use of brand names. Teflon is another example, seen in products as diverse as frying pans, paint and neckties. Remember, this is branding being used by suppliers of raw materials in other people's products – branding is not just for fast moving consumer goods.

The buyer's principal interest in this quadrant is security of supply – keep those plastic bags in stock. This might lead to all sorts of approaches – a demand for frequent deliveries, long-term contracts, or perhaps a willingness to sit on high levels of stock. The watchword is *security*.

Suppliers can expect to be treated with respect – they are, after all, quite important. Perhaps they will be asked to guarantee security of supply, but they are not likely to be given huge amounts of the customer's time. The good news, of course, is that they shouldn't expect to be too pressed on price. No buyer will risk closing the factory for a 1 per cent discount from such suppliers. You might also expect to find a great deal of buyer inertia when considering any change of supplier, provided that the current suppliers behave adequately.

In order to make and sell butter, Unilever purchases a huge number of items, from salt to milk to packaging materials. One very important supplier is positioned about as far top left as it is possible to be: the supplier of the butter flavour. The flavour is a vital ingredient in the final product and accounts for less than 1 per cent of the total cost. This supplier is expected to provide absolute security of supply, without fault, and so long as they continue to deliver a completely consistent, fault-free product, then Unilever will continue to value them and reward them accordingly. Both supplier and Unilever refer to the Unilever 'fat man' (Figure 9.4) in recognition of this fact.

The fat man represents the total costs of all materials purchased by the Unilever butter business. On the same scale, the small heart represents the flavour component and that is worth remembering – small but it is the heart. Nobody, both sides recognize, is going to have a heart transplant for the sake of a price discount!

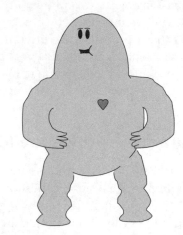

Figure 9.4 *The Unilever 'fat man'*

Strategic partners – top right

This is where the suppliers might expect to be welcomed in with open arms. They matter, and they have lots of money spent on them, so the customer should be prepared to give them time. More than time, they should be wanting to establish relationships on all levels – partnership KAM, perhaps even synergistic KAM for the most significant of all.

The demand for more contact might come from the customer; a desire to meet with senior management to discuss longer-term issues, or to be more closely involved with product specification at the R&D level.

That is not to say that the supplier should be expecting an easy ride. The customer will be placing heavy demands. There is a lot of money at stake, but the rewards will be good for both parties. This is where hard-working suppliers can become very successful.

Examples of such suppliers? Big brand consumer goods. The retailer sells vast quantities and the brand is a vital factor in that turnover. But the supplier doesn't just walk in and take the order. They will be expected to spend a lot of time with the retailer; preparing promotions, tailoring ranges, analysing sales data – perhaps even practising *category management,* a particular type of strategic partnership peculiar to the retail industry where both supplier and retailer join in focusing time and energies on identifying and meeting consumer needs from the broadest standpoint (the whole product category, not just the particular supplier's brand). The practice is particularly prevalent in the confectionery trade, where big brand suppliers such as Mars collaborate with retailers to prepare shelf layouts and promotional calendars and will work together on the launch of new products. (Also see Chapter 26, section on category management.)

Textbook partnering

One of the most highly publicized examples of such a partnership is that between Proctor & Gamble as supplier and Wal*Mart as customer, in the United States. Both had reputations as fairly 'confrontational' negotiators, based on the strength of their positions, but in the late 1980s they decided to work things a new way. Wal*Mart began to provide P&G with information on the sales of P&G products, detailed stuff – volumes, returns, profit, regional variations – all of huge value to the supplier. Wal*Mart then allowed P&G to take responsibility for managing their stock, placing orders, determining levels, even allocating space in store. The benefits were huge.

For Wal*Mart's part, they removed 'stock-outs', reduced transaction costs and passed such savings on to customers through an 'everyday low price' policy agreed with P&G.

For P&G, they got very close to a customer that represented 10 per cent of total revenue. The company was able to produce to demand, based on the excellent forecasts the information facilitated, and learnt a great deal about the challenges and dynamics of the retail industry.

Tactical make easy – bottom left

There are plenty of fish in this sea – lets say stationery suppliers – and the total spend is not huge. What clever purchasers want here is an easy buy. They don't want to spend hours haggling with competing suppliers. This is the box where suppliers might expect to be granted sole-supplier contracts, with tough performance standards and speedy exit if they fail to meet them.

It is also the box where many purchasing organizations are turning towards e-commerce as a means to simplifying transactions. If 80 per cent of their time is spent in such areas, removing the salesperson can remove a lot of the noise. Purchase through the Internet continues to grow. Allowing staff to use purchase cards rather than placing 'indents' through the purchasing department is on the increase and proving very effective, provided that the contracts are set with clarity in the first place. Remote ordering through EDI and telemetry are more complex solutions requiring an *increase* in time spent by the seller and buyer in setting up such systems but, once in place, they can prove very attractive and time-efficient for both parties (Chapter 27 looks at the impact of the e-revolution in more detail).

Today, the bottom two boxes are where the e-revolution is impacting most on supplier–customer relationships. This is the place for quick wins

The really big wins are still to come, in the top two boxes

One of the things that purchasing organizations are finding once they position suppliers in this bottom-left box is that they have a number of suppliers of broadly similar products. A good example for any large company would be stationery items. By grouping these suppliers together, through supply base rationalization, not only are there huge savings in transaction costs, but the scale of purchase is also increased to the point that time spent on shaving a few percentage points off prices is now well worth the effort. In other words, while individual suppliers might have been positioned bottom left, grouping of suppliers and subsequent rationalization shifts a supply type to bottom right.

One result of ICI's use of this positioning model was the establishment of a sole-supplier arrangement for stationery items, using purchase cards to allow individuals to buy direct without going through the purchasing department. The result was significant savings in purchase price and transaction costs.

While one result of positioning a supplier in this box may be to ask them to reduce the frequency and level of people contact (replacing this with e-commerce solutions), an alternative outcome might be to ask for *more* of the supplier's people time – asking them to carry out transactional tasks previously handled by the purchasing department. Such self-management and self-regulation can reduce transactional costs enormously, but it does require a high level of trust and confidence in the supplier.

Tactical profit – bottom right

Again, lots of fish in the sea and a lot of money at stake, so carry a big stick and see what you can get out of your suppliers. This is what some buyers might call the 'good old-fashioned fun' box, where blood sports are still in vogue.

If suppliers find themselves in this quadrant, they can expect to be talking price and perhaps not much else.

SO, WHO'S THE KEY SUPPLIER?

Don't leap to the assumption that only suppliers in the top-right quadrant can be viewed as key suppliers. Certainly they will be regarded as important, and perhaps have a head start, but there is more to this. So what is the requirement?

Behave appropriately

This is another of those very simple concepts that doesn't take much to say but, if missed, you and your company can go through untold agonies of frustration and wasted time.

So, don't skip past this next sentence too quickly. It's rather a 'Napoleon' of a sentence: short, but important.

> *To be regarded as a key supplier, you need to behave appropriately to your positioning in the eyes of the customer.*

If the customer sees you in '*tactical make easy*', be supremely easy to do business with. Make sure things flow – install remote ordering systems, communicate through e-mail, don't overburden them with your presence. Be there when required and keep out of the way when not. Don't try to force complex relationships on the customer, unless they lead to easier transactions. Show willingness to take on those administrative tasks that perhaps traditionally have been the buyer's – think about offering to set, *and* police, your own standards (but don't be too pushy!). If you behave this way then perhaps their easiest option will be to award you with a sole-supplier contract. What better definition of a key supplier?

If the customer sees you in '*tactical profit*', be the sharpest on the block. Make sure your costs are the lowest in the business and pass on your efficiencies to the customer. Stay keen on prices and keep close to the movements in the market – you can put prices up when conditions allow. Of course, only do all of this if you really *do* want to be considered a key supplier by this customer. The alternative is to be more opportunistic with them and accept that they will be the same with you. Another alternative is to seek a way of marking yourself out, finding a differentiation that will raise your significance to the supplier. This will not be easy. Finding the differentiation is only half of the battle; communicating it convincingly to customers that have already positioned you as 'bottom right' will be tough.

If the customer sees you in '*strategic security*', never ever let them down. Be the most reliable in the business, or else maintain your hold on the customer whether it be through your brand name, your technology, your service, a long-term contract or whatever. Be prepared to consider proposals that tie you in – consignment stock, serviced ordering and so on – provided you *do* wish to be with this customer for the long term.

If the customer sees you in '*strategic partner*', act like one. Spend lots of time with the customer. Establish all the relevant points of contact, particularly at senior level, and focus on the long term. Devote time and energy to understanding their needs, issues and culture – and make sure that you

117

continue to come up with the goods. Bring them your new ideas, first. Above all, get the relationship right. A '*tactical make easy*' supplier that gets it wrong will be a nuisance, but a '*strategic partner*' that gets it wrong will be a disaster.

IS THERE ANY ESCAPE FOR SUPPLIERS?

Behave appropriately, but plan your escape…

Are you inevitably stuck with the customer's pigeonholing? In the short term, probably yes, but don't let that stop you *planning* to move. Three things should be remembered:

- The customer's perception of your position is more important than the fact. Work on the perceptions as much as trying to alter, or argue the facts. Perhaps they place you in the bottom-left quadrant, whereas you know that your unique technology actually places you top left. Don't expect to be able to just tell them. Take every opportunity, and every potential contact, to slowly drip feed the information required for them to change their view. Wait patiently for the opportunity to demonstrate your incomparability.
- Everything is relative. Your immediate contact might view you as bottom right, but their boss watches a larger picture that might place you more towards the top left. You may have to demonstrate different behaviours at different levels of the customer. Take advantage of a more senior perspective, but don't expect the MD to take a great interest in your next supplier team meeting – and don't make the mistake of going behind the buyer's back!
- If you are stuck left of the line, because spend is low, but you provide superb value, then perhaps you need to persuade the customer that there is more to life than spend. The 'value' model discussed in the next chapter would probably suit you better, but proceed with care. Remember, the customer chooses how to measure their suppliers, not you. The 'value not price' argument is a strong one, but you should recognize that it is not always an easy one for the customers to evaluate and they may be suspicious of your motives. Of course, the true supply side manager, focused on value in the chain, ought to be on your side on this one – they are probably already thinking in terms of this second model.

Moving north…

Lets suppose that you are positioned in the bottom right hand box but aspire to the top right. If we consider an analogy it might help. I am your customer and you are selling me petrol for my car. I spend a lot on petrol but couldn't care less whose it is – truly a bottom right positioning.

You try to increase your significance to me by several means, and historically we can see what these have been – Green Shield stamps (for those who go back that far), free glasses, product performance claims, additives, loyalty cards, on site shop, branded on site shop, on site coffee shop, on site cash dispensing machine, and so it goes on.

Some of those grab me, some of them don't. I never have gone for loyalty cards, but the cash machine works for me – I buy my petrol where I can get my money more conveniently, and so it wins my loyalty.

What is happening here is that the supplier is expanding their offer, sometimes through the product, more often in this case through services offered. And each time the offer is expanded, the competition catches up of course, and so the supplier must look for the next thing. It is rather like a series of concentric circles growing out from the original core product (see Figure 9.5), each seeking to increase their significance to the customer.

Where does KAM come into this? In two important ways.

Firstly, if I was a key account of this supplier they would surely want to identify which of these various 'expansions' did the most for me, and then shout it out loud so that I heard. I hope they wouldn't try to shout them all at me – some I care about, some I don't.

Secondly, the very practice of KAM is what helps the supplier to identify these wider concentric circles in the first place, using the KAM relationship to stimulate and develop their product and service offer.

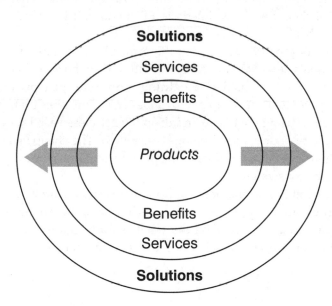

Figure 9.5 *Building significance*

10

Measuring value

WEAKNESSES OF THE SPEND MODEL

Why do purchasers measure spend? Perhaps because they *can* measure it, but that isn't to say it is the only, or the best, measure. My mother gave me some sound advice when the time came to leave home: 'Always buy a good pair of shoes and a good bed; you'll spend half your life in one and half in the other.'

Well, she got the ratio wrong, but the principle was right – never skimp on the essentials; it will always catch up with you in the end. Of course, she was advising me to consider something more than just price; she was talking about *value*. That cheap pair of shoes again, the ones that split at the vital moment causing me to trip and drop the priceless vase I was carrying would be pretty poor value, all things considered. The cheap bed that loses me sleep, gives me backache, makes me grumpy and loses me my job would be fairly disastrous value.

The argument is a strong one, but how many buyers are in a position to measure true value? Supply side managers have it in their remit – to look at the impact of their purchases on the whole supply chain, but more often than not it remains up to the seller to provide the evidence.

MEASURING VALUE

A tale of two copiers

The buyer of office equipment for a multinational company has virtually decided to give a sole-supplier contract to a company that sells low-priced photocopier machines. The savings seem to be big. The supplier undercuts most of the current suppliers by up to 8 per cent and, for a sole-supplier deal, will give a further 3 per cent discount.

Luckily for the buyer, as it turns out, there is one last presentation to be considered, from a relatively high-priced supplier but one that has done some homework.

The supplier has found out how many reams of paper the customer will put through these machines in a year – and it is huge. Much of the paper is relatively expensive high-quality paper bearing the company's letterhead.

From extensive research of the various machines on the market, the supplier is able to present a convincing case of how its machine, through its superior reliability, will use far less paper than its competitor's machines, particularly when compared to the lowest-price machines such as those under consideration by the buyer. The reason is down to how much paper is wasted by the lower-price machines in mis-feeds, smudging and the general mayhem that goes on inside cheaper photocopiers.

Added to this, the mis-feeds often lead to down time and, not infrequently, the need for a service engineer. The lower-priced machines offer only minimal service cover before extra charges are applied, so the true costs in use might start to rise significantly over time.

This is, of course, the key to the matter – the true costs in use. The true value of a product or service is only determined once it is in use. If you never intend to wear that cheap pair of shoes then the cheaper the better! Supply side managers are asked to measure *costs in use*, *total acquisition costs* and *life-cycle costs* – different definitions of this all-important concept.

'Cost in use' ... ... a key to measuring value

The supplier is able to put forward a case that demonstrates how its machine will deliver the 'lowest-cost printing solution' for the customer, as opposed to the 'lowest-cost copiers'. After all, they point out, what are you buying – copiers, or what they do for you?

The buyer places the order with the higher-priced supplier, sending a note to their boss explaining why they have gone for a higher-price option. A victory for a principle that all sales people will recognize: people buy benefits, not features – but this one very nearly didn't!

There are four key points to be made:

1. The fact that the buyer feels the need to explain their decision. Buyers are measured on purchase costs and savings over previous years, so such a purchase is not an easy decision for them to take. The suppliers that argue value in use must remember this and proceed with care. Wherever possible, they should aim to involve in the decision those who see the full costs – the stationery buyers, the office managers and the users.

2. A supply side manager might have been measured differently – on the savings brought to the business as a whole (the true value of the purchase), which might have made for an easier decision.

3. The supplier had to come up with the argument and the justification. The purchaser, as is so often the case, was not in a position to do the necessary homework.

4. The winning supplier *had* done their homework. Somewhere in the customer's organization they had found some valuable information – they had some good contacts.

An irony of this sort of case is that good sales people have been speaking this way for years, only buyers haven't always been in a position to listen. If they really are measured on purchase cost savings, and nothing more, then they *should* buy the cheaper photocopier (if getting their Christmas bonus matters to them).

A tale of two hospitals

Two competitors are each trying to sell an x-ray machine to a hospital. One costs £400,000, the other £550,000, and they apparently do much the same job.

The buyer, an old-fashioned type with no time for procurement strategies or supplier positioning models, calls it a 'no brainer' and goes for the cheaper machine. The buyer feels pleased about a good day's work that saved the hospital £150,000.

Over the next two years the x-ray machine is serviced eight times, each time at a cost of £10,000, plus it required a major overhaul costing £20,000. Oddly enough, the buyer doesn't care; they are not responsible for servicing costs, which come out of the radiology department's budget.

The machine has broken down on two occasions, resulting in major patient logjams, a lot of ill will towards the hospital and one *very* expensive court case for negligence. Oddly enough, the buyer doesn't care; they are not responsible for patient-processing targets and they rarely go to court or read the newspapers.

The hospital down the road is practising supply chain management. It bought the more expensive machine. The service contract requires only two services a year, each at £10,000, and the machine has never broken down. The hospital has no patient logjams, and no bad press.

Hospitals increasingly have to fight for their customers, like anyone else, and what brings customers in is a feeling that they will be well cared for. Not surprisingly, people want to go to the hospital that isn't in the newspapers.

Summarizing value

The customer will see value in terms of what the supplier, their product, or service, can do for their business. A cheap raw material that results in a massive product recall would be a low purchase-cost option, but also very low-value option. The difficulty for the supplier, and also for the customer that attempts to measure in this way, is evidencing that spending more on the raw material would remove the risk of recalls.

Getting value is, in this sense, rather like buying insurance – you don't realize its worth until you need it. And, of course, we all know how easy it is to ignore the arguments of 'future value' we hear from those 'silver tongued' insurance sales people.

'Value in use' is a result of experience. For both parties, trial and error will form part of the measurement process. As a supplier, stay patient; wait for the opportunity. As a customer, look for suppliers that will help you take the risk out of trialling.

So, it depends on how the customer measures things in terms of price, cost or value. But the supplier has a key role in presenting the case. Some customers will need to be 'helped' towards this more complicated measure of supplier performance. The seller has to juggle the purchase-cost needs of the buyer with the total-cost needs of the company. The juggling is that much easier where the purchasing function already uses something like the value-based supplier positioning model.

THE RISK/SIGNIFICANCE/VALUE MODEL

This is the hardest model for any business to prepare and, perhaps not surprisingly, given the effort involved, few in the past have bothered. This is a great pity for, as we have seen in the previous two tales, both supplier and buyer have much to gain from this approach. The model is illustrated in Figure 10.1.

The vertical axis of the first supplier positioning model remains the same; we have replaced 'relative spend' with 'total value', as defined in the preceding section.

Figure 10.1 *The risk/significance/value model*

Managed supplier

Suppliers should expect to be under close scrutiny, 'managed' to deliver more value. Access to the customer will be controlled, information will tend to flow more as demands than shared insights and, as a result, it might be difficult to make much progress – something of a catch-22. The supplier must realize what is at issue and start working on value propositions. Slowly, the effort *will* be appreciated, even if at first it misses the target.

Partnered supplier

This suggests open doors, perhaps even open books if value really is the issue at stake, and not costs and prices (see below). As ever, the warning for suppliers is not to become complacent.

Welcome supplier

This suggests that there is an opportunity for the supplier to win more business, to become a larger supplier with greater significance, and so develop into a partnered supplier. The door is always open, but learn how to use this privilege to the *customer's* benefit – don't abuse it.

Arm's length supplier

Here, you will only be called upon in times of great need. Not a good starting point, of course, but don't despair: times of great need are just the moments when you can prove yourself by demonstrating your ability to get the customer out of a hole – a pretty high-value outcome.

OPEN BOOK TRADING

Buyers have always tried to get cost breakdowns from suppliers. This is a very old-fashioned, but highly effective way of getting price reductions. The trick is to get the supplier, often through an indiscretion, to disclose the costs of various parts of their package – perhaps the delivery costs, the packaging costs, or even the costs of the sales people. Then, choose part of the product or service that you can do without and demand a discount for this new 'stripped down' package.

The tale of the sales force

A supplier of a big brand name consumer product found their back against the wall with their largest customer, a national retailer. The salesperson was being told that they 'never did anything' to help their customer and it was about time things changed.

Being trapped – the wrong way to handle open book trading…

Being in a corner, the salesperson 'broke' and said, 'But that's not true, just our merchandising sales team alone costs us at least £100,000 a year'.

This was true. Indeed, the merchandising sales team was of high value to the customer – they took orders, stocked shelves, built displays and handled complaints. But that was not the point and, a few weeks later, the salesperson was summoned to a meeting with the buying directors.

'We have been considering your services to us,' they began, 'and we have decided that we no longer require your sales team to take orders in our stores. We will do it ourselves, starting next month, and we would like you to compensate us for our extra work, from the £100,000 that we will be saving you.'

This was not strictly true as the sales force covered other customers as well. Rather than saving £100,000, costs might actually increase, compared to sales achieved. But nor was that the point. The sales force was removed and a substantial payment made to the retailer.

The story gets worse. After a few months, it was clear to the supplier that sales were declining. The retailer was not as diligent in their duties as the supplier's sales team and the salesperson was forced to go back to the directors.

'Can we put our sales team back in?' was the plea.

'Of course. They can start tomorrow,' came the answer, 'but don't expect your money back…'

The right response?

So, where does this leave an increasing trend in purchasing practice to ask for 'open book trading'? This is where suppliers will give full breakdowns of

Trick or treat?

costs, raw materials and services and the customer might also disclose their own costs of using the product or service received.

Is this a new term for an old trick, or is it a genuine attempt to secure greater value from the combined supply chains? There are two things that can be said about this.

First, the suppliers with the most to fear from open book trading are those that have activities or costs within their own chain that do not give value to the customer. If we were feeling harsh, we might say it was their own fault if they got caught out – and buyers often feel harsh.

Suppliers in the top-left quadrant of the value model might experience the worst of this new demand and would doubtless be in fear of meeting it. This will not make for good relations and the whole thing could end in ruin. Much better to start working on improving the value delivered and ironing out the 'wrinkles' of activities that only add cost.

Suppliers in the top-right quadrant might even welcome the request. They have little to fear and much to learn of the customer's own chain.

Rather like the arguments for carrying identity cards, it is said that the only people with anything to fear are those who wish to conceal their identity for some 'dissident' purpose. But it is also the case that 'honest' people might object to the notion through feelings of independence, pride or 'honour'. Fine sentiments, but no way to run a KAM relationship.

The second point is that the supplier must, of course, use their judgement. We are dealing here in the realms of trust, a most important notion in the buying and selling arena, but one often forgotten or underrated. The third supplier positioning model, based on trust rather than spend or value, is useful in considering this question, and will be examined in the next chapter.

Focus on all the costs

If a buyer is focusing on your costs, they may just be after a lower price and this is simply a tactic on their part, or they may actually just care about costs! Where the latter is the case, respond by focusing on theirs. This isn't a question of tit for tat, it's about being honest and open – there are costs on both sides of the relationship. The question should perhaps become – which will be the more appropriate and the more beneficial to tackle?

In a truly mature relationship, if you are asked to go down the route of open book trading, you should also be asking to go down the route of openness about the customer's costs in use.

If you can truly measure those costs, and can also measure the impact you can have on them, you are fast entering the realm of value selling, and a principal aim of many KAM strategies.

Selling value

Suppose you sell pumps, large scale industrial use pumps, and they sell at $40,000 a time. Over five years each one uses the best part of $250,000 worth of electricity. Now, which would do the customer more good – giving them a 10 percent price discount, or investing your budget in developing a pump that was 10 percent more energy efficient?

The former saves them $4,000 today, the latter saves them $25,000 over five years. Only some customers will value that, and that is an important point – value is in the eye of the beholder. Don't expect a customer with cash flow problems to think the energy efficiency argument a good one.

Then there is the point of who in the customer cares about this. What if the buyer just buys pumps, not electricity? If it doesn't impact on their budget or their performance measures then perhaps they wouldn't care so much about you saving them $25,000? Of course, if they are a 'supply chain manager' (see Chapter 8) they should care a great deal, but what if they are not? Remember the idea of the snail from Chapter 3? This is the time to be targeting the factory manager, or whoever gets the electricity bill, and persuading them to pressure the buyer to buy your pump.

Selling value in this way comes in several steps, and they all matter:

1. Understand the customer's needs.
2. Identify what matters most to them right now – what are their challenges and headaches?
3. Understand their definitions of value received.
4. Understand their cost structures and financial performance measurements.
5. Construct your value proposition based on the above.
6. Find the people who benefit most from your proposal.
7. Sell to the 'snail', not just the buyer.

11

Measuring trust

Perhaps your customer is not able, or willing, to exert the effort to measure either spend *or* value. Perhaps they 'position' suppliers in a far more subjective way – a *feeling*…

The trust model is therefore far more subjective; it considers those hard to quantify factors of trust and confidence. As a result, it is rather more a 'seat of the pants' model, and given most people's preference for working that way, one more widely used – at least subconsciously.

The title of this chapter is, of course, rather misleading. The model does not attempt to 'measure' trust, rather to recognize its importance in the relationship. Even to think of this as a formal model is perhaps misleading. While the spend and value models may get put on to paper, this one, more often than not, remains in the head or the heart and plenty of experienced sales and purchasing professionals will say it is all the more important for that – and I would agree.

In most sales situations, especially big money ones, trust, confidence and what we might call 'rapport' are very important (see Chapter 27, 'Selling to the individual'), perhaps even the vital determinant of success. As it is difficult to *measure* such things accurately and quantifiably, it is worth pausing just for a moment to reflect on the following: supposing it is hard to measure the important things – that doesn't mean they don't count. And just because you can measure some things, that doesn't necessarily mean that they are important.

Answering the telephone before the fourth ring has become one of the mantras of professional customer service and it has certainly gone a long way to improving customer relations. But how much more important is the voice that answers the call, the tone, the words used and the degree of helpful assistance? The number of rings is measurable, the rest is much harder to turn into statistics; yet which of the two is more important in building trust?

The level of trust and confidence in the supplier is a factor often underestimated by sales people, perhaps because of the sometimes theatrically contrived postures taken up by buyers. Who could believe that they actually cared about such stuff?

Trust matters more than you will ever be able to measure

The truth of the matter is that they *do* care, very much indeed. Independent surveys of what customers want from suppliers regularly place 'honesty' or 'reliability' at the top of the list – so why don't they say this to the seller's face?

There are many reasons, ranging from, 'It's not an easy conversation to have', through to, 'This is my perception, not a judgement based on facts'. As any salesperson of experience will say, the customers' perceptions will almost always count for more than any evidence or facts that might argue against it. Let's not forget that we are selling to human beings.

What we are looking at here are customers that assess suppliers on a combination of factors ranging through a proven track record, honesty, reliability, a sense of substance, a judgement on ethical standards and a matching of moral values. These are not easy to quantify and any attempt to measure trust is best left, in the end, to an understanding of the power of *'feelings'*.

When Boeing, or any other aircraft manufacturer, sets out to tender for a major contract then of course price matters, as do quality and service, but the sales team knows how much time and care they should take on establishing the right kind of relationship from the very start. The whole process of tender, specification, design, manufacture, delivery, testing and refinement might spread over years. No customer wants to head into such a process with a supplier that they cannot get on with, that they don't like or don't trust.

THE RISK/SIGNIFICANCE/TRUST MODEL

Figure 11.1 depicts the trust model. The labels on the boxes may not seem very different from the value model, but what is perhaps of more interest here is the sort of relationship you might expect as a supplier viewed in each of these four ways.

Figure 11.1   *The risk/significance/trust model*

Partnered supplier

Perhaps likened to a marriage. Like any good marriage, there are ups and downs and it needs continual effort and attention from both parties to maintain the trust and confidence of the relationship. The real test, like a marriage, is how it stands up to hard times. The best marriages have ways of building strength and cohesion through adversity.

Problem supplier

Having started the analogy, we might liken this one to a 'promiscuous' relationship. The customer is ever on the lookout for alternatives. Despite your obvious attractions, there is something not quite right about you, at least not to chance a full-blown commitment. Without proper attention, an apparently loyal customer will 'snap' (see Chapter 3) when a better offer comes along.

Occasional supplier

Be prepared for 'flirtatious' buying behaviour. The customer may give you their time, but rarely the order. As in life, this is a position full of frustrations.

Non-supplier

Plain and simple, a 'frigid' buying behaviour.

Winning trust

Without a basis for trust, and without some reason for recognizing a supplier's significance, you have, effectively, a 'frigid' relationship. If it is a new customer, and you an unknown supplier, then this is where you begin. If you aspire to partnered supplier status then in what direction should you travel?

After all the 'it depends', a general principle holds for most cases. Aim to win trust and confidence *before* trying to prove your significance. Another chicken and egg: how to win trust and confidence if they don't do business with you; they won't do business with you unless they recognize your significance to them; they are reluctant to see that significance if they don't have trust and confidence in you. Nobody said this was going to be easy.

As ever, patience pays. Recognize that it is the small things that win the customer's confidence. The way you behave, the way you keep your promises – to send a brochure by the next post, or to call them back in a week with some figures – these are the most important things at the outset of any relationship. Persistence, balanced by large doses of empathy, is the best approach. Don't talk about what *you* want or what *you* need, talk about what *they* might want and *they* might need.

Once you have won these early confidences then, and only then, will the customer be prepared to listen to your proposals. Go in too early with assertions of what you can do for them and they will simply not be listening, possibly because they may not believe you.

The rewards of trust

The pursuit of a customer's trust and confidence is not simply a question of business ethics or morality – it is the pursuit of competitive advantage. Trust is like a reservoir of goodwill from which both sides can take, provided it is topped up regularly.

The battle between supplier and customer for 'control' of a marketplace can sometimes see trust pushed to one side. The retail market has often been such a battleground. In recent years retailers have fought back against what they have seen as the undue dominance of the big brands. The disputes over loss leading (where retailers sell brand leaders at prices below cost in order to entice customers into their stores) have moved on to wrangles over the sale of low-priced branded products imported into the UK from outside the EU. Armed with market data culled from their point of sale scanners and wielding ever more sophisticated own brands, many retailers have maintained a fairly consistently anti-supplier stance.

Not so M&S, which throughout the 1980s and 1990s put a high value on their supplier relationships, particularly the question of trust. Important suppliers were given key cards to the M&S offices, allowing them open access to buyers, and to others. This may seem a small point, but it was part of a supplier management culture based on trust and reciprocity – compare it to those retailers that still 'welcomed' suppliers in small, white, cell-like offices on the *suppliers'* side of the reception desk.

M&S benefited by having suppliers that didn't hide their own savings from the customer, and the suppliers benefited from loyalty, that is the principal of reciprocity. Trust must work both ways, and the rewards must flow both ways. In 1995, M&S introduced a new kitchen product, only to find that the supplier had miscalculated their costs and were making a loss on supplying something that was now a great success for M&S, with a price fixed in the M&S catalogue. Many a retailer would have called that an education, but M&S went about helping their supplier to re-engineer the product to lower costs, while they themselves reduced their margin. The result? A long-term relationship with long-term profitability on both sides.

But take care not to become reliant on trust alone; sellers and buyers alike beware. Changes inside or outside the relationship can alter the picture in a very short space of time. When M&S hit problems with sales in the late 1990s, particularly with clothing, it was the suppliers that suffered most. Long-term relationships were broken despite high levels of trust and rapport. It would be too easy to lay the blame entirely at the door of M&S, it is the case that relaxed relationships can sometimes breed over-relaxed suppliers. In pursuit of trusting relationships, 'cosiness' is a very poor substitute for hard-headed realism.

When trust goes out the window

I have heard plenty of sales professionals crying 'foul' over buyers they thought were 'tame' who then suddenly turned on them. Their use of language suggests that perhaps there was something less than two way trust going on here, but whatever, such appeals often show an innocence that we must not permit, as innocence breeds all sorts of problems.

There are two things to say here – the danger that trust breeds complacency, and the danger that complacency blinds us to the real world.

Complacency

You don't bring me flowers... anymore...

Selling is sometimes like courting. It all begins with a view from afar, and then moves slowly towards contact, at which point the pace quickens amid treats, gifts, and armloads of flowers. Then comes the marriage and the honeymoon and slowly the flowers start to drop off. The months and the years pass and suddenly someone comes home with a bunch of flowers – and the response? OK, so what have you done?

The real world carries on…

So you have perfect trust and openness and then suddenly the buyer demands a price cut or else you will be out. Sales people can react to such things with all the surprise of a jilted lover, which rather suggests that they have not been paying attention. Such sudden demands usually result from something – poor trading conditions for the customer, a lost customer for the customer, cash flow problems after an expensive acquisition or investment – the very sort of things that the key account manager should be fully aware of.

The skilled key account manager will know when the time is right to speak to the customer about what help they might need – the perfect timing being just before they speak to you! That way changes to arrangements don't lead to breaches of trust, indeed they work to strengthen it all the more.

12

Supply base optimization

The natural result of all this 'spend mapping' and 'supplier positioning' is the customers' desire to 'manage' their suppliers, or supply base. In broad terms, supply base optimization answers two questions: (1) Which suppliers will best help us? (2) How must we help them?

This might involve reducing numbers, finding new suppliers or resurrecting sleeping ones. It might even involve actively developing the capabilities of some suppliers.

The aims are varied: improved efficiency through lower transaction costs, greater leverage, greater control and improved value received. But, whatever the motivation, this is a trend that will affect all suppliers. This chapter will look at two broad directions: (1) reducing supplier numbers; (2) developing suppliers' capabilities.

REDUCING SUPPLIER NUMBERS

Supplier rationalization is a phrase to strike terror into the hearts of most suppliers. Of course, if you are on the list of survivors then it could be good news, but that hardly makes you sleep easy at night while the process is under way.

Done badly, such activities can create havoc for both supplier and customer. Confidence can be blown and performance can suffer. A nervous supplier is rarely the best supplier. Doing it 'badly' might mean any number of things: in a hurry, without warning, without supplier consultation, without defining the rules, without reference to the supply chain, or worst, to a hidden agenda.

Done well, the outcome can be good for all, even for the non-selected suppliers who at least have a clear understanding of what it will take to be selected. Doing it 'well' might mean: planned, with clear objectives, communicated to all involved, with the support of suppliers and for the benefit of the whole supply chain.

There is an analogy with 'downsizing', the trend of the 1980s and 1990s where staff levels were radically reduced, particularly at middle-management levels. We all know of horror stories where key people were removed, essential expertise was lost and basics like customer service began to crumble. There are also cases where such actions transformed a business from near death to prosperity. The difference usually lay in how the exercise was carried out.

For the supplier faced with the prospect of rationalization, the most important thing is to be talking, early, to the customers concerned and to be asking some crucial questions.

Questions, questions, questions

- Why are they reducing numbers? Leverage, performance improvement, lower transaction costs, true alliances?
- What are the target outcomes? Final numbers, specific performance measures, lower costs, better value?
- What standards will they apply?
- What are the givens and what are the differentiators? What must any supplier do – what might make a supplier stand out from the crowd?
- Will they be 'selecting out', or 'selecting in'? Removing the chaff, picking the winners?
- How do we stand right now?
- What must we do to meet your standards?
- How long do we have?
- What can we expect in return for meeting your standards?

Don't fight supplier rationalization, you can only lose. Seek to understand the rules and play to win

The earlier you talk, and the broader the range of contacts (remember, the 'diamond' relationship is about ensuring long-term security and customer retention), the more chance you will have of surviving such rationalization. With appropriate skill and subtlety, perhaps you can even influence the setting of standards and performance measures by which the decisions will be taken, to suit, of course, your own performance advantages.

The worst thing to do would be to curl up in a ball and await your sentence, good or bad. The process of rationalization can be just as daunting for the customer as it is for suppliers and those suppliers that can actively help with the process will stand well in the pecking order.

Potential downsides

Be aware of their objectives and also be aware of some of the potential downsides of rationalization. These might be useful, not to use as arguments *against* the customer's intentions, but to demonstrate your concern to help them get the best outcome:

● Is it just a fashion, to be reversed in a few years' time?
● Where will all the 'rationalized out' suppliers go – the competition?
● What if you kill a supplier?
● What if, as times change, you need them back?
● With the advance of e-commerce, do you need to rationalize?
● Will the remaining suppliers be as capable as they claim?
● Are you increasing your risk exposure?
● Can the smaller list be managed and policed, or will local buyers simply ignore it?

Is the trend waning?

If downsizing was the trend of the late 1990s, we have seen some evidence of its reversal in more recent times. Will supplier optimization follow a similar path? If we remember the objectives of reducing supplier numbers – efficiency, leverage, control and value – then if alternative ways of achieving this appear, we might expect the trend to reduce or even reverse. One such alternative is e-commerce (see Chapter 27). GE is one example of a business that has seen e-commerce as a route to greater purchasing efficiency and control and now, rather than reducing suppliers, they are expanding their supply base through this new medium.

When considering your own future with a customer that has a supplier optimization programme in process, you will need to walk carefully between two principles. In theory, it should be the ends and not the means that will determine the outcome; if you can offer greater efficiency through e-commerce, why should they delist you merely in pursuit of a numbers game? But, in practice, you must also adhere to their current thinking, which may have more regard for the immediate means – the programme itself.

RATIONALIZATION & CENTRALIZATION – *CONTROL AND PROFITABILITY*

The trend towards fewer suppliers has usually gone hand in hand with the trend towards greater centralization of purchasing, and for similar reasons – control and greater profitability through better deals and reduced purchasing costs.

The question – is centralization good for a supplier? – may appear to depend rather on the supplier's starting point. If it's you that is being narrowed down to, perhaps that's OK, but what if it costs you in terms of margin?

Or is this the wrong sort of question? I think so. If the customer is centralizing and rationalizing then you only have one choice – help them. Consider how difficult it is for them – they have their own internal problems to cope with – the last thing they want is an uncooperative supplier. What they really want is someone who will help them succeed in what is a tough challenge.

A business based in fifteen different European manufacturing locations decided to centralize its purchasing of packaging materials, including 205 litre metal drums. They also decided to source from just one supplier rather than fifteen. The result was a handsome discount.

Don't get held over a barrel...

Unfortunately, the buyer was not aware that each site had designed its loading bays to hold precise numbers of these 205 litre drums, based on the height of the drum used. When the decision was made to centralize and rationalize the chosen drum just happened to be two centimetres taller. Not a lot, but stacked three or more high all of a sudden the right numbers could not be got into loading bays across Europe. The extra costs of storage space ended up being more than the savings on the drums in the first place! Not such a smart buying decision. But should we blame the buyer? Rather we should blame the suppliers for not seizing their opportunity. Once they knew what was afoot, surely one of them at least should have moved to help the buyer make the right choice. There were of course options – source different sized barrels by location, get the locations to alter their loading bays, source a shorter barrel, and doubtless you can think of plenty more.

Moral of the story? The key supplier is the one that helps the customer achieve what they want, in an intelligent and economical way. Don't fight centralization, make it work for you by using your local expertise to the buyer's benefit.

DEVELOPING SUPPLIERS' CAPABILITIES

Perhaps in the past there was a tendency for busy but dissatisfied buyers to wait for the 'right supplier' to find them, or hope that existing suppliers would make the improvements required. Of course, they would do their best to cajole, to press, perhaps even to demand those improvements, but their responsibility ended there, passing it into the hands of the supplier.

Supply side managers might see their responsibilities differently. As well as cajoling, they might now determine to actively help key suppliers to improve. For some suppliers, this might result in a rather different kind of relationship where they are managed *by* the customer. This is not uncommon in the retail industry where major retailers effectively manage some of their own label suppliers: the customer sets the standards and the specification; they manage the forecasts and so the production schedules; they initiate new product developments; and, perhaps of greatest significance, they manage the suppliers' margins.

The style and resultant activities of such a relationship might depend on the box occupied in the supplier positioning model. Let us go back to the original risk/significance/spend model from Chapter 9.

Bottom left – tactical make easy

The motivation might be to develop a supplier to be a capable sole-supplier. It might need help with integrating its processes with the customer, particularly any form of e-commerce. Perhaps the customer might even install an EDI system that allows the supplier direct access to their customer. In return, the customer will set tough performance targets and will expect penalties to be paid for shortfalls.

Top left – strategic security

The customer will be concerned about future security and will often go to great lengths to improve the reliability of key suppliers. UK supermarkets wanting to sell organic produce have found that many potential suppliers do not have the commercial set-up to cope with their demands. Sainsbury's, in their drive to develop this market, has taken active steps to improve such suppliers' capabilities, particularly their business processes, and has offered training and investment through organic supplier 'clubs'.

Top right – strategic partners

Joint investment in development projects might be expected to form a part of these relationships. A customer eager to see a faster flow of new products might help their supplier with their financial investment by providing people, giving guarantees of business, or offering themselves for pilot trials. In return, they will expect some form of special arrangement, perhaps exclusivity.

This gets to the very nub of relationships in this box: the supplier has undoubted privileges, but they come with attendant responsibilities. The customer may let you get very close to them, provided you agree not to supply their competitors – anyone who works closely with companies such as Coca-Cola or Procter & Gamble will recognize this theme.

Through the 1980s and 1990s, Marks & Spencer led the way in the retail trade, managing some of their strategic partners to the point that those suppliers thought, talked and acted like Marks & Spencer – true synergy. Some suppliers became very reliant on Marks & Spencer, put their trust in the customer's judgement, and allowed their customer to determine their ranges, quality standards, service levels, even their margins. Was this good for suppliers? Many benefited enormously – some still do – but others found themselves severely burnt when Marks & Spencer's fortunes were reversed in 1999. The decision to look to cheaper, more varied and more creative suppliers for clothing hit some of their incumbent 'partners' hard.

When a customer manages their suppliers to the extent that Marks & Spencer have done, they gain much from the control, but they also risk a significant loss – the loss of an 'independent' suppliers' flair and innovation. When a customer takes on all the responsibility for things such as their supplier's product development, then they have to get it right because there isn't anyone else to come up with the ideas.

A successful relationship in this box must recognize the potential perils as well as the benefits of such closeness – only then can it guard against them.

Bottom right – tactical profit

Not the most fertile ground for trying to develop suppliers' capabilities – strong-arm tactics are usually easier and may well be more effective. One area might be to help suppliers increase their scale, and so their efficiency, by carefully managed increases in volume in return for steadily decreasing prices.

13

Culture and values – becoming a strategic supplier

The tale of two hospitals from Chapter 10 involved two elements to do with value, one obvious, the other more subtle.

The obvious measure of value involved servicing costs, costs of overhauls, perhaps even the cost of the court case. These are tangible things and the maths soon becomes clear – my mother was right, you should always buy the best shoes you can afford; they're cheaper in the long run.

The more subtle sense of value was around the fact that the hospital sinks or swims based on their reputation. I once heard a hospital manager say, 'If the customers feel they can trust us then they don't begrudge having more expensive coffee in the waiting room.' He went on to say, 'They don't even mind if they have to pay for things that other hospitals do for free – but do badly.'

The more subtle, or broader, sense of value that might be used to assess a supplier's offer usually has something to do with the broader aspirations of the business – their *business strategy*. Of course, providing the sort of value that helps a customer implement their business strategy is 'a good thing'.

A supplier may become regarded as a key supplier because they behave appropriately against the expectations of the customer – the KAM will certainly need to identify the 'obvious' measures of value. To become a strategic supplier, the KAM will have to identify with the subtle measures as well.

To do this they will have to understand the culture of the customer and the values that drive it. More than this, the KAM will need to orientate their own business so that their operations in front of the customer match with the customer's values. If we see the achievement of strategic supplier status as a development beyond key supplier status then it will be ignorance of the more subtle sense of values that does most to deny the supplier the accolade.

Key, strategic, preferred, honoured... what's in a word?

Maybe nothing. Your customer may use entirely different words, or none at all. No matter, the definition of 'strategic supplier' as used here is simply a supplier that manages to have a positive impact on the very heart of their customer's business.

This chapter attempts to give a short (_very_ short) summary of some foundations of business strategy and how they might reflect in the values held by the business. The purpose is to help key account managers identify the values driving _their_ customers, and be better placed to match them.

WHAT ARE THEY UP AGAINST?

In Chapter 3 we looked at Michael Porter's model for assessing the competitive forces on a business in order to understand our own competitive position. We might attempt to do the same for our customers: what forces are they trying to resist, what barriers might they raise, or what obstacles do they seek to overcome in order to achieve their strategy?

The supplier that understands their customer's competitive position, and acts to enhance it, advances themselves several places in the queue for 'strategic supplier' status. To do this, the supplier must first be able to identify the customer's business strategy; a task not so easy as it may sound. It will take more than just asking the buyer. How often have you complained of not knowing your _own_ company's strategy? Then why should your customer's staff be any better informed? Such understanding will require a breadth of contacts, particularly at a senior level.

BUSINESS STRATEGY

Business strategy is a vast subject, countless textbooks explain its intricacies, and much time is spent on its development. The following is intended merely as a practical tool for identifying with your customer's business strategy and its implications for your key account planning.

Business strategy, at the level we wish to understand it, might be said to be the outcome of three questions, each with its own issues and each with its own simple model to aid understanding (see Table 13.1). The result is a set of specific aspirations, values and approaches that will define the activities of the business.

Table 13.1 *Business strategy questions*

Questions	Issues	Model
● What to sell and where?	● Products, markets and risk	● The Ansoff Matrix The Product Lifecycle
● Why will people buy?	● Competitive advantage	● Michael Porter's Competitive Advantage
● What makes your business hum?	● Leading business system or driver	● Treacy and Weirsema's Value Drivers

Business strategy is reflected in purchasing strategy – if the supplier knows what to look for

As we have seen (Chapter 8), in a business that practises supply chain management you would expect to see the business strategy reflected in the purchasing strategy. This in turn determines their expectations from suppliers and provides the key account manager with insights into providing genuine value. The more that can be understood of the customer's wider aspirations and strategy and how these are manifested in the business's culture and values, the better.

The rest of this chapter will take each of these three questions in turn, using the appropriate model as a guide to uncovering the answers and illustrating how those answers might impact on a supplier.

WHAT TO SELL AND WHERE? THE ANSOFF MATRIX AND RISK

For any business wishing to grow, there are four choices with regard to what it sells and where, expressed by the four boxes in the Ansoff matrix (Figure 13.1), named after its developer:

- Sell more of existing products into existing markets – *market penetration*.
- Sell existing products into new markets – *market extension*.
- Sell new products into existing markets – *new product development*.
- Sell new products into new markets – *diversification*.

Provided that there is more business to be had in your existing market (you do not already 'own' 100 per cent) then market penetration is usually the safest strategy. You already have a presence, you know the requirements and you can measure your activities with some confidence.

As your chosen growth strategy moves around the matrix, from penetration to extension, to NPD and, finally, to diversification, the risk of failure increases. Why does risk increase? With each step away from your existing market and your existing products you are moving further into the unknown.

Of course, some risk is necessary if you wish to grow, but any sensible business will always seek to manage or contain that risk as far as it can. There are many things that can be done to manage risk:

- market research;
- market testing;
- joint ventures with experienced partners;
- take on experienced staff, or training;
- seek help from the suppliers.

This last point is, of course, of great importance to the budding strategic supplier.

Reducing the customer's risk

If the customer's business strategy involves market extension, NPD or diversification then the purchasing function can do a great deal to help reduce or manage the increased risk by calling on their suppliers for help. That help might come in a variety of ways, depending on what sort of growth they seek.

Risk is good, if you can help your customer to manage or reduce it

Figure 13.1 *The Ansoff matrix*

Market extension

Your customer is seeking to enter a new market with their existing products. Let's say it is in the sports clothing business and you supply them with textile dyes. The new market that the customer has their eyes on is the fashion clothing market – they believe there will be a demand for their products as teenage fashion wear.

The staff realize the risks involved – what do they know about the fashion business? – and they are sensible enough to look for help. Suppliers that also have experience in this new market may be in a good position to advise them. There are some specifics that will be required from the suppliers – an ability to keep up with the growth, perhaps a need for different dyes, but it is the help beyond those things that will earn them the greatest respect. Information on market size and dynamics, distribution channels, pricing, consumer trends – all of this will help the customer reduce the risk of their new venture.

The opportunity to be more involved with the customer's marketplace is almost always one to be welcomed by a supplier and the more they can become involved, the more likely they will be viewed as a supplier of strategic importance.

New product development

Your customer has publicly stated their aim of launching 30 new products in the next two years – a *lot* of risk. Depending on the type of business, success rates for NPD can be as low as single-figure percentages. You supply fragrances to the perfume and cosmetics industry, one where NPD success rates are certainly in the lower teens and the costs of a product launch run into the millions. If your activities as a supplier can help improve the customer's chances of success by only a few percentage points then you will matter to them – a *great* deal.

What does the customer need? A supplier that can be trusted with confidential information. A supplier with an innovative R&D department. A supplier that can move quickly, to tight deadlines. A supplier that can help the customer reduce the time to market. A supplier that is prepared to take on some of the risk.

The importance of matching the customer's values is paramount in this scenario. You must speak the right language, as well as coming up with the goods. If you speak to your customers about incremental growth, bore them with your ability to deliver three times a week and offer them extended credit provided they don't ask for any short-notice services, you should not be surprised to be shown the door.

The main issue is likely to be sharing of risk. You will be asked to work with the customer at the early stages of NPD, before the merest sniff of a sale. You will be asked to commit time, energy and perhaps even money to a venture that could fail. Willingness to cooperate could well be rewarded by the recognition that you are a strategic supplier – one that helps the customer achieve their strategic goals.

This is not to say that the supplier must always leap in with both feet to any request for help. Remember the 'sad tale' of the ink supplier from Chapter 6. Such requests will test your judgement and your knowledge of the customer. You must judge how successful another company will be at launching a new product – judging your own is hard enough and, of course, this company is your customer. How far should you be involved? How far _can_ you be involved? Who will control your destiny?

Avecia LifeScience Molecules is a very successful supplier to the pharmaceutical industry. One of their greatest challenges is knowing how much effort to put into a piece of work for a customer setting out on a new drug development. Will the customer's drug succeed? There is a mountain of tests, regulatory approvals and efficacy trials to get through. It could be years before any appreciable volume of business is established. 'Jam tomorrow' is a common call to action. Much of the success of Avecia LifeScience Molecules is based on their ability to make these judgements – Avecia practises partnership KAM.

Reducing your own risk depends on your ability to assess your customer's level of risk

The questions that need answering are hardly the sort that can be discussed by a seller and buyer across a negotiating table. These are issues that involve the whole of the supplier's key account team in their relationship with the broadest range of contacts on the customer's side. The 'diamond' model of partnership KAM is a prerequisite for such judgements and decisions and so a prerequisite for success in this high-tech industry.

Diversification

Customers involved in this activity, provided, of course, that they are aware of what they are taking on, might ask for a combination of the sort of help described above.

The risks are so significant in this type of activity (a record producer that decides to be in the airline business, or a cigarette manufacturer that decides to enter the fashion apparel market) that most businesses will seek significant help and support from their suppliers. This might even extend to full partnership in the form of joint ventures or licensing arrangements.

Virgin manage their high-risk strategies by using expert suppliers

The Virgin formula (record producer, to airline, to hotelier, to soft drinks, to railways, to investment manager – diversification with a vengeance!) is to minimize risks through close partnerships with key suppliers. Virgin brings the brand name, the supplier brings the market expertise. The supplier is expected to take on a good deal of the risk (in some cases, the majority) and should they fail in any way then Virgin retains the right to step in. This is not an activity for the faint-hearted.

The success stories become the stuff of legend, but, of course, the gutters are awash with the failures. The challenge for the KAM is knowing when to back and when to back off. The judgement will require an intimate knowledge of the customer and their capabilities and, should you decide to proceed, the closeness of the working relationship will require a close mirroring of culture and values.

WHAT TO SELL AND WHERE? THE PRODUCT LIFE CYCLE

Partly as a consequence of the disciplines of supply chain management, buyers are increasingly interested in understanding the life cycles of their own company's products or services – something that was previously the preserve of their marketing colleagues. The results of their analyses of these Product Life Cycles (PLCs) can have a significant impact on their expectations of suppliers.

Figure 13.2 shows a standard PLC, with the introduction followed by growth, moving into maturity and then into saturation and decline. The company's marketing department will, of course, be working hard to give new life to products as they approach maturity, and these efforts may often cause the purchasing department to put new demands on suppliers.

Figure 13.3 suggests some typical concerns for the customer at each stage of their own product's life cycle. These will increasingly be voiced through the purchasing department, and will impact on the kind of response expected from a good supplier.

Understanding where the customer is on its product life cycle gives big clues as to what it might expect from suppliers

The stages of the Product Life Cycle

Introduction

We have seen from the Ansoff matrix (Figure 13.1) the high risk involved in new product development, and it is at this early stage of life that most flops occur. Suppliers are targeted for all kinds of help before the introduction to

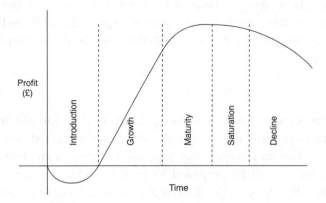

Figure 13.2 *The Product Life Cycle*

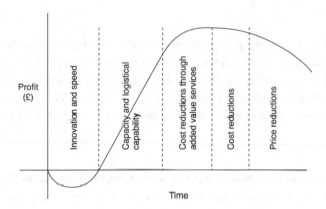

Figure 13.3 *The PLC – expectations of the customer from a 'good supplier'*

maximize the chance of success, but at the critical moment of launch one requirement stands out above all others – timeliness.

The speed to market is of prime importance in highly competitive markets, as days can make the difference between exclusivity and 'me too', and success or failure. A supplier that misses deadlines at this point is signing their own death warrant, and sometimes being too early can be as bad as too late. The target is: on time and in full.

Growth

When a product moves into the growth phase, the biggest problem is often dealing with its success. Forecasting is one thing, but nobody wants to hold back a runaway success just because the forecast was for less. Suppliers are chosen based on their ability to keep pace with growth and those that frown and complain when forecasts are exceeded will not be doing themselves any favours at all.

Maturity

If the marketers are unable to ward off maturity then the purchasers will turn to a different kind of remedy – the search for increased efficiency and cost control. The lazy buyer may just ask for price cuts, but the more thoughtful buyer will be prepared to look for opportunities to receive greater value. For the supplier, this might mean developing a service offer that reduces costs for the customer. Added value services are at their most popular at this stage and, if they can help the customer to revive the product into a new period of growth, then they will be welcomed at a premium.

Saturation

By this point, the writing is probably on the wall for this product and the buyer will be looking to reduce costs by the most straightforward means – price. The future value in the product is not sufficient to justify more complex solutions that might involve new investment. The supplier that can guarantee price cuts projected into the future will be given a lot of airtime.

Decline

The product is on its way out, but the customer still has to keep it going with minimal effort. A supplier that is happy to keep going at the lowest of prices with declining volumes, and also to help by policing their own activities, placing their own orders and the rest, will be very welcome. Why should a supplier be so obliging at this late stage of the customer's PLC? Unless the customer is about to disappear there will, of course, be other products at earlier stages and the supplier would hope to be rewarded for their loyalty and assistance by a generous share of the more interesting projects.

Avoiding the lowest common denominator

There is a particular challenge for a supplier that does business with a customer that has different products at all stages of the PLC. It is very easy to lose focus on the different circumstances and needs, and to then succumb to the lowest common denominator – price pressure. If a buyer wins a price concession from you on a product at saturation or decline, then why shouldn't they chance their arm at one for a product in the growth stage?

The supplier must be very sharp on precisely what kind of value they contribute at each stage, and do their best to keep the buyer equally sharp.

Observation and identification in the real world

Understanding the issue of the customer's PLC is one thing, but being able to spot what stage a product is at is quite another. We are right back to the discussion in Chapter 3 about understanding the customer's market; only through such an understanding can we hope to be able to identify a product's position in its life cycle.

There may also be another clue, one that also takes us back to Chapter 3 and the discussion about the *'opportunity snail'*. It may well be that, in working with a customer to help them launch a new product, the main points of contact will not be with buyers but with R&D. Once the product is launched, and hopefully heads up the growth curve, we might find ourselves having more contact with the operations departments – production and distribution. It is at maturity that we can expect the professional buyer to enter the scene. In other words, the people we see can sometimes tell us something about the customer's concerns based on the stage of the life cycle.

Avoiding maturity

Products don't have to mature, they can be rejuvenated, relaunched, repackaged, enhanced, even replaced. This raises three important issues for the supplier:

PLCs are not pre-programmed, suppliers take note

1. Should they be pressing the customer into these actions?
2. If so, who should they be pressing?
3. When is the right time?

The answers will, of course, depend on a host of factors, but more often than not they will be: 1) yes; 2) marketing; and 3) as early as possible. Don't wait for the customer's product to reach maturity before suggesting a means to give it a new lease of life – things take time to happen.

WHY WILL PEOPLE BUY? PORTER AND COMPETITIVE ADVANTAGE

Michael E Porter, in his book *Competitive Strategy*, outlines the competitive forces that bear on a business (see Chapter 3) and goes on to argue that competitive advantage – the reason that people will buy your product or service – comes from one of two sources:

- Being the lowest cost supplier.
- Being a differentiated supplier.

Success comes from the ability to focus the whole business on whichever route is chosen. Failure results from a business that vacillates between the two, or has functions or departments that argue with each other as to the right choice.

The implications on suppliers and their activities are clear, but only if they understand what their customer is trying to achieve.

Lowest-cost suppliers

This does not mean cheap or slipshod. It does not mean that companies will sell at the lowest price, though they will be able to do this should the need arise. A successful practitioner of this strategy once said to me, 'The trick is to be the lowest-cost supplier, but not let the customer know that!'

It means that they aim to supply at a lower cost than their competitors. They will look at the total costs of supply, purchasing, manufacture, distribution – the total supply chain – and take appropriate actions in each case. Dell Computers have taken huge costs out of the supply of computer hardware as a result of their significant use of the Internet as a sales medium. The answer may be investing in state of the art production facilities, or management systems. Wal*Mart, the huge US retailer, has invested more than any other retailer in information systems and the result has been hugely reduced operating costs. It might result from buying cheaper raw materials, but it could equally result from buying higher-quality materials that reduce wastage, prevent recalls and speed the production process.

For the supplier, the *value in use* argument is vital. Often, the easiest, and the laziest, way to reduce costs is to get the supplier to reduce price. I once had a customer that called their suppliers the 'soft underbelly' of the market, the place you could always poke with a sharp stick. Poor suppliers will succumb to such pressure. A good supplier, a key supplier, perhaps even a strategic supplier, will seek to reduce their customers' costs by more creative means. This may involve changes to specifications,

A customer pursuing a lowest-costs strategy will be looking for suppliers that will help achieve that goal – not necessarily the cheapest

improvements to quality, changes to service, more technical support and, maybe, just maybe, a *higher* price.

Lowest costs can also come from economies of scale and if this is the customers' route to success then they will need suppliers that can cope with the volumes required. An ability to grow alongside the customer will be important. Economies of scale can come from dealing with a few big suppliers just as much as they come from large production runs. This, of course, is the very stuff of supplier rationalization (see Chapter 12).

Differentiation

The customer that sees its route to success through building points of difference from its competitors will be seeking suppliers that can help them achieve this.

It will be important for suppliers to understand what differentiation their customers are seeking to bring to the market, to enable them to make an appropriate offer.

Let's consider the aspirations of a large printing company. The printers want to offer an exciting, innovative range of unique 'finishes', achieved through the type of paper used. They don't expect huge volumes from this venture, but they *do* see the benefits of what they call the 'halo' effect, as customers' perceptions of their standard services are enhanced as a result of these 'new technologies'. They have dozens of paper suppliers, but the right one for this job will be hard to find. It must be a supplier with an ability to develop new products. It must be prepared to offer them exclusively. The volumes for these new finishes may be small. But the supplier that *will* do all this will be held in great esteem and might very well expect to see some rewards through other parts of their business with the printer.

WHAT MAKES YOUR BUSINESS HUM? TREACY AND WEIRSEMA'S BUSINESS VALUE DRIVERS

What makes the business hum? In other words, what values distinguish it and drive it? How do staff know what to do each day – what values drive them and their decisions? What aspect of the business leads to its success – general all-round ability, or is there something more specific?

Treacy and Weirsema, in their book *The Discipline of Market Leaders*, identify three key business drivers. All may be present in any successful business, but in *really* successful businesses, one or other of these drivers tends to stand out, distinguishing the business for their staff and for their customers.

Table 13.2 *Example companies demonstrating Treacy and Weirsema's value drivers*

Driver	Examples
Operational Excellence	Federal Express, McDonald's, IKEA, Dell, Wal*Mart
Product Leadership	Microsoft, 3M, Merck, Intel, Nike
Customer Intimacy	Kraft, Quest International, Airborne Express

Operational excellence is about doing what you do, well. It is about effective processes, smooth mechanics and the efficiency with which products or services are brought to market. Efficiencies of production, economies of scale, uniformity and conformance, accurate forecasting, slick distribution, fast response – these are the sort of things that might be important to a business seeking operational excellence. Such 'excellence' can bring significant competitive advantage in a market where reliability is important or price is competitive. In the main, businesses in the mass market – the no-frills, low-hassle, low-price arena – will be driven by this value.

One size fits all

IKEA achieves huge efficiencies through their logistics chain, from manufacture to store and, in store, the self-selection, self-collection formula completes the operational excellence of the supply chain, reflected in excellent value for customers. International uniformity (Swedish product names like *Gutvik* and *Sprallig* make it all the way to Australia), modular ranges and a carefully honed (limited, but it doesn't seem so) offer are some of the watchwords.

Product leadership is about producing the best, leading-edge or market-dominant products. Businesses with high rates of innovation and patent application often have this value at their heart. It is hard to imagine a successful pharmaceuticals company that is not driven by this value. Investment in successful NPD is the key to success; the market for 'nearly there' or 'almost as good as the best one' drugs is rarely good. One of the biggest threats for a business driven by this value is that of falling behind and it is necessary to continually push the boundaries of performance – and be *seen* to be doing so.

Customer intimacy is the ability to identify with specific customer needs and match products and services accordingly. What distinguishes the customer-intimate business is their stated determination to develop close customer relationships and to act on the resultant knowledge at all levels of their operation. They will probably have a wide menu of products and services and the ability to mix and match these to suit individual customer requirements – or perhaps they will go further than this and offer a totally bespoke service. There is a limit to how many customers this can be done for and a customer-intimate business will think carefully about segmentation and key account identification. Something else that often distinguishes a business driven by customer intimacy is their willingness to share risks with their customers and to expect a concomitant share of the rewards.

Quest International (part of ICI) supplies fragrances to the perfume industry. Each of their customers' products is unique and the fragrance is equally unique – there are few off-the-shelf solutions. The perfumer's art is as much one of black magic as chemistry and Quest must be able to identify with this. Customer intimacy is essential for success; absolute identification with the customer's needs and the ability to focus the whole organization on meeting them. Many of Quest's customers are driven by product leadership – branding is all – and Quest must be intimate with *that* value driver in order to be regarded as a key supplier. Their success is evidence of a broader observation: truly customer-intimate suppliers must be able to identify with value drivers in their customers that are quite different from their own.

Every customer, every product, and every project is unique

Implications for the business

Those businesses with clear business strategies will probably also exhibit a clear preference for one of these values or drivers. Those businesses that are less able to define where they are headed and how they will get there might exhibit a vague mixture of these values, often to their cost. It will be clear that the drivers could be in conflict with each other, particularly if different functions adhere to different values. A customer-intimate sales force promising product and service variations may be in open conflict with its own production and distribution departments if those functions are driven by operational excellence.

If a successful business makes clear its leading business driver then it is easy for the functions within that business to focus their activities accordingly. If customer intimacy is the goal then that doesn't mean the factory should throw operational excellence out of the window. What it *does* mean is that the business should seek to identify *appropriate* operational excellence – perhaps measured by customer satisfaction rather than occupacity (the efficiency with which plant is used to ensure maximum output)?

The tale of the burger

A friend of mine once worked behind the counter at McDonald's, a supreme example of an 'operationally excellent' company. Their ability to replicate the product unfailingly, on every continent of the world, is a remarkable achievement. My friend was young and keen to make a good impression so,

'Good ideas' that ignore the customer's drivers are bad ideas

one morning, as a sign of his initiative, he took a bottle of his mother's best home-made pickle in and placed it on the counter. Every customer was offered a free scoop from the jar to add to their burgers. My friend did not last long with McDonald's. This was the wrong kind of initiative. Now, if he had found a way to improve the uniformity of the buns, or reduce the cooking time of the fries by 5 per cent, then perhaps he would now be on the board.

Implications for the KAM

If, and this is a big if, the purchasing function operates in line with the business strategy, and you are able to identify the business strategy in terms of Treacy and Weirsema's drivers, then you might be able to better predict what issues will be considered of importance. By acting positively on these issues, the supplier increases their chance of being viewed as a strategic supplier.

For the purchasing function, Table 13.3 illustrates some examples of what *might* apply.

Table 13.3   *Practical applications of Treacy and Weirsema's drivers*

Value Driver	Purchasing Focus	Ideal Supplier
Operational excellence	Logistics, inventory, e-commerce	Excellent systems
Product leadership	Supplier partnerships, lead times	Leading R&D, innovative
Customer intimacy	Supplier relationship working in the chain	Flexible, responsive, expert

Suppliers that show an interest in understanding such things about their customer will usually be regarded in a good light. Asking the right questions, of the right people, will bring hugely valuable information. It is unlikely, however, that a full understanding will be possible 'across the buyer's desk'; this is a task for the KA team, gleaning snippets of information at every point of contact and piecing those snippets together for an *intimate* understanding of the customer and their market.

Do we enhance their competitive position, and *should* we?

In discussing the answers to each of the three questions – What to sell and where? Why will people buy? and What makes your business hum? – we have been seeking to understand our customer's business strategy and how we as suppliers can help to achieve its implementation. In essence, we are seeking means to enhance our customer's competitive position, whether by raising barriers against competing forces in their market or by providing the means for them to hurdle over the barriers raised by others. This seems straightforward enough, until we consider the impact this will have on our *other* customers.

Is it the purpose of KAM to aid certain customers to prevail over others? If we are very confident in our identification of key accounts then maybe the answer is yes. We are, of course, right back to the purpose and objectives we set for implementing KAM. How much did we see it as about picking winners? How many 'winners' can there be? Must we be fair to all, or are some customers more equal than others? These are issues we will return to in Part IV.

Of course, in some industries this is an area where large customers, those with dominant market positions, will try to influence their suppliers through persuasion and pressure. Suppliers to Coca-Cola, Kellogg's or Hewlett Packard will know how difficult it is to be a key supplier to these while also actively chasing their competitors.

Does it matter what *you* are?

This chapter has been about understanding what makes the customer tick and how identification with that will enhance your ability to become a strategic supplier. The very same questions – what to sell, why will people buy and what makes your business hum – can, of course, be asked of your own business. In particular, the understanding of value drivers is important to any business embarking on a KAM strategy.

The principles and disciplines of KAM might tend to suggest that a KAM strategy requires a customer-intimate driver. While that would certainly add force to the KAM ambitions, it is entirely possible for KAM to exist and thrive in a business driven by operational excellence or product leadership.

The customer relationship can be 'intimate' in any scenario; it is how that intimacy is turned into actions and commitments that may vary. A supplier driven by operational excellence will seek activities that both meet customer needs and suit their own strengths and abilities – matching market opportunity with business resources. The same can be said of the business driven by product leadership. Nobody would argue that a business with a brilliant list of product innovations could survive without nurturing their customer relationships (at least not for long – see Chapter 6, 'The bad story').

The supplier's own value drivers will influence the way that KAM is practised

It is certainly the case, however, that a CI culture and a KAM culture have a lot in common. Both recognize the importance of customer relationships as the foundation of knowledge and so competitive advantage. Both recognize the need to focus the whole business on to the customer. Both CI and KAM, to be fully effective, must become cross-business processes.

In Chapter 4, we identified what KAM might actually feel like, with two features standing out:

- KAM will change the nature of the relationship with customers, both in its complexity and in its purpose.
- Key account managers and their teams will take on a much greater responsibility for the impact of their activities on their own business and must aim to align their business colleagues behind those activities.

In a CI-led business, both of these features will have full rein. Indeed, they will need to if the business is to be true to its values. In an operational excellence-led business, there may be some restrictions on the scope of these two features. There may be little point establishing complex in-depth relationships with a customer (at least to the same extent as the customer-intimate business) if your operational excellence depends on an entirely standardized offer. Indeed, there is scope for creating frustrated customers if all you succeed in doing is raising expectations for change.

The bad story from Chapter 6 made clear how product leadership cannot stand alone from close customer relationships if those 'clever' innovations are to be relevant. Simply imposing your brilliance on the customer is not enough.

(See Chapter 16 for the implications of competing value drivers within the supplier's business.)

THE CULTURAL MATCH

To be regarded as a strategic supplier, must the supplier be in the same mould as the customer – must they be alike on a cultural level?

The answer is no, plenty of successful relationships exist between absolute opposites, particularly on the global stage. However, it is fair to say that such relationships can sometimes have their moments of doubt, when both sides might wish for something more than that tangible demonstration of business value; when the customer wants to feel they are working with 'like' souls. A preference to work with suppliers from the customer's home country rather than from abroad is in this sense often more than a simple matter of the efficiencies of geographic proximity.

To be viewed as a truly strategic supplier, it may be necessary to practice some level of 'cultural mirroring'. If this is not possible or desirable on the supplier's part then it may be necessary to review how far this particular relationship can develop.

By understanding the customer's business strategy and acting to make a positive impact on it, the supplier will in some way have developed a closer 'cultural match' with the customer. That cultural match might be observed on several levels, from things as simple and as observable as dress codes through to the complexity of organizational culture.

Some factors are easier to match than others, and some are more deserving of the attempt than others. Remembering to dress up or down when visiting the customer is simple enough (and the way to avoid much discomfort), while changing your organization's structure to mirror the customer's is a much bigger throw (and may not even be necessary).

Table 13.4 is a list of the kind of areas that you might need to examine (with some inevitably vague definitions against a notional spectrum in each case), first to understand the customer's culture, and then to assess the likelihood or desirability of a match. How far you go will be entirely down to your own circumstances, capabilities and ambitions. There is no golden rule, other than to observe and understand – once that is done, the necessary actions become much clearer.

Table 13.4 *Some factors to consider when looking at 'cultural matching'*

Dress code	Informal	Formal	Uniform
'Entertainment'	None	Internal only	From suppliers
Meeting venues	Customer's	Neutral	Supplier's
Meeting style	1:1	Ad hoc	Teams
Organizational structure	Hierarchies	Teams	Flat
Management control	Open	Federal	Centralized
Management style	Empowered	Process led	Individualistic
Internal communications	Informal	Ad hoc	Formal
Career development	Ad hoc	Fluid	Structured
Time horizons	Short	Medium	Long
Attitude to risk	Averse	'Shared'	Entrepreneurial
Growth aspirations	Low	Medium	High
Growth methodology	Organic	Mixed	Acquisition
Growth strategy (Ansoff)	Penetration	Market ext/ NPD	Diversification
Competitive edge (Porter)	Lowest cost	Mixed	Differentiated
Value drivers (Weirsema)	Operational excellence	Product leadership	Customer intimacy

Part III

Preparing For Key
Account Management

What will it take? Goals and obstacles

There will be a list of issues that confront you depending on how far you and your business are already orientated towards KAM:

1.   Where do you want to get to? What are your goals?
2.   What obstacles stand in the way?
3.   What new attitudes, behaviours, skills, systems, organization and resources will be required?
4.   What changes, activities and commitments will be critical to your success?
5.   How will you manage the change required?

GOALS

The key account management and key supplier status models (see Chapters 5, 9, 10 and 11) are designed to help you and your team to identify your current positions and articulate your goals. They provide a common language. Remember, *everyone* in your organization must be able to identify with these goals – everyone must speak the same language.

The models will also help to describe and guide the journey involved, providing important signposts and comforting milestones of progress made. It may seem obvious, but it is very important to start with an assessment of where you think you are – not everyone may agree. Remember the joke about the man asking directions from the 'local yokel': 'Arr, I knows where youz be's a wantin',' came the reply, 'but if I wuz youz, I wouldn't be startin' from 'ere.'

Goal 'hierarchies'

There will be KAM goals for individual accounts, but there must also be KAM goals for the whole business. For instance, is the business using KAM simply to identify the most important customers, or is a 'KAM culture' being sought – perhaps a process for driving and directing the business?

The wider the scope of the goals, the more radical their impact on the business and the greater the requirements for change; then the greater the obstacles and opposition that might be expected. The following chapters attempt to outline those obstacles and indicate what skills, systems, organization, resources and change management will be required to overcome them.

Part IV will then look at the kind of definitions for key accounts, and others, that will be required to help the whole business align behind the KAM concept.

OBSTACLES

The obstacles to KAM are rarely out there in the market place – it's not the customers or the competitors that stop you. The obstacles usually sit within the supplier's own organization. The following list covers those most frequently found, though of course your own list will be unique to you – please don't be nervous about adding some more!

The deadly sins

Poor skills

- Resistance from the sales team
  - Fear of change
  - Inappropriate skills
- Inappropriate people or skills
  - A non 'streetwise' supporting team

Poor systems and processes

- Failure to measure the impact
  - — Poor measurements of account profitability
- Conflicting measure of performance across departments/regions
- Clashes of objectives and priorities across functions
  - — 'Inappropriate Operational Excellence'
- KAM as bureaucracy
  - — 'Telephone directory' account plans
  - — Meetings, meetings, meetings…
- Poor disciplines for internal communication

Inappropriate organization or structure

- The Silo mentality – *functional managers as 'Barons'*
- Multiple or competing supplier business units
  - — Whose Key Account is this anyway?

Failure to make it happen

- Top management 'cop outs'
  - — Short-termism – *failure to respect the need for investment*
  - — Failure to identify the key accounts
  - — Failure to align the business
  - — Failure to empower the key account teams
  - — Abandoning the concept in times of crisis…
- Complacency and inertia
  - — No dissatisfaction with the status quo
  - — Existing processes no longer appropriate but too deeply imbedded

Failure to make the hard choices

- Too many Key Accounts
- No plan for servicing the non Key Accounts
  - — Failing to free up the energy required
  - — Service Creep – every customer gets the package designed for the key accounts

The day I meet an organization that suffers not one of these sins is the day I hang up my trainer's boots…

I have not listed them in any order of severity (they are in fact in the order that they will be addressed in the following chapters), and in different circumstances what constitutes the 'worst sin' may vary considerably.

Some of the above are problems encountered once the journey is underway – KAM as bureaucracy for instance – while others will stop it even starting – Complacency and Inertia being a particular killer.

The list is daunting, and perhaps it should not be expected that even the most successful applications will be entirely free of some of them.

Perhaps your task at this stage is to determine exactly what does stand in the way (are you starting, or are things in progress) and which need to be tackled earlier, and which can be left for the moment.

Sign the pledge ...   Don't get hung up about curing everything before you start – rather like Alcoholics Anonymous, recognizing you have the problem is half the battle.

What will it take? Skills

THE CHANGING REQUIREMENT

Before we get too far with this it should be noted that when asked, the sales professionals currently engaged in the task of KAM have often proved to be the worst judges of what skills they require to do this job!

Why this state of affairs? Largely because they differ so much with what the customer thinks is required. Cranfield Business School has done a good deal of research into what the customer looks for in a key account manager, and the answers have been surprising (at least for those KAMs!).

Instead of selling skills, negotiation skills, presentation skills and the like, the customer values integrity, trust, the keeping of promises, and an ability to get things done in the key account manager's own organization.

The supplier really does have to leave behind some of the beliefs and attitudes that have perhaps served it well enough in the past, and here is an irony, sometimes served it very well!

Figure 15.1 lays out the skills required in what we might call the traditional sales task, compared to the key account management task.

It has been quite possible to find the skills for the traditional sales task all within the one person, indeed the absence of any one of these skills usually becomes quite apparent from their performance.

How about the skills for the KAM task...?

- **Traditional Sales Task**
  - Product knowledge
  - Interpersonal skills
  - Presentation skills
  - Negotiation skills
  - Self organization
  - Time management
  - Territory management
  - Independence

  Possible in a
  top class sales person

- **The Key Account Task**
  - Strategic planning
  - Business management
  - Project management
  - Team leadership
  - Strategic influencing
  - Innovation & Creativity
  - Managing diversity
  - Co-ordination

  Possible in a
  well formed KA team

Figure 15.1   *Changing skills and capabilities*

Key Account Managers and the obstacles

Chapter 14 laid out the deadly sins. What is the expectation on the Key Account Manager's skills with regard to their handling those sins?

Some HR functions insist that all Key Account Managers must be top level influencers able to remove any internal obstacles. Others think it best to remove the internal obstacles first and accept that Key Account Managers are mere mortals after all. I leave you to deliberate the choice.

Man or Superman?

If the absence of a particular skill in the traditional sales representative was easy to spot from their performance, how much more serious is the absence of any particular capability listed under the KAM task (Figure 15.1)?

Key Account Managers are important people, but their team is even more important

And yet do you know anyone capable of all that lot? It is a breadth almost certainly beyond the scope of one individual, and therein lies the importance of the Key Account Team. Provided that the team can provide this range of skills and abilities (where better to look, for instance, for project management skills, than R&D?), then there is no need for the Key Account Manager to become some kind of super-being. I'm sure that this is a relief to all, and not least to the HR department who had been despairing of ever finding such rare creatures.

This doesn't mean that the sales professional can just carry on doing what they have been doing and as they have been doing it. Instead it raises perhaps the biggest change that any sales person will be asked to make on taking on the role of KAM. To use a musical analogy – they must be able to put down their violin – whatever their virtuoso ability – and pick up the conductor's baton. Their role is to conduct the orchestra. Their ability to motivate others, to delegate tasks, and to co-ordinate a team sell becomes paramount.

The key competencies

Many organizations work with competency models, and there are many models, so the following is a rather general statement on what my own observations have shown to be the most vital competencies for the key account manager to possess. The list could be long in theory, but for any practical use it is important to edit hard – I have limited myself to four:

1. The ability to form, motivate, and direct a team of people in a 'team sell', while those people probably do not work directly for them (in a line management sense), are perhaps senior, and are certainly more expert in their own area. **Do you have what it takes?**
2. A focus on creating value for the customer. This involves seeing opportunities, marshalling internal resources to meet them, and presenting powerful propositions.
3. The ability to build long term relationships based on trust. This involves an ability to assess complex decision making processes, the ability to network, and the ability to work in a cooperative and consultative way.
4. The ability to enhance profitability through an understanding of the supplier's own business models.

THE TEAM'S SKILLS AND ABILITIES

The challenge of new skills and abilities does not stop with the key account manager. The KA team members will have their own challenges. If people from traditionally 'back-room' functions are to be involved with the customer on an increasingly independent basis then they too will have to develop a range of new skills and abilities. These might include:

- commercial understanding – a 'streetwise' appreciation of their environment and responsibilities, particularly in front of the customer;
- interpersonal skills;
- persuasion and influencing skills;
- presentation and negotiation skills.

To some extent, people from these previously 'back-room' functions will have to take on many of the skills of the salesperson – or at the very least become customer focused and commercially aware. This is, of course, every bit as important as getting the skills of the key account manager up to scratch, but behind the challenge lie many obstacles.

For one, these people might not want to – plenty of people go into R&D, production, or IT precisely because they *wanted* a so-called 'back-room' job.

Equally, the key account manager may have gone into sales because they wanted a job with 'independence', away from the responsibilities and politics of head office. They might view this new role with some distaste, or even apprehension. We are dealing with more than just skills, but with people's attitudes and behaviours.

ATTITUDES AND BEHAVIOURS

New skills do not just appear because job responsibilities change, or because people are sent on training courses. Skills do not develop in a vacuum.

Before new skills can be taken on, those involved need to understand what is required of them, why it matters, and how they might benefit from the change. A man that has spent a lifetime in the role of family bread-winner does not become an ideal house-husband just because he loses his job. Almost certainly, those asked to adopt new skills will also need to adopt new attitudes and behaviours. So, what is the difference between attitudes, behaviours and skills?

Attitudes and behaviours are deeply entrenched and rarely respond to simple exhortations to change. A skill can be learnt, but will not be applied unless there is a desire to do so. (Men can be very slow at learning how to cook, iron and wash up – much slower than learning the skills of, say, driving, fishing and gambling!)

Attitudes are the most deeply entrenched, and will take longest to change – if at all. Behaviours result from attitudes and, although we can all 'play act' to some extent, our true colours will eventually show through. Skills are merely the tip of the iceberg.

Let's just consider one example, from a salesperson's perspective.

Selling versus collaborating

A traditional sales rep might have been used, over the years, to receiving annual sales targets, a range of new products and an instruction to go out and sell. In order to succeed (and survive) the following attitudes and behaviours (good and bad) might have been in evidence:

- My job is to make the customer want what we have.
- I work in my own best interests and if that doesn't suit the customer, I will let my company know through periodic sales reports.
- Achieving my sales target is my number one objective.
- I will aim to do this with minimum disruption to my own organization.
- I will do this single-handed (because I have to!).
- If I encounter internal opposition, who am I to argue?
- If I encounter customer opposition, I need to sell harder.
- Success will result from my own energy and my ability to present and negotiate.

It may be very different for key account managers. To begin with, it is quite possible that they will be responsible for setting their own targets. On top of this, any new products they have to offer will have emerged perhaps as much as a result of their own lobbying as of any marketing departments say-so. For them, the word 'sell' will have a different ring. Success will depend on a rather different set of attitudes and behaviours:

- Not: my job is to make the customer want what we have, but *our KA team's job is to develop an intimacy of relationship that allows us to fully understand our KA customer's needs.*
- Not: I work in my own best interests and if that doesn't suit the customer, I will let my company know through periodic sales reports, but *it is the KA team's responsibility to seek an alignment between our own and the customer's interests (where this is not possible, perhaps the customer cannot be a KA).*
- Not: achieving my sales target is my number one objective, but *satisfying the customer in a profitable manner is our number one objective.*
- Not: I will aim to do this with minimum disruption to my own organization, but *we will aim to do this by involving and directing the organization as appropriate.*
- Not: I will do this single-handed (because I have to!), but *the KA team will achieve this.*
- Not: if I encounter internal opposition, who am I to argue? but *if we encounter internal opposition, we must understand why and seek a way forward, continually aiming to align the business behind our KA objectives.*
- Not: if I encounter customer opposition, I need to sell harder, but *if we encounter customer opposition, we may well be doing the wrong thing.*
- Not: success will result from my own energy and my ability to present and negotiate, but *success will result from our ability to work in collaboration with the customer and to harness the resources of our own organization.*

New ways of thinking – not easy, but essential for success

If the traditional reps were tempted to see themselves solely as messengers, with perhaps an occasional lobbying on behalf of their customers, then key account managers must at least take on the role of 'champion' for their customers. Moreover, they must become the responsible managers of the total relationship between the two organizations.

This sort of change cannot be expected to occur overnight. There are many requirements:

- It *will* take time.
- It *will* require the support of senior management – particularly when there are setbacks.
- The *whole* business must be aligned behind the goals and concepts of KAM.
- Such change has to be managed – *someone has to be responsible*.

Chapter 17 will ask the question that may already be on your lips – are our existing sales people the right ones for the KAM job?

Chapter 18 explores the principles behind managing change of this nature and Chapter 30 offers a timetable and development track for key account managers and their teams.

What will it take? Systems and processes

The attempt to get all the systems and processes required for KAM in place before the journey starts would be a wasted one in all likelihood. The nature of the requirement will be determined to a large degree by the nature of your own particular journey and experience. There is a lot to be said for learning as you go in this regard.

That said, there are some things that almost all businesses need to consider at an early stage, and this chapter will discuss those more general system and process requirements (or will refer to other chapters where they are tackled in more detail).

Making it easy to do business with you

Of all the vendor ratings, of all the customer satisfaction surveys, the issue that comes out most often as a key to success for any supplier is 'making it easy for the customer to do business with you'.

If you wish to practise KAM, then securing key supplier status is important, and if you wish to be a key supplier then you must be easy to do business with. This simple notion should be shouted loud and clear every time that you consider a system or a process – *will it make us easier to do business with?*

KAM systems, the Golden Rule

The following short analysis looks at five broad categories of systems and processes:

- Customer Classification
  — Identifying the key accounts – *The KAISM*
  — Customer Distinction
- Information
  — Measuring Key Account Profitability – *Cost to Serve models*
  — Customer Information – *CRM (Customer Relationship Management)*
  — Knowledge Management
- Communication
  — E-Mail – internal/external
- Operational
  — Forecasting, Logistics, and Supply Chain Management
  — E-Commerce
  — Key Account Plans
- Performance Measurement
  — The Performance Map

CUSTOMER CLASSIFICATION AND CUSTOMER DISTINCTION

This will be dealt with in detail in Chapters 21 and 22. In essence, it is important to identify just who the key accounts are, and to classify the other customers by criteria that will help us to create unique sales and service packages for each category of customer. The task doesn't stop there however, it is even more important that the process used for this classification is understood by everyone involved with KAM, across all functions – it needs to be simple and transparent.

INFORMATION SYSTEMS

Measuring profitability

There are very few rules of KAM, but measuring profitability by account has to be one of them

Chapter 7 has stressed the need to measure account profitability. You will certainly need to engage the support of your business accountants and IT people if this is to be done successfully. Make them part of the team and ensure they understand the importance of what you are asking them to do. Don't expect to just hand them a brief – or if you do, don't be surprised when nothing happens.

Measuring profit by customer may require a substantial overhaul of the current sales and profit reporting systems – perhaps a substantial investment of time and money – and almost certainly a change to some accepted wisdoms and conventions. The reasons for doing so will have to be very clear before you are allowed to proceed.

The tale of the 'Italian Job'

The Italian office of a multinational supplier of high performance plastics was urged to drop one of its larger customers when Head Office in Holland declared that they made a loss in selling to them. Once the customer was duly 'lost', a new profit reporting system was adopted that showed how the now 'ex' customer would have been one of their more profitable. How so crazy?

The old reporting system didn't calculate profit by customer, but did record that the Italian office sold below the Head Office transfer price for products made in Holland. When Head Office looked at the Italian office's books, the customer showed a loss.

The new system abandoned transfer pricing and recorded profit to the whole European group, based on real costs. The Italian office turned out to be one of the 'leanest and meanest' of their European offices, and the product concerned turned out to be one that enjoyed high economies of scale in manufacture (never reflected in the transfer price), and on top of all that, the customer had always paid ahead of time.

The Italian office was asked to 'reinstate' the 'lost' customer. They are still trying....

Customer information

If a true 'team sell' is to be achieved, then a wide range of people will need to know about the customer, and have access to the increasing wealth of knowledge about that customer. Old style visit reports are unlikely to fit the bill, indeed, they are likely to become a bureaucratic nightmare. The KA team will need access to a more ambitious customer information data base. This is not the place to recommend alternatives – there are numerous such systems on the market, or perhaps you will need to develop your own – but only to urge that consideration is given, at an early stage, to this vital ingredient of KAM.

CRM – Customer Relationship Management.

The salesperson is trained to be on the lookout for a range of information – customer needs, buying criteria, perceptions – and to feed this back to those in a position to do something with it – the R&D department, production, distribution, marketing. Such is the theory, but we all know how often such knowledge stays locked in the salesperson's head, or is lost in a string of miscommunications, or is simply ignored by the head office folk who clearly know better.

CRM seeks to use a variety of different systems and software packages to harvest this kind of information from the host of electronic interactions with customers, whether these be visits to the supplier's website or the transactions of e-commerce. Every interaction with the customer has the potential to provide information about their needs, their buying behaviour, their perceptions, their concerns and their frustrations.

The Internet allows various techniques to be used. Analysis of the customer's *clickstreams* as they work their way around your site and into your system can reveal how they go about making their choices – do they look for information first, do they check for alternatives?

The 'virtual sales assistant' is a technique that allows the customer to ask questions, and in so doing reveal much about their interests, their certainties, their doubts and their priorities. Some sites allow customers to interrogate 'virtual customers', to seek 'opinions' of the product or service, and through this interaction the customer will display a whole range of concerns, attitudes and perceptions. This is no different in principle than utilizing the traditional skills of the sales person. We might equate the analysis of the *clickstream* with the sales persons ability to read body language, only now we see the potential for harvesting these observations on a massive scale and using them to modify the proposition. (It is an irony that marketers will now happily listen to what the sales people have to say, provided that those sales people remain reliably virtual!)

Such information is kept in what is referred to increasingly as the *data warehouse* and at this point the amount of information could be mind-boggling. Without sophisticated analysis techniques such as *data mining* we would soon be pining for the 'old fashioned' market researcher with their clipboard. Data mining involves a range of techniques for identifying patterns of behaviour from sales information and other transactional histories. The concept of 'signalling' is one such, trying to recognize customer intentions from their transactional behaviour – perhaps a willingness to pay more for speed, or a desire to set a specification.

And in practice...? That's the theory, but what about the practice. Simply installing a new system will do nothing for the supplier or the customer. This mode of doing business requires trained staff, clear objectives and genuine value for the customer – elements of the equation all too often ignored by companies that think they can hand the responsibility of all this over to the IT experts. The answer of course is to integrate these IT experts into the key account teams hoping to utilize these new systems.

The M for 'Management' in CRM is perhaps misleading. People will still manage the relationship, the system will provide the information. That is true at least for key accounts. Chapter 21 looks at other classifications of accounts, and CRM may well have more of a role to play in the more active management of what we will be calling *maintenance* and *opportunistic* accounts.

Knowledge Management

Capturing information is one thing, turning it into knowledge and using it to enhance performance is quite another.

What many organizations are calling 'Knowledge Management' is becoming a vital source of competitive advantage in the market – those companies that can not only 'discover' valuable information, but then also disseminate it to those that need to know, ***and put it to positive use***, have a significant advantage – knowledge is indeed power.

The challenge is to find the combination of systems, discipline, and skills that will form the core of a Knowledge Management culture (Figure 16.1).

Figure 16.1 *The core of knowledge management*

And the culture itself? Knowledge is power, but power for the organization, not the individual. That is the main cultural challenge. The organization must develop a means of capturing information and ideas, editing those ideas, sharing them with the right people, and putting them into action. The KA team is the means of capture, and they will also be responsible for ensuring the rest of this challenge is met, as demonstrated in Figure 16.2.

Figure 16.2 *Knowledge Management in practice*

BP – Knowledge Management and the *Virtual Team Network*

BP has had enormous success through its development of what it calls a Virtual Team Network. This is a Knowledge Management system, process, and culture, all wrapped into one, and is still permeating the global BP organization. BP has claimed improved profits of $30m in just the first year of operation, but whatever the numbers, there is no doubt that it has made a lot of positive difference. This is primarily a PC based system, where staff have access to the BP Intranet, and can use it largely as they see best. Global project management is a particularly valuable application, with the ability to share information and more importantly, knowledge (the application of that information), across business units, countries, with customers, and with suppliers.

Success results from five key ingredients:

1. Clear business objectives communicated to all.
2. A flat organization allowing easy and open access to senior management.
3. The encouragement of 'breakthrough thinking'.
4. The drive to create value.
5. Information Technology – PC accessed Intranet, video conferencing, etc.

The philosophy of the BP Intranet is to allow staff to use it as they wish – creating their own home pages – 'let a thousand home pages bloom'. Launched with a relatively small group of users in 1995 (the pilot scheme saw a £7m investment), very quickly staff have found access to information, expertise, unknown colleagues working on similar issues, and the idea grows, with more people requesting access to the scheme. By 1996 business units had to pay to become involved, and they came in droves, voluntarily.

One of the most ambitious elements, and particularly relevant to the KAM scenario, is the way major projects are being handled through these 'virtual teams'. Major contracts are conducted through desktop conferencing, and suppliers are involved in a highly creative way. Suppliers are asked to form an 'alliance' on a particular project, working together with BP. More than this, the alliance of contractors is asked to manage the project with much less direct supervision from BP than ever would have been the case pre 'virtual teams'. This is what BP call 'breakthrough thinking'.

For me, the most intriguing aspect is the impact of this 'breakthrough thinking' on how BP now select their contractors and suppliers. If they are to participate in such activities, they must exhibit strong motivation towards working collaboratively, with the customer, and with other suppliers and contractors. They must be highly trustworthy, and they must be very IT literate.

If BP was one of your Key Accounts, would you match up to this vendor rating?

Oiling the wheels of key account management

Having blazed the trail of knowledge management in such fields as exploration, now BP is bringing those skills to the application of key account management. All the training in the world will be of only little use if those involved in implementing KAM are not given the necessary systems support, particularly where customers are global, multi site, and receiving a range of complex product and service solutions. BP's 'Platinum' system, based on lotus Notes and used in its Specialised Industrial Business Unit, provides the account teams with a full range of support, including:

- customer data, and not just the figures, but including details on their needs, motivations, purchasing styles, and key drivers;
- a smoothly oiled system *(what else would you expect from a lubricants specialist!)* for setting actions and monitoring activities across global account teams;
- performance measures, including the all important cost to serve data and the resultant measurement of account profitability.

One of the most impressive parts of the system, perhaps the most important, is the way in which individuals can sponsor changes and improvements to the system found through its use in practice, changes that can then benefit all users, world wide.

COMMUNICATION

As the KAM relationship approaches anything that looks like the 'diamond' of Partnership KAM, it is possible that the KA team, or indeed the business, can suffer a breakdown through a communications overload. As more people talk to each other, and more reports of those meetings flow, and more data is gathered and shared, then there is a danger that KAM can become a monstrous bureaucracy. There will be an urgent need to develop new systems, and new disciplines, for managing communications.

Making remote communications work

You have spent a lot of money on getting the systems in place, but how much have you spent on training people to use them – and I don't mean what buttons to press...

The technology exists, that is not the issue, it is how the technology is used that matters. Whether e-mail helps or hinders is down to the users. How many messages do you have when you return from a week away? (Going away for a fortnight is now just too daunting!) It wasn't the system that sent you this headache – it was people. If video conferences are a yawn (and all the easier to sleep through) then to blame the time lag on the picture or the poor quality of the sound is to miss at least 80 per cent of the reason – it's those people again.

In the old days, being one of the buyer's 'speed dial' buttons on their telephone was said by some sales people to be a mark of achievement – now it's being given access to their intranet. That being so, a proper and disciplined use of the medium is even more important.

When managing global key accounts, or accounts with a wide geographic spread, it is very likely that your own team will itself be based in several different locations. It must be able to work as what me might call a *virtual team* with remote communication the norm and physical get-togethers the exception.

Continuing improvements to video conferencing technology make this ever more easy (though by no means simple) and e-mail quite simply makes it possible in the first place, but there is still no replacement for a physical meeting of the team, as often as is possible, and certainly once a year. The social element of the team is very important and the simple fact of putting faces and personalities to names is hugely beneficial. Any new member of the team tends to remain an outsider until such time as they meet their colleagues face to face.

All that said, for most of the time the discussions will be at a distance and e-mail will be the vital link. It will be as well then to understand some of the pros and cons of this medium, and to agree some team 'rules' on its use.

E-mail – the pros and cons

The advantages of e-mail are many, ranging from its low cost to its immediacy, and including its ability to make time zone differences of little significance, the fact that a written record is kept of all discussions, and the ability to include the customer in the net.

The down sides should be recognized and faced up to. It is still a relatively impersonal medium and a desperately easy one through which to cause offence or confusion. Most of us do not write as clearly as we think we do, and worse, we tend to express our written feelings with much greater bluntness than we would dream of doing face to face. Quite simply, if there is any chance of upsetting folk in your team then e-mail is the surest way to ensure that you do!

The spoken word is not the same as the written, and there is scope for much misunderstanding. Consider the case of a manager seeking advice from the training department on how to develop one of their team members. They feel that this person is a bit rough round the edges, lacking sophistication in their behaviour, and they send a summary comment – 'lacks polish'. The return message suggests a self teaching course of Linguaphone cassettes…

It is a great medium for detail and nitty-gritty but not yet ideal for complex debates or for negotiation or persuasion. Unless you have some special extenuating circumstance, never try to negotiate a price increase with a key account by e-mail and never ask a question by e-mail where the answer 'no' will be unacceptable, but all too likely.

Finally, if this is a global team, don't forget the language issue. Face to face we realize the limitations of each other's understanding but when separated we too easily take it for granted that everyone understands all that is said.

It is a good idea to agree as a team what we might call a communications charter – a rule book of guidelines on how to behave. This is something that you might tackle at your first physical gathering.

The 'Communications Charter'

The issues to agree on might include:

Address groups – do we want all communications shared across the whole team or will the unthinking use of address groups lead to overload? Start a campaign within your team against the receipt **and the sending** of junk mail.

Confirmations – when someone asks for something to be done, must the recipient reply to say they are doing it, or can it be taken as read?

E-mail or telephone – what sort of conversations should we try to have by telephone, or video conferencing, rather than e-mail?

Attachments – take note of the fact that users based at home can have their line occupied for huge chunks of time with complex PowerPoint presentations and the like as attachments – be sensitive.
Length of messages – messages should be edited ruthlessly – don't send long rambling 'streams of consciousness'. Of course, this takes time; George Bernard Shaw once sent a long letter to a friend and closed with an apology, *'I am sorry for sending you such a long letter, I didn't have time to write you a shorter one.'*

Finally, a piece of advice from Lord Chesterfield to his son in 1747 – *'Do as you would be done by'*. He wrote a letter of course, but such brevity would have made him a natural for e-mail!

OPERATIONAL SYSTEMS & PROCESSES

Forecasting & logistics

The implications for the business of what we might call 'full blooded' KAM are sometimes daunting. The impact on lead times, the demands for flexibility, the impact of 'bespoke' offers; all of this could turn a business from profit to loss if the right operational processes and systems are not in place.

At the top of most lists will be a system that provides accurate, updateable forecasting, and of course, the best forecasting systems are ones that involve the customer. The more intimate the customer relationship, the closer you will get to accurate information. Perhaps of more importance, the closer you work together, the more you know of the customer's *doubts*, the key to *real, long term* forecasting, rather than relying on their public pronouncements – usually of enormous growth. A forecasting system that allows an element of judgement, a percentage certainty of a particular order, for instance, is one that will suit the intimacy of a KAM environment.

Consider who forecasts are for. This may seem obvious; they are for production and distribution people, so that they can plan their activities. But if they are to actually base their operational decisions on those forecasts, then they will want to have faith and trust in them. A manufacturing unit that sees forecasts as the 'wild blue yondering' of irresponsible sales reps is unlikely to take much notice, and so those sales reps feel less inclined to update their forecasts, and the downward spiral begins – garbage in garbage out. Forecasts must be 'owned' by all, and they must be continually reviewed and updated. Whatever system is adopted, it must allow for that joint ownership, and flexibility.

Also close to the top the list will be systems to provide slick logistics. Those businesses that are looking at Supply Chain Management – the co-ordinated management of supply from purchase, through manufacture, through sales and marketing, to distribution – will already be well down this line. If your business is not looking at this, then the move towards a KAM environment; with its greater focus on specific customer needs; will make it all the more necessary.

E-Commerce

Chapter 27 goes into detail on this increasingly important aspect of modern business practice. E-Commerce provides opportunities to improve business processes, particularly those between supplier and customer, to a degree not thought possible only a few years ago. Not only will E-Commerce solutions speed transactions, they will capture information in a way that will allow both supplier and customer to work together in improving those transactions.

Key Account Plans

Chapter 31 will look at this important process for turning the theory of KAM into practice. Key Account Plans must above all else be practical documents – short, and to the point. There is no room for 'telephone directory' sized documents filled with diagrams that simply show you have read a text book!

PERFORMANCE MEASUREMENT

Of course, just as new skills (discussed in Chapter 15) are insufficient without the right attitudes and behaviours, so will new systems fail if there is not a wider understanding of their aims and purpose. Installing a system to measure profit is one thing, but without an agreed definition, across the business, of what profit *means*, the system is all but useless.

We are beset by conventions in measuring and reporting performance, but there are two common conventions, or limitations, that can be particularly damaging to the implementation of KAM. Firstly, what I call the 'burden of the year'; and secondly, the clash of competing measurements, as is often seen between functions.

The burden of the year

Do you rely on astrology in your business? Is the phase of the moon of significance to you? Do you look out for Mars or Venus entering your star sign? No, so why is it so important to you that it takes 365 days for the earth to go around the sun? Our ancestors began to formulate calendars with months and weeks as a means of measuring the passage of time, but now it would seem that the 'burden of the year' has become a means of measuring us.

In some very fast moving industries, the food industry for one, the year is far too long a measure. Comparing performance in annual 'chunks' risks missing the ups and downs within a twelve-month period that are the very dynamics of the industry. Whereas, if you are in the business of selling steel mills, then a year can be the flicker of an eye, and nobody should get too depressed if any twelve month period is rather lean.

The point, of course, is that the period of time for measuring performance should be set by you, not the sun, the moon, or the calendar.

KAM can be a long-term process. Developing a particularly complex customer relationship may take time, the benefits may not accrue immediately, and performance after a year may look fairly dull. It would be tragic if annual requirements caused you to pull back at this point, simply because you were not able to measure performance over a longer period. Remember the notion of 'life time value' (Chapter 7).

Retailers, with their access to sales data through EPOS (electronic point of sale – or, if you prefer, the till) can measure performance by the week, or the day, even the hour. They will often take decisions on particular new products after only a few days' sales. If you supply the retail industry, then your own performance measures must be able to reflect this speed of decision making.

Whichever the need, longer or shorter periods of measurement, your accountants and IT people will doubtless relish the challenge, *and* rise to it, if you involve them in the team.

Competing performance measures

A very common obstacle to KAM is the existence of performance measures that work against a customer orientation. These measures often reside in the functions that support the KAM effort. Consider two examples.

Production measures

A production manager might be measured on 'occupacity' – the efficiency with which they use the plant to ensure maximum output. A Key Account Manager might approach that manager with a 'customer focused' request – to produce a modified product. Let's say that this might involve closing the production line, a re-tooling, a relatively short production run, another close down, another re-tooling, and then back to where we left off. Should the Key Account Manager be surprised if the production manager sends them packing?

Logistics & distribution measures

By their very nature, logistics and distribution functions crave regularity and order – 'operational excellence'. 'Customer intimate' Account Managers who come with short notice orders that help the customer out of a hole are not always welcomed. Let's suppose a business has an 'understanding' between sales and distribution that orders can be met within two weeks of being placed. Not only that, but with a two week lead time, 100 per cent 'on time in full' will be guaranteed. Perhaps this 'understanding' has worked well for a few years.

Times change, and the customers change. The newer customers demand shorter lead times, it is the trend in the market, they do not wish to hold stock – just in time is becoming the order of the day. Perhaps *their* customers are demanding the same of them? The whole distribution chain is changing.

The Key Account Manager, intimate not only with the customer but with the customer's market, is keen to meet the new demands. But distribution call these new orders 'rush orders', and feel no obligation to meet them. They were not part of the original 'understanding', and so are outside the performance measurement for their department. The result is chaos.

Some sales people (those gifted with silver tongues) are better than others at getting their 'rush orders' accepted, but in doing so, put at risk the company's ability to meet the more standard orders. The result? Nobody is happy.

What is required is a concerted approach by sales and distribution to understand what is required in the market, to develop forecasting and logistics systems that will deliver it, and to agree performance measurements to monitor the system. Distribution will still aim for 'operational excellence', but in a customer focused context, not in a vacuum – what we might call 'appropriate operational excellence'.

The answer to the problem in each of the two examples lies in how that production manager or logistics manager is measured; which brings us to the tale of the basketball player.

The tale of the basketball player

Anyone that follows professional basketball will know about the host of statistics that surround the game. There seems to be a measure for every single aspect. Players' performances are measured with merciless accuracy – that is the nature of the professional game.

Two measures stand out – 'baskets', and 'assists', that is, how many times they put the ball through the hoop, and how many times their 'play' helped *another* player put the ball through the hoop. Couldn't some functions be measured on 'assists'?

The Performance Map

There is a lot to making KAM work, you will have realized that by now and we are still only half way through the book! That means there is a lot to measure, and a lot to monitor. What would be useful is a map that shows where we have to go, where we are now, how far we have to go, and what is the best direction to take. This in essence is the Performance Map (Figure 16.3).

The map uses a simple piece of software to lay out the elements on the KAM journey that are of importance in your own circumstance. The steps relate to each other in logical sequences, for instance – two specific require-ments might be a Key Account Plan, and an analysis of the customer's Decision Making Process (Chapters 23 and 24) – but it is unlikely that you will have prepared a decent plan without first having done that piece of analysis.

A questionnaire is used to assess your capability at each step, and the results plotted on the map using green and red lines to indicate good and bad performance. The result is a highly visual picture of where you have strengths – the way you have come – but also where you need to improve performance – the way ahead.

Further information on using the Performance Map can be obtained by contacting the author at INSIGHT Marketing and People Ltd (see chapter 32).

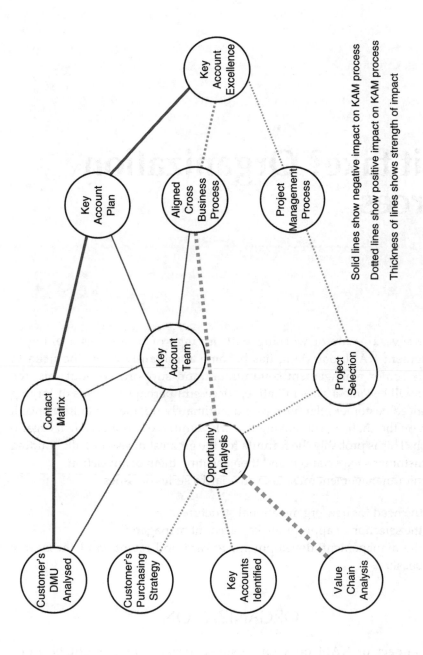

Solid lines show negative impact on KAM process
Dotted lines show positive impact on KAM process
Thickness of lines shows strength of impact

Figure 16.3 *The Performance Map (A much simplified example)*

17

What will it take? Organization and resources

After several years of working with a range of businesses seeking to implement KAM, one thing has become abundantly clear: the need to secure senior management commitment and support. Without this, the effort will become a sales initiative, successful perhaps in terms of forging enhanced customer relationships, but ultimately doomed to failure once it takes on the challenge of making it work within the supplier's own organization. This is probably the formula for the greatest disaster of all: building the customer's expectations and then cheating them of any action.

Senior management must take on board a series of issues:

- the need for new organizational structures;
- the selection of appropriate key account managers;
- the management, development, reward and retention of these 'rare beasts'.

ORGANIZATION

The impact of KAM on your business organization might be quite profound, especially if you intend it to be! If the implementation of KAM is intended to establish a customer-focused business, without 'silo mentality', with performance measures relating to the customer's satisfaction and with the business decisions driven increasingly by key account needs, then expect the organization to be turned upside down.

Turn the organization upside down

Take one requirement – all functions must now share the same values of customer focus and customer satisfaction. How can they do this if the business is still organized in traditional hierarchies and silo-like functions?

One option, if you intend turning it upside down anyway, is to start that way on paper – turn the organization upside down – quite literally, as in Figure 17.1.

In traditional hierarchies, the management sits at the top and the people with customer contact sit lower down, often at the bottom. In a KAM hierarchy, the people with customer contact (whether sales people, customer service, distribution, or whoever) are placed right at the top, with the lines of management beneath.

So what? The message is perhaps mainly symbolic, but well expressed by one new manager when he took over a major company that he felt was arrogant and distant from its customers. This was how he addressed his first meeting with the senior management team:

If you can't be rid of silos, at least turn them in the direction of the customer

'If in your job you don't actually meet with customers, then you had better make damned sure you support someone who does.'

The symbolism continues – the KAM team is empowered to act on behalf of their customer. The task is then to turn the symbolism into action.

The point being made with upside-down structure charts (or perhaps we should start to call them right-way-up charts) is that the management structure should exist to service those who service the customers. The same

Traditional Hierarchies   KAM Hierarchies?

Figure 17.1 *Turning the organization upside down*

187

point can be made for the functions: they exist for the customers, not for their own definitions of operational excellence.

(Going back to silos: the world seems a very different place and you soon change your habits if, instead of being a baron sitting on *top* of your silo, you find yourself viewing the rest of the company from the bottom of it!)

Customers will have little understanding or sympathy for suppliers' structures or for organizations that might mean something to the supplier but have no positive impact on the customer or, worse, seem to operate as obstacles to progress. It is interesting to note that whereas in the past a good supplier would always try to secure an 'organogram', or structure chart, of their customer, it is now quite normal for customers to ask suppliers to provide details *and explanations* of *their* structures. This is seen as something that a good supply side manager should aim to influence in managing their supplier.

Multi-business, multi-unit, multi-site suppliers might find some sense in having separate sales teams for the same customer, but often the customer does not see things the same way. Duplication of contacts is bad enough, but if this complexity also leads to different terms, conditions, service levels and the rest then the customer will not be satisfied. The pressure will be on to change the organization in response to customer demand – not a bad motivation, but it is always best if the organization can pre-empt such demands and look at their own organization from the customer's perspective first.

Letting the customer determine your structure?

You are probably doing this, to some extent, already.

If the customers in your market demand low, and decreasing, prices then a structure allowing a focus on reducing the costs of supply will probably have formed. If the route to lower prices is through economies of scale then manufacturing will perhaps take a lead role, driving the business through forecasting and supply chain processes. Both sales and purchasing might be subservient, focused on volume-related issues, whether with big customers or big suppliers. We might expect a business driven by operational excellence and structured accordingly.

If, on the other hand, the customers demand high-tech products with 'added value' services, a different structure will have formed, perhaps allowing a focus on 'staying ahead of the field'. We might expect to find R&D in a prominent position in such an organization and it will be their project-based processes driving the business. Sales might uncover the needs, but R&D will be the arbiters of what goes and what doesn't. We might expect a business driven by product leadership and structured accordingly.

As well as having described two of Treacy and Weirsema's three business drivers (as discussed in Chapter 13), we have also described here the fundamental choice facing a business seeking competitive advantage, as described by Michael Porter (also Chapter 13) – lowest-cost supply or differentiation. This one decision, if you have taken it and avoided the swampland of the 'inbetweeny', will already have determined much of your structure and organization.

Avoiding meltdown

Should KAM be allowed to take it still further? Should the business be driven by the demands of key accounts? Should cross-functional key account teams determine the objectives and activities of the functions they represent?

This is perhaps the biggest 'it depends' question of the lot, and few generalizations are likely to be relevant to your own situation. Perhaps all that can be said is that if you have applied the thinking suggested by this book to your market and your customers then you will be in the best position to judge!

We should try to go a little further, but be warned, we are entering 'hypergeneralization' territory!

If your business success comes from high market share for a standard product, uniformity, economies of scale and big production runs (operational excellence – see Chapter 13) then it could be that accommodating too many individual customer demands might put that at risk. That is not to say that we should not practise KAM, but that the emphasis is on the 'relationship management' side, not on the 'committing the business' side.

If your business success comes from bespoke offers for precisely articulated needs (customer intimacy – see Chapter 13) then both sides of the KAM story should come into play – intimate relationships and a committed organization.

Your own structure will never be perfect, but if you wish to practise KAM, then you will consider your customer's organization as much as your own

Whichever the case, the selection of those key accounts is vital. In the former, we can only spread our team resources so far; in the latter, we can only work on so many different activities at a time.

We can perhaps console ourselves that we will rarely need to decide, in full, one way or the other. The challenge of business management is coping with perpetual change – nothing is forever. That is not to say that we can afford to drift, but that we *can* consider such decisions as a development over time.

Let's take a company that operates in three countries and has three separate business units. For good reasons, historically, they have chosen to organize geographically, by countries. Local relationships have been seen to be important and local variation and flavour has been of greater significance to success than any 'global' standardization. But, over time, this structure has started to give problems. The needs of customers have become more specific, more challenging, and they have caused a rise in business unit-specific activities. Each business is starting to take on their own approach, their own values. With a country-based structure this gives some problems; there is inevitable duplication of effort and, at the same time, a dilution of its impact.

A move begins towards a business focus and, at some point, the organization is changed to reflect this – three business units overlaying the country structures and perhaps, in time, replacing them. With this structure, there is more scope for developing supply chain management processes (almost inevitably business specific, not country) and for developing a key account management strategy (see Figure 17.2).

How far you will go towards the KA teams directing your focus will depend, but they will provide a bridge through any transitional phase

As time goes by, different strains are felt in the new structure. The development of supply chain management and key account management practice has raised the level of customer intimacy in the businesses and there is a need to review the structure in order to meet new goals. Perhaps the global customer has become a reality and some of these are supplied by more than one of the business units. KA teams become the route to KAM as a cross-business process, perhaps even a cross-company process. In time, it may be the KAM process that emerges as the most significant structural device – a truly customer-intimate development.

Figure 17.2 *Moving towards a business-specific focus*

Whatever the outcome, we should seek to avoid revolution – it rarely works in business, being either too hard to instigate or too difficult to control. We should also seek to avoid black and white – the complexity of working in a matrix of reporting lines may seem crazy at times, but the days of simple straight lines are long gone. In Chapter 15, we identified 'managing diversity and ambiguity' as one of the skills required by a key account manager. It is very much this kind of ambiguity to which we were referring.

Making significant structural changes to a business can be traumatic. Merging different business units that might occupy different sites, or have very different cultures, perhaps even see each other as competitors, can take years. The KAM process can act as a bridge between units in such circumstances, either as a precursor to merger, or *instead* of merger.

Whatever the resultant organization, the important thing is to give KAM some teeth.

From silos to customer focus

Figure 17.3 shows a traditional silo structure with all the problems of aligning internally focused functions and activities towards the customer.

What is the right structure? This depends upon the circumstances, as there is no precise blueprint to help you, and in any case one thing is for sure, it will never be perfect. Let's suppose an organization only has two customers. One of those customers has a highly centralized organization dominated by the purchasing function and strong supply chain management, while the other customer is a loose federation of regional sites, some led by manufacturing, others by marketing, others by logistics, and so on. Unless the organization divides into two businesses, however it is structured, it is likely to be wrong at least half of the time!

Figure 17.3   *The silo structure*

Figure 17.4 shows not so much a structure as an aspiration, with service functions providing the core, operating in support of those parts of the business with direct customer contact, whether that is key account teams, marketing or CRM systems.

Figure 17.4   *The customer-focused structure*

Key Account Selection

If the business organization and structure *is* to be determined by the demands of key accounts then the *selection* of those accounts is critical. Not only that, but selection into categories or segments with common needs that allows a business to be customer intimate while retaining critical mass. Part IV goes into more detail on the relationship between market segmentation and the identification of your key accounts, with advice on how to avoid the 'meltdown' of a business pulled too many ways by their customers.

HUMAN RESOURCES

Chapter 15 will have made it clear that a good key account manager is a rare and valuable animal. Many businesses have looked at their existing sales force and found it wanting, turning instead to outside recruitment. While this might secure the necessary skills, it should be noted that it doesn't always make for an easy initiation for the new recruit. The existing sales people probably see the role of key account manager as their natural next step and may be less than cooperative with anyone that bounces them off the promotion track.

Death of the salesperson?

Does the ideal key account manager have to come from a sales background at all?

This comment is not meant to frighten sales people and is certainly not to suggest that they cannot handle this job, but many organizations are finding that the 'traditional' sales representative, employed for their independence and their 1:1 skills, is not necessarily at the front of the queue for the key account manager's job. Recalling the musical analogy from Chapter 15, if the key account manager comes from the sales team, then they must be able to put down their violin – whatever their virtuoso ability – and pick up the conductor's baton. Their role is to conduct the orchestra and that being so we must add another observation: 'The best violinists don't always make the best conductors.'

The need for planning, coordination, and project management skills, and the increasing requirement for influence within the business, may lead the organization towards people who already have those skills and abilities. Perhaps they might come not from the sales team but from one of the support functions. In such a case, training will play its part in adding the selling skills, or perhaps the obvious sales activities can be performed by a salesperson within the team?

Certainly, when the 'diamond' partnership KAM relationship is considered, and it is identified that a particular function holds the key to building that relationship (let's say that the future is all about new product development and the need for a lot of R&D input), then it is becoming more common for the key account manager to come from that particular function.

The profile of key account managers in a company like Avecia has changed dramatically during recent years. As the selling circumstance has become more technically and scientifically demanding, the level of personal qualification has risen, so that it is increasingly unusual to find a key account manager that does *not* have a PhD. Moreover, their background is more likely to have been in R&D than in traditional 'commercial' roles.

Is it easier to take a PhD chemist or an experienced engineer and train them as sales people than it is to take an 'ace' salesperson and add the qualifications or the expertise? There are those that might argue either way, but at least it is food for thought. Perhaps the answer becomes clearer when we remember that the key account manager is not a 'super salesperson', but a coordinator of the team's capabilities. Selling skills must exist in the team, but they don't have to be the sole preserve of the key account manager, indeed, it is much better if they are not.

How senior?

As each year passes, so the seniority of key account managers increases...

In many implementations of KAM, the key account manager is taken from a level of management senior to the existing sales team, perhaps even senior to the sales managers. Indeed, the role of the traditional sales manager is as much in question here as that of the traditional sales representative. A key account manager will in many cases respond directly to the business management team, not through a 'sales silo'.

This is most evident where the objectives for KAM cut across business and functional lines – perhaps an intention to establish 'global key accounts' in a multi-national, multi-business environment. In such a case, the key account manager will need the credibility and authority that comes with their seniority and experience.

... and sometimes it starts at the very top

In South Africa, Kohler is a leading supplier of packaging materials, and is organized into distinct business units focused on each main packaging technology, such as card, film, can and so on. When Kohler decided that they needed to appoint key account managers to coordinate the activities of these separate units, in front of customers like Nestlé that made use of all of the units, the appointments were made at senior levels, for example, plant manager, divisional director, etc. The role was one that required knowledge and experience of the inherent barriers and an authority to overcome them.

For some new appointees, the 'sales' orientation of the new role seemed a problem at first. Either it raised new expectations of them or, for others, it might even have appeared a downgrading of their seniority. In fact, as far as the top management at Kohler was concerned, the role of key account manager was among the most important in the company and would be rewarded accordingly. The message finally got through, and most senior managers were keen to be involved in the new direction.

Sponsors in the board room

The challenge of the internal role – aligning the business to respond to the enhanced understanding of the customer's needs – has led many businesses to appoint senior managers, perhaps even from board level, as key account 'sponsors'. They don't manage the account on a day-to-day basis and are wise to steer clear of any interference in the activities and decisions of the key account manager. Their role is to facilitate the internal changes required with regard to issues such as organization, resources and any clashes of priorities. Such appointments are also symbolic, expressing the commitment to KAM at a senior level, and they have one last potential virtue: if the senior manager is also the head of one of the support functions, or one of the business units, and they sign on to the principles of KAM, then that is at least one less 'baron' with a 'silo mentality' to worry about!

Directors as KAMs?

Sometimes its more than being a sponsor, and a senior manager will take on actual responsibility for a specific key account. They will retain the services of a key account manager, but they take on a more active directing and supervisory role. This is particularly common when those accounts are global and the supplier works in a number of different territories. There are of course plenty of pros and cons to such a move.

Potential disadvantages

The potential disadvantages include – the danger of becoming sucked into the daily detail, becoming a 'super rep', confusing the KAM over who is responsible for what, confusing the customer with the same, and perhaps worst of all, demotivating the KAM.

Potential advantages

The potential advantages are simple, but significant – their seniority and clout helps to make it happen!

Sales people in the team

At this point, some people might be worrying that the possible appointment of a non-sales person as key account manager not only risks losing accumulated skills of the sales force, but ignores the continuing need for top-flight selling skills in front of the customer. There is no reason, in the partnership KAM model and beyond, why some of the individual points of contact should not be sales people.

The key account manager is the conductor, and may well have as their principle contact not a buyer but a *supplier manager*. There is still a need for the virtuoso 'first violinist' salesperson in front of the buyer. Perhaps the customer is a multiple-site business, ie the key account manager is responsible for head office contact, but there is still a need for a salesperson at each site, perhaps facing up with buyers, operating with a combination of central direction and local autonomy. There is still a need for top-flight selling skills.

Global accounts

In a global key account, there will almost certainly be a need for regional account managers with regional sales responsibilities, or they may have sales professionals within their own regional teams. The global account manager may also have a global sales role, but it is often to their advantage if they can remove themselves from the nitty-gritty of the sales negotiation and raise the nature of their customer relationship to a more strategic level. The supplier side of the diamond might look something like that shown in Figure 17.5.

Figure 17.5   *The global key account team*

There is sometimes a confusion about points of contact in global accounts that Figure 17.5 should help resolve. A truly global customer (that is, one not just situated globally but also operating globally) can easily be frustrated by the regional operating differences of a global supplier. Their protests can sometimes be wrongly interpreted as a request for 'one point of contact rather than all this diversity'. They are unlikely to be requesting this, and should one point of contact in the supplier attempt it, then they would doubtless collapse under the strain (although their air miles tally would be very impressive). What the customer is probably trying to say is that they want one point of control, one point of coordination, and that is the global key account manager. It is their task to gather their global team, including regional sales people, and direct these multiple points of contact along some uniform processes.

From all of these discussions, we might conclude that KAM is certainly not the death of the salesperson, but for some it asks for a marked change of direction.

The tale of the sports commentators

I was told a story about sports commentators in South Africa that illustrates the point. Sport was not broadcast regularly on South African television until well into the 1970s – radio being the normal medium. When TV started to broadcast more frequently, it needed commentators, so it took them from the radio – well-known and respected voices. There was, however, a problem. After years of reporting every move on the pitch and every swing of every club, bat or racquet, the radio-trained commentators found it hard to adapt. Quite simply, they spoke too much and soon infuriated the audience who could see quite plainly what was going on with their own eyes. The solution, at least in this case, was new people with new perspectives and different skills.

New lines of reporting and responsibility

As KA teams begin to establish themselves, people from the functions will find new calls on their time. As well as their functional responsibilities, as KA team members they will also have customer-specific responsibilities. What about time management and priorities? What about objective-setting and annual reviews? It will become normal for people to have objectives for their jobs that come from more than one point – their function and their customer. In time, not having a customer objective, whatever else your role, will become so unusual as to be cause for concern!

In the long run, the customer part of the job might grow to become dominant and they might even become full-time on one key account. In some cases, formal KA teams with their own reporting lines will be the solution, while in others, the ambiguity of *matrix management* will rule. There is no one template for handling the complex reporting lines, the *solids* and the *dotteds*, even the 3D of matrix management; the only right answer is what works in practice. Whatever the outcome, the transition will be one that requires constant attention with regard to the human resources employed. Be aware of this need from the start; the HR department has its role to play – welcome them to the team!

KAM and downsizing?

Some businesses see KAM as an opportunity to reduce the size of the sales force – replacing regional structures of field-based reps with a small team of key account managers supported by a customer service office of tele-sales people. This may be a possible outcome, but, as an objective for KAM, care should be taken that objectives, resources and opportunity (see Chapter 2) are not getting out of balance – is it really possible to service your customers that way (opportunity)?

KAM may result in fewer sales people – but don't let cost cutting become the motivation for one of your most vital business decisions

One arena where it certainly *has* been possible is that of food manufacturers serving the UK supermarkets. Centralized purchasing has caused dramatic *downsizing* of sales teams: Birds-Eye Walls have reduced from a team of hundreds to around 40; Anchor have a team of around a dozen to handle the entire grocery trade. But not all suppliers saw the trend and many hung on to large sales teams much longer than they were required. The result was an uncompetitive cost burden, not to mention head-office buyers annoyed by local reps still trying to influence decisions at store level.

The KAM-orientated business must look with great care at any trends towards centralized purchasing and assess the impact on their sales force requirement. They must not reduce field teams too early (losing out to competitors still active at that level) nor too late (losing out to more cost-efficient competitors). The solution? Consultation with the customer is essential. What do they require? (It is surprising how few suppliers think to ask.)

The food industry was one of the first to be affected this way; others are seeing it only now. Pharmaceutical companies have some of the largest sales teams, calling on local GPs. Will this be the most efficient way to sell these products in 5 or 10 years' time? The development of multi-practice GP purchasing groups is perhaps an indication of the future – and more significantly there are signs that the professional buyers employed by these groups are interested in more than glossy brochures. Getting the message to the prescribing doctor will require new approaches.

KAM and reward and recognition

Much time and creative thought has been given by sales managers to the reward and recognition of their sales people, using every kind of package from straight salary to 100 per cent commission and all stops in-between.

Reward in the KAM environment requires a new kind of creativity. The solutions must be designed to suit your own circumstances, and must above all else be designed to support the business objectives, but the following four questions might stimulate your own debate:

1. On what criteria should reward be based?
2. Do you reward the key account manager or the team?
3. If the key account manager is a senior salesperson, how should their reward compare to other senior managers?
4. Given the 'rarity' of good key account managers, how do you keep them without promoting them beyond the job?

Reward criteria

Sales volume is unlikely to be the best measure, although it is certainly the easiest. Better measures will be those that emphasize the key account as an investment. Profitability is therefore to be preferred, but it is much harder to measure. Lifetime profitability, as described in Chapter 7, is even better. There should also be measures that relate to the nature of the task, such as building a customer relationship. Customer satisfaction ratings might form a part of such measures. Finally, probably the best measure of all is what progress is made towards the objectives set down in the key account plan. This linkage of reward to objective setting, planning and successful implementation will also help establish the responsibilities of key account management on the same kind of level as business management, which is precisely where they should be.

The manager or the team?

This one is very simple: it must be the team. This requires the formal creation of a team with clear goals, roles, obligations and work plans for each member and for the team as a whole. Up until the point that such a team exists, the reward might be related in part to the account manager's ability to form the team, this being presumably one of the objectives of the key account plan.

The sales ladder

The RAF came up with a neat solution to a problem not so dissimilar to that posed by questions 3 and 4. If you joined the RAF to fly planes then you could do so up to the rank of squadron leader, but after that if you wanted promotion you had to take a desk job. This was a significant problem for those who had joined the RAF to fly.

The solution was to allow those officers who wanted to continue flying to proceed up a salary ladder that paid them the same as ranks two or three above them, while still remaining a squadron leader.

ICI has a similar solution for their best R&D people that want to 'stay by the bench', called the 'scientific ladder'. This allows for increases in reward without the need for a move into general management.

Could a 'sales ladder' do the same for key account managers?

Sales awards

A final point on recognition – sales awards. Although I'm not a particular fan of such awards, if you do make use of them it is no surprise if they usually find their way to the salesperson who won the most exciting piece of new business that year. In the key account management environment, you might like to consider two changes. First, give the award to a team, not an individual. Second, consider giving the award to the account team that has retained the most business in difficult circumstances – a real test of key account management skills in a mature market.

18

What will it take? Making it happen

So, let's suppose that by now you have a clear idea of what is required. You know what skills, attitudes and behaviours must be developed. You have planned for new systems and a new organization. Now all you have to do is make it happen!

You have some choices, including:

1. Jump in and get going – perhaps a training course in project management, perhaps a new e-mail system.
2. Be a little more structured and focus on one thing at a time – perhaps a full-scale overhaul of the cost reporting system.
3. Proceed by stages through a process of alignment and change management to the implementation of some first practical steps.

Hopefully, the folly of options one and two are clear. The activities in themselves may be done well, but nobody listened, nobody changed and nothing happened… But what do 'alignment' and 'change management' mean?

ALIGNMENT AND MANAGING THE CHANGE

Perhaps you are crystal clear on what you wish to achieve and why, but who else cares? You are going to need the support of the whole organization – the functions, the management and the people involved directly with implementing KAM in front of the customer. Alignment is the process of getting them to see the vision the same way as you and doubtless modifying your own vision as you proceed, listening to the views of others, taking on new perspectives and so evolving a KAM policy and practice that all will sign on to.

This will almost certainly involve a series of activities more complex as the size of the organization and the significance of the change increases. In practice, you may be involved in meetings, persuasion, negotiation, seminars, workshops, newsletters and more, but to keep things simple we will focus not on the methods used, but on the principles behind them.

Cross-business alignment is vital if you want to avoid the frustration of KAM being simply a 'sales initiative'

Creating a KAM business environment will certainly involve a great deal of effort – yours and others' – and will almost certainly involve a great deal of change to ideas and practices that may be long established and well favoured by many in the organization.

Why do people change? Why do they buy new products, sign on to new ideas or change the habits of a lifetime?

The notion of a *change equation* will be of great help in understanding both the process of change and how you can manage it. The 'equation' starts with something that Thomas Edison realized in his pursuit of invention and innovation: *Discontent is the first necessity of progress.*

THE CHANGE EQUATION

People don't buy new products just because you tell them they are good. People in the bed industry talk of beds being a 'distress purchase'. Customers buy beds because their old one has a spring through the mattress, or is too small, or too hard, or they wake up with a back that feels like it's encased in cement. In other words, they had a need based on some dissatisfaction with what they had already. The same applies to buying a car; the old one is too expensive to maintain, too unreliable, too slow or doesn't suit your new aspirations or ego. Whatever the reason, dissatisfaction with the current position is at the root.

Perhaps the most important 'model' in the key account manager's collection?

Figure 18.1 *The change equation*

I have used buying a product to illustrate the notion (Figure 18.1), but the equation applies equally to new ideas, attitudes or behaviours. People are most likely to change if:

1. They are dissatisfied with how things are now.
2. They have a vision of some better way of doing things in the future.
3. There are some simple first steps that will get things under way.
4. All of the above is greater, both in reality *and in their mind*, than the costs of change – and remember, cost is not just money, but time, ego, status and so on.

Establishing dissatisfaction

For an organization to align behind the notion of KAM, there will need to be some pressing reasons – dissatisfaction with the current situation. Where organizations set out to implement KAM and fail, it can usually be pinned on a *lack* of dissatisfaction with how things were before. Once the effort and the pain involved become clear, it is all too easy to fall back on doing it how we used to – 'after all, it wasn't so bad…'

Chapter 14 listed the 'deadly sins' that stand in the way of successful KAM. Number 8 was 'complacency and inertia' and it is in the light of making it happen that we can see why this is perhaps the deadliest of them all.

What sort of dissatisfaction are we talking about?

- Are we losing sales?
- Are competitors gaining ground?
- Are profits falling?
- Are we missing new opportunities?
- Is customer dissatisfaction growing?
- Are there any examples of failure?
- Could the customer be made happier?
- Is our organization 'creaking'?
- Are internal squabbles leading to customer failure?
- Even if things are OK now, will this be the same in the future?

Perhaps your desire to implement KAM is particularly visionary – all is well at present, but *you* see how times will change. This makes managing change a little more difficult – there is no dissatisfaction with the current situation. Your task will now be to project dissatisfaction into the future, perhaps demonstrating how things could turn out if KAM is *not* adopted. It is a technique that any insurance salesperson knows well: 'Have you considered what will happen to your family if you die?' they ask cheerily, practising the principle of *anticipation*.

Anticipation demands an ability to discuss possible futures and the worst sort of complacency that can stand in your way in such situations is the phrase that should be banished from any company wishing to survive beyond the end of their nose: 'If it ain't broke, don't fix it.'

Sharing the vision

Stirring up doom and gloom is not of course the aim – thoughtful concern would be a better target. Scared or depressed people are no easier to change than the smug and complacent ones. But 'thoughtful concern' is only the start of the change process and you will soon be an unwelcome *Cassandra* if that is all you generate. Alongside the concern must come the vision of how things might be. The key to alignment is securing a *shared* vision of that future.

This is where the purpose and objectives of KAM must be made clear, with some understanding of what is involved:

- What will KAM do for us?
- What benefits will we get?
- What benefits will the customer get?
- What will KAM look and feel like?
- Will it be worth the effort?

First practical steps

Despite the advice of some business 'gurus' that the role of leaders is to foment upheaval and chaos, it is usually best to avoid revolutions wherever possible. Rather, it will be necessary to agree some first practical steps to get things going. These do not have to be dramatic – almost better if they are not. A sensible start might be a gathering of interested parties to identify objectives, obstacles and what we might call the *critical success factors*.

CRITICAL SUCCESS FACTORS (CSFs)

These are the things that you and your business will need to do, or have in place, *in the broadest sense*, in order to make progress on your KAM journey. If a business is to be truly aligned behind KAM then it will need to agree these CSFs at an early stage.

A possible process

1. Gather a wide cross-section of interested parties – heads of functions, potential practitioners, etc.
2. Ensure that sufficient dissatisfaction with the current situation is apparent to all and that KAM is regarded at least as one of the potential visions for the future.
3. Ensure the principles of KAM, its purpose and practice, are understood.
4. Identify the objectives for KAM and the obstacles to progress – your own list of 'deadly sins'.
5. Identify the 'things that must be' if those obstacles are to be overcome – your critical success factors.

Some tips, and some warnings

- Use an independent consultant or facilitator – it is important to escape from the confines of current thinking. You *do* need to sort out the wood from the trees.
- Stay objective, but don't ignore people's perceptions and feelings – remember, you are trying to change attitudes and behaviours.
- Listen to all views, including those in opposition (never exclude the possibility that they might have a point!). Alignment will involve compromise, modifying your own vision, perhaps even improving on it.
- Seek alignment across *all* functions and departments.
- Involve senior management at the earliest stages.
- Remember, *you* have probably been thinking about this longer than they have. Don't expect instant alignment – be patient.
- The alternative to alignment is the probable stillbirth of your KAM plans.

CSFs – an example list

The following is a list of CSFs, identified by a real business at the early stage of embracing the KAM philosophy. The list was reached after an analysis of the particular problems and obstacles that stood in the way of KAM implementation in this business:

- KAM must be a cross-business process, supported at senior levels, with objectives and responsibilities that supersede those of individual functions or departments.

- All team members must understand and share the purpose and objectives of KAM.
- The KA team must understand and sign on to their purpose as increasing customer prosperity, and so our own competitive advantage, in order to secure key supplier status. They must focus on the customer's processes, and the customer's markets.
- There must be a system for cross-business communication (including the customer) and the necessary skills and disciplines to make it work.
- Team members must have the right skills and understanding to carry out a customer-intimate role – interpersonal skills and commercial awareness are top priorities.
- We must all understand the dynamics of team working.
- We must have enhanced skills of project management.
- Attention to detail. We require relevant, customer-focused operational excellence from all functions.
- There must be a system for measuring progress on the KAM journey and for assessing the benefits to our customers and ourselves.
- There must be a written and easily updateable KA plan.

Taking the time to plan and prepare

Books like this are always urging you to spend time planning and preparing. Faced with the urgent need to be *doing* things this is not always so easy, but the importance of careful planning for KAM implementation cannot be overstated.

If you *are* about to turn your business upside down, it pays to know what might be lurking underneath. Anticipating obstacles and problems before they arise will pay dividends. Waiting for a crisis to arrive and then proceeding on the grounds that people will react if they really have to, is an unwise policy – people in crisis tend to freeze, like rabbits caught in headlights.

The tale of the tortoise and the hare

I suspect you know this one…

Part IV

Identifying Key Accounts

19

The 10 step process

Many businesses are put off the notion of KAM simply because they find the task of selecting the key accounts too daunting. The problem is of course, who don't you select? Such businesses are right to be cautious, but wrong not to persevere.

What is required is a process that helps to navigate the journey, while avoiding the potential bear traps that lie in wait. This is the 10 Step Process shown in Figure 19.1.

A new kind of journey plan ...

The 10 step process is shown as a flow chart, indicating that while the steps do form a broadly linear process, there are several points at which you will need to go back to some earlier decisions, using your steadily increasing knowledge to challenge some of the assumptions behind those decisions.

This is of course a good thing, and it does allow you to make a start somewhere without prejudicing all future decisions. Some would argue, and with much justification, that you should start with Step 5, the marketing plan and segmentation, or perhaps Step 3, the assembly of a project team. Either is fine, if you wish it so, provided that you really do start with a clear marketing plan, or that a project team can easily be assembled as the first step in the process. Whatever the case, the flow chart will take you back to Step 1 from either of those starting points.

Chapters 1 and 2 address these points, essential foundations to get right. Steps 4 through 10 are covered by the next chapters, 20 through to 22. The rest of this chapter will deal with step 3.

Step 1. Know your objectives

Step 2. Understand your resources

Step 3. Assemble the selection team

Step 4. Map the *real* opportunity

Step 5. Segmentation first….

Step 6. The key account selection matrix

Step 7. Identify the *Customer Attractiveness* factors

Step 8. Know your *Relative Strengths*

Step 9. Classification, Selection & Communication

Step 10. Customer Distinction Strategies

Figure 19.1   *The 10 Step Process*

STEP 3 – ASSEMBLE THE SELECTION TEAM

Getting the right people to work through this process is perhaps, along with step 5, the most important part of the process. It is tempting, maybe even it sounds obvious, to get the sales team to do this, but that way lie problems.

First, sales people naturally have positions to defend, and careers to build. Everyone wants their own accounts to be key, surely that way lies promotion? Of course in truth maintenance accounts are just as important to the health of the business, and may be vital for today's profits, but most eyes tend to turn towards the key and key development accounts.

Second, KAM requires the support of the whole business, and if the selection of the key accounts is left only in the hands of the sales team, how might that be viewed elsewhere? Perhaps you already think you know your key accounts, maybe you are certain, but what if the rest of your business doesn't seem to see it your way.

I learned this lesson in the first few months of my selling career. I sold decorative paint to independent retailers, and as an eager young rep out in rural East Anglia – where I was warned there would be little I could do to rouse customers from their comfortable slumber – I determined to identify those customers worthy of the most attention, my key accounts. After poring over my sales statistics and pushing pins of different colours into a map of my territory I went off to inform my local distribution depot, absolutely certain of my analysis.

For ten minutes or so I briefed them on the key accounts that they must now give extra attention to, and then reeled with amazement as they contradicted almost every customer identified. For me, a sales rep, a key account was one where I could expect a large order as the result of my call. For my distribution colleagues this was the sin of sending eager young reps out in the first place! For them, a key account was a customer so regular and so consistent in their order pattern that they could form the backbone of their workload planning.

We agreed to differ and I went away wiser on one very important issue – it was highly unlikely that key accounts could be identified by single criteria and certainly not from the narrow perspective of any one function. Fortunately, I was dealing with rather small independent retailers in a quiet corner of the country, not the global customers that might have determined our whole future. There is a time to learn by your mistakes, and a time to get it right.

Getting everyone to agree...

The ideal team?

The ideal team is only ever ideal for the purpose for which it is formed. There is in fact a dual purpose for this team:

1. To identify and select the key accounts based on a combination of intimate customer knowledge and a clear vision of future strategy and goals.
2. To give that selection sufficient authority for it to mean something across the business. Selection without implementation will be meaningless.

How senior?

Consider two scenarios.

In the first, the team is a group of senior managers who approach the task very much with their eyes on the recently agreed five year plan. 'Vision' abounds, but 'what', say the sales force, 'what do they know about our customers?'

In the second scenario, it is a group from sales and customer service that make up the selection team, and their efforts reflect their intimate knowledge of the customers. 'Fine', say the bosses, 'but what about tomorrow's customers? Where's the vision?'

The ideal team must aim to combine vision and knowledge. Knowledge will exist in a lot of places and any attempt to gather it all together in one team would result in an unworkable monster. Perhaps the solution is a core team, probably with a bias towards 'vision', who call on the knowledge of others as and when it is required.

The more senior the team, the more likely that their conclusions will make an impact – and that is surely the purpose of this whole selection activity?

Identifying key accounts is the responsibility of the senior management team.

20

Segmentation

The golden rule:
Segment your
market first – then
identify your key
accounts

Perhaps there are already some alarm bells ringing in your head with regard to implementing KAM in your organization. Not only will it call for enormous effort and significant change, but there are also some other potential problems:

- If KAM implies some kind of special treatment for one customer compared to another, does this mean you will be helping to put some of your customers at an actual disadvantage, perhaps even out of business?
- If customer intimacy implies not only understanding your different customers' specific (and more than likely varying) needs, but also acting on them, how will you avoid being pulled apart at the seams by the competing activities?
- How do you hope to focus your organization on anything if the rules of the game seem to be: 'Every customer is unique; there are no *standard* standards'?

The answers to these and many similar issues will be found by taking a few paces back from the coalface. We need to put KAM back into its wider context: the management of markets through some process of segmentation.

By doing this we will happen on one of the happier outcomes of KAM, the marrying of sales and marketing planning. Forget the notion, popular in the 1970s, that sales is simply the tactical front of the marketing department with sales managers subservient to marketing managers. Forget also the equally unhelpful drive to make the key account manager dominant over every other function in the business (including marketing!). And banish the notion that KAM is a sales initiative that seeks to 'do something' to the customer. Instead, we will see how KAM and market segmentation come together to ensure a greater focus of effort, on a strategic level, and the avoidance of the sort of problems outlined above.

First, let's just consider one more problem.

THE PROBLEM FOR SUPPORT FUNCTIONS IN AN UNSEGMENTED BUSINESS

Functions, left to their own devices, are often tempted towards extremes. Either they campaign to drive every cost, frill or excess (their perception!) out of their activities in the pursuit of an almost anorexic 'leanness', or they aspire to deliver a Rolls-Royce when a 'humble' Ford would do. Left to their own devices means, of course, managed separately from the rest of the business and from the rest of the supply chain at a distance from the market and, worst of all, at a remove from the customer.

Requests for variations from the norm, as determined by the particular support function in the absence of any other guidance, not only lead to perceived inefficiency, but also to confusion. See it from their angle. How is it that one salesperson is calling for fewer frills and a standardized product when another is berating us for a lack of new product development? How is it that one customer will place orders with a fortnight's notice while another claims it will go under if it doesn't have a 24-hour response? How is it that what has kept the majority of customers happy for years suddenly becomes unacceptable to a group of customers and sales people that seem to have found louder voices than the rest?

The core of all these problems is the same. This is a business that sells to customers with different needs; different because they operate in different ways, with different challenges and aspirations, perhaps even in different markets. The problem is that this business does not distinguish its customers in any way; not by their size, their style, their function in the supply chain, their end-customer or their use of your product. To this business, all customers are equal and, of course, since they are always right, they must all be treated the same.

Functions asked to service customers in such an environment will always have a hard time of it. Tell them that you intend setting up a KAM process that will focus even more intimately on specific customer needs and you might expect a rebellion!

WHAT IS SEGMENTATION?

There are many excellent books on segmentation and this short chapter is by no means a suitable alternative to the full treatment such books give this very important issue. Its purpose is simply to show how a KAM strategy can, and must, fit into the business marketing plan and in particular its segmentation plan. An overview of what segmentation is, and how it is done, is required to set the scene.

What is a segment?

Let's start by defining what we mean by a market segment.

> "A market segment is a grouping of customers with similar buying needs, attitudes, and behaviours."

It is important to stress the last two words, 'attitudes' and 'behaviours'. If we only looked at needs we would be severely limiting our options. We all *need* food, and if that was our only consideration there would be only one segment in the food market – food! Of course there are dozens of segments because beyond mere need we display an amazing array of attitudes to the stuff, and exhibit an equally large range of ways of going about buying and using it. Each of these facets of behaviour or attitude provides a potential market segment. Just consider a few of those in the food market:

- Eating out – restaurants, cafés, fast food, food on the move, vending machines
- Eating in – breakfast, lunch, dinner, entertaining, barbecues…
- Business – canteens, hotels, institutions, catering, airlines…
- Retail – supermarkets, wholesalers, cash and carry, delicatessens…
- Branding – brands, own brand, no brands…
- Health – low sodium, diet, low fat, high fibre…
- Diet – vegetarian, vegan, organic…
- Ethnic – Indian, Chinese, Italian, Moroccan…
- Family – 2.4 kids, single parent, retired, single….
- Experience – cordon bleu, first time cooks, professionals…

Add to this list the range of food fads, local tastes, traditions, income levels, time to cook, lifestyles and more, and you can see that the list is huge.

Here we come across the first joy, and the first headache – it's about making choices, and that is the art and the science of segmentation.

The 'viable' segment

There are some helpful first thoughts – is this idea of ours for a segment 'viable'? Segments should stand up to a few simple tests.

- Is it large enough to justify focused attention?
- Are the customer's needs attitudes and behaviours similar enough to be aggregated together?
- Are the needs attitudes and behaviours specific enough to be distinguishable from other segments?
- Is it possible to design an appropriate *marketing mix* for the segment? (see below)
- Is the segment *reachable;* can it be identified, measured, analysed, communicated to, and sold to, *discretely* from other segments?

Positive answers to these questions will start to suggest that you are looking at a viable segment.

Segmentation and the Marketing Mix

Segmentation is a three step process:

1. Deciding on what basis to 'slice' the market into segments.
2. Choosing those segments that you wish to be active in.
3. Targeting each of those active segments with a unique *marketing mix*.

The supplier aims to influence demand and gain competitive advantage through the application of the marketing mix, often known as the four P's – the product, the price, the promotion, and the place, illustrated in Figure 20.1.

Figure 20.1   *The marketing mix*

By preparing a different and specific marketing mix for each segment, the business ensures that it will meet the needs of each grouping of customers in a more focused way. At the same time, it enhances its opportunity for maximizing profits through premium pricing, or differentiation, or the offer of a lowest cost option – whatever the dynamics of the particular segment demands.

In theory, segments could be as small as each individual customer, with their own unique needs, attitudes, and behaviours, but in practice it is helpful to aggregate customers together under some more general definitions. This enables the business to divide its activities up – enough to meet the market's needs, but not so far that they are pulled apart at the seams.

Airlines – a class act in segmentation

The airline industry provides an excellent example. The division of customers into classes; first, business, economy, and stand-by; each with its own needs, similar enough *within* the class for aggregation, and different enough from the next for discrete treatment through four different marketing mixes. The result? On a flight from London to New York, passengers will be paying anything from £200 to £6000, for the same seven hour flight!

THE BENEFITS OF SEGMENTATION

There are many benefits to be had from good segmentation:

- An enhanced understanding of the market dynamics, particularly with regard to market chains (see Chapter 3).
- An enhanced understanding of competitor strengths (the competition will differ by segment), and so the opportunities for competitive advantage.
- Greater understanding of the needs, attitudes, and behaviours, of customers.
- A better chance that you will see how to develop the capabilities of your business in order to match those needs.
- A basis for organising and structuring your business – focusing the whole supply chain on the customer.
- Improving your ability to manage the marketing mix, in a customer focused way.
- Enhancing your opportunity to add value, gain competitive advantage, and build barriers to entry for competitors or substitute products.

- Enhancing your opportunity to create, maintain and defend price premiums.

The purpose of segmentation is to focus your limited resources on to those opportunities that will take you where you wish your business to be, and represent the best chance for you to gain competitive advantage.
Failure to segment will at best result in missed opportunities, and at worst, result in the inability of your business to gain competitive advantage and long term security.

METHODS FOR SEGMENTATION

Segmentation based on historical sales is likely to be too narrow-minded and too short-sighted – a recipe for tripping over. In order to avoid this outcome there are a number of steps to take, designed to ensure that you understand the *whole* market and not just the bit you happen to occupy:

1. Market mapping: identify opportunities; identify 'levers'.
2. Who buys what, how, when and where?
3. Selection of segments and positioning through the marketing mix.

MARKET MAPPING

A good start will be to draw up a *market map*. This is a diagram illustrating all the routes to market for your product or service; what we might call the 'market channels'. The example (Figure 20.2) shows the main routes (much simplified) for a manufacturer of adhesives, industrial and consumer.

The map presents some options and choices for segmentation, some clearer than others. The next stage is to follow a process of focusing in on the best possible means of segmentation.

Opportunity Analysis

- Note the size of the market and the percentage share at each 'junction' along the different channels. This will normally be done as percentages of sales volume, although using sales value or profit may be more illuminating.

Figure 20.2 *Market map*

- Note the size of your own business, and the percentage share, at the same points.
- Note your competitor's size and shares at the same points.

Doing this will help you to compare your historical performance to the total opportunity and who you are up against in each area. Segmentation must start with the whole market, not your historical sales – otherwise, not only might you miss opportunities, but you will also ignore potential threats.

Where to segment – leverage points

There are many choices, each with its pros and cons. At this point, statistics will get us only so far – we must now engage our brains.

Examine the market map for what we might call *leverage points*. These are points in the chain where critical purchasing decisions are made. Decisions are made at every point, but where are the big ones, the fors and the againsts, to buy or not to buy?

- Are decisions made globally, regionally or locally?
- Do distributors make the choice to present your products to the market or do they simply service demand?
- Is it the channel that makes the important choices or the end-user?

Push or pull?

If your product or service has a strong reputation, a good brand name and a decent market share, you might expect to be in what we would call 'pull' marketing. Your efforts in the marketplace create a demand that pulls customers into the channels of supply. Without such reputation and market position you will be more used to 'push' marketing, persuading the channels of supply to use your products and services. Reality will combine both push and pull, but it is useful to understand the relative balance at different points of the chain.

Segmenting by end-consumer might be easier and more effective for a pull strategy, while a push strategy might call for segmentation by channel of distribution.

The closer to the end-user you can segment, often the more powerful the impact, but, of course, remembering the test questions from the start of this chapter, will it be a *viable* segment?

Getting a full understanding of these leverage points goes beyond market size and percentage shares – it requires a whole new set of questions to understand the dynamics of how your market works.

In our example of a market map, based on a real map used by a manufacturer of specialist adhesives, the main leverage points might be found at:

- manufacturers of medical products;
- builders and DIY consumers;
- specialist distributors to the automotive, electrical and engineering industries.

Already we are finding that the leverage points are at different points towards the end-user in each of three main areas – medical (close to supplier, but beyond the distributor), building and DIY (close to consumer) and specialist industrial uses (the distributors).

We might then expect to find that the way the buying decisions are made, and can be influenced, would be different in each of the three cases. We are perhaps beginning to identify three 'segments' – medical, building and industrial – but there are more questions to be asked.

WHO BUYS WHAT, HOW, WHEN AND WHERE?

In the excitement of all this analysis, it is good to remember a simple truth: *markets don't buy anything – people do that!*

We need to understand the buying habits at each junction and of each potential grouping of customers, particularly if we aim to segment by end-user or consumer.

There will be a lot of trial and error in your attempts to find the right basis for segmentation and, for each possible 'cut', you should be aiming to understand:

- attitudes and perceptions;
- motivations;
- needs;
- buying behaviours.

In our example, we might expect to find the following sorts of differences, at three different leverage points:

Medical manufacturer – has some very precise specifications for the product and expects a good deal of help from suppliers in delivering bespoke solutions. Buys in large quantities, with long-term contracts. The 'R&D buyer': price is of little significance.

DIY consumer – no expertise in the product, but looking for something they can rely on. Influenced by advertising and brand names, buys in small quantities, irregularly, and wants to find it freely available in DIY superstores. The no-hassle, 'convenience buyer'.

Specialist distributor to the engineering industry – wants to be able to present the best solutions to their customers. Wants a range that meets the spectrum of demand and wants buying terms that give a large enough margin to justify the technical support they offer to customers. The 'commercial buyer'.

Some more examples

Adding value through segmentation

A fertilizer manufacturer found their product to be in slow decline in a mature market. They decided to segment as a means to finding new offers, testing first the more obvious 'cuts', for example crop type, geography and seasonality. Finally, they hit on the simple truth noted above: wheat didn't buy fertilizer and nor did East Anglia – it was

Figure 20.3 *Segmentation by type of farmer*
Courtesy of Professor Malcolm McDonald

farmers every time! Farmers came from different backgrounds, with widely differing attitudes, aspirations and buying behaviours. Once the manufacturer started to explore these factors, they began to understand (almost for the first time) what *really* made people buy their product, or not. The final segmentation was done on the basis of attitudes and needs, the traditional family farmer, for instance, having a rather different outlook from the graduate of agricultural college managing a large estate. The resultant marketing mixes helped the manufacturer target their product better, add more relevant value, structure their own operations to suit customers' needs and gain a significant increase in profits.

A paint manufacturer in the domestic DIY market had long segmented on the basis of product types – coloured paint, white paint, gloss paint, emulsions and so on. More ambitious segmentation had looked at inside and outside use, even decoration, protection and hygiene as specific end-uses or purposes in buying, but the resulting segments were never clear enough to design a hard-hitting marketing mix. Turning to attitudes and behaviour, the manufacturer identified that there was a major division among domestic paint purchasers – those that planned and those that applied. The needs of each group were quite different and the marketing mix applied was also quite different. *Planners* had to be targeted early in the decision process, through magazines and TV, while *appliers* could be targeted in store, with advice and information.

Segmentation with attitude...

Finding all this out

In the last example, the paint supplier knew in great detail how much of each type of their product they sold. This had led initially to segmentation by product type – the easy option, but often a dangerous one. By imposing their own internal constraints (their product range) the supplier reduced their ability to understand the true market environment. To segment by planners and appliers called for a different kind of data, obtained from new market research. Market research and segmentation must go hand in hand.

MAKING THE CUT

Once attitudes and behaviours are better understood then you can go back to the market map and look again at leverage points. Is it the channels of supply, or is it the buying behaviour of your end-users that drives the purchasing decisions and would best allow you to design an effective marketing mix?

In our example of the adhesives supplier, let's suppose that the market research identified an even more mind-boggling range of options than our first map. The supplier is beginning to realize that the dynamics of these three main areas are very different from each other. So different that it goes back a stage before segmentation – these three areas represent three different businesses: medical, building and DIY, and industrial.

Depending on the scale of the supplier, we *might* be looking at three businesses to be segmented, or we might be looking at three segments to be divided into more manageable sub-segments. We will suppose that it is a large enterprise and the building and DIY business is established as an independent entity. The process now starts again, in more detail. More research, more searching for leverage points and more understanding of how customers buy.

Looking for the final basis for segmentation will almost certainly involve a mix of factors. The building and DIY 'business' is finding that DIY consumers purchase in very different ways from professional builders. They compared a range of bases for segmentation (Table 20.1).

Table 20.1   *Bases for segmentation*

Base	Builders	DIY consumers
Size of purchase small	Large volume, large packsize	Small volume, packsize
Frequency of purchase	Weekly	Annually
Technical specification	High	Low
Price elasticity	Price sensitive	Price insensitive
Major influence on purchase	Builders' merchant staff	Advertising & brand

The outcome was a decision, not only to create two segments, but also to create two separate brands. The needs and attitudes were so different in the two groups that the marketing mixes had to be kept quite discrete. The extra costs of developing a new brand were far outweighed by the ability to service the needs of these two segments effectively and with significant competitive advantage. Before segmentation, it had never been possible to manage all the activities required to meet the needs of such diverse customers.

Segments and sub-segments

With two distinct segments, the search could go on for sub-segments in each. Here the 'test' questions raised at the start of the chapter – is it viable? – need to be applied. Perhaps DIY consumers can be divided into 'hobbyists', 'amateur builders' and 'anti-DIYers', each with their own sets of needs and attitudes; the amateur builder looking for *serious* products, the anti-DIYers wanting something that will do the job for them. If the groups are large enough, if the messages can be targeted and if profits can be made, these sub-segments will be helpful in applying more focused marketing mixes.

The 'Adopters Curve'

This particular method of segmentation has a lot of attractions to those interested in identifying key accounts. The reason being that the same criteria can be used to identify both the target segment and the target key account.

When a new product is launched there is usually a vanguard of ardent enthusiasts that jump on board, sometimes almost regardless of the

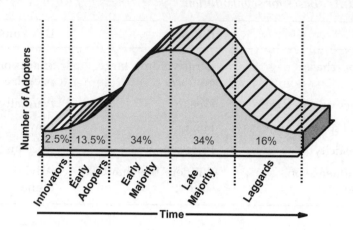

Figure 20.4 *The Adopters Curve*

From Everett Rogers, Diffusion of Innovations (New York Free Press)

product's merits. Often it goes no further and the product dies, remembered only as a fad supported by a clique of fanatics.

If a product is to succeed it has to go beyond that narrow following and find a wider audience. It has to progress beyond the *innovators* to find the *early adopters*. Everett Rogers captured this concept in his much quoted 'adopters curve' shown in Figure 20.4. The curve shows how most new products or ideas go through stages of adoption, first by the innovators, a small but enthusiastic group, then by the early adopters who help make the product something of wider appeal. The early majority provide the volume sales that drive down costs and turn the product into a mass market one such that the late majority come sweeping in to buy. Laggards are those that resist till the very end, or perhaps never succumb.

A classic example of such a development is the electronic pocket calculator. At its invention it was bought as an advanced scientific instrument, predominantly by businesses and institutions, doubtless requiring approval by the capital acquisitions committee. It was not long however before a new segment of the market opened up, spurred on by government legislation. Once it was approved that calculators could be used in 'O' level maths exams every little Johnny and every little Jane rushed home to demand their parents bought them one. Cumbersome instruments, often with a mind-boggling array of functions from cosines to reciprocals, this new demand from the *early adopters* brought prices tumbling down. Before long the pocket calculator was an established item for business people and this *early majority* helped drive prices even lower until calculators were being given away free as promotional items; the *late majority* was engaged.

An interesting feature of the model is the role of the innovator, sometimes a positive force, but not infrequently a drag on the market's uptake. The Internet is a case in point. Early users of the Internet were portrayed as 'nerds', sad characters with no social life who sat up late at night surfing the net in search of other such lost souls. Whether true or not, this image of the early users served to hold back wider acceptance of the Internet, perhaps for as long as two years.

As a model for segmentation the adopters curve holds much promise, and also as a method of identifying key accounts. If your offer is new, leading edge, challenging, even risky, then you will need to find your key accounts among the innovators and the early adopters of the market. If your offer is well established, secure, safe, perhaps even a little staid, then it will be to the other end of the curve that you may need to look.

Be wary however of the innovators who may be easy to sell to but will suck up your resources and may prove fickle and promiscuous when the next new thing comes along. Early adopters and early majority types may be your most secure targets in the long run.

SEGMENTATION AND KAM IDENTIFICATION

Hopefully, it is becoming clear why an understanding of segmentation is vital to any business aiming to implement KAM.

The business must have a planning hierarchy, from business plan, to marketing plan, segment plans, and key account plans, as illustrated in Figure 20.5.

This is not to say that the entire process is top down. Invaluable inputs will come from the bottom up or the balance between objectives, resources and opportunity (Chapter 2) will not be found; but segment plans must be subsets of marketing plans and key account plans should be subsets of those segment plans.

Making sure that you avoid 'sizeism'

Without segmentation, the selection of key accounts will tend to suffer from *sizeism*. The next chapter will show how comparing the attractiveness of customers and assessing your strengths in their eyes will provide a basis for identifying key accounts. Without segmentation, most markets are too large and diverse for this to be workable; what seems attractive in one part of the market is not so important in another and so the scale of business becomes the only truly comparable factor – hence *sizeism*. The 20 per cent of customers that supply 80 per cent of the business will be the key accounts.

Figure 20.5 *Business plan hierarchy*

In our adhesives company, the largest sales are to the specialist distributors serving the industrial markets. Without segmentation, these would have been the company's key accounts, full stop. Having segmented, it finds that some of the DIY multiple retailers in the building and DIY business are certainly candidates for a key account approach. The same issue can be repeated at this level – within the building and DIY business. The DIY multiples make up 80 per cent of the sales, but there are some builders' merchants that do significant business in their own segment, or sub-segment of the market. Segmentation allows the supplier to recognize the importance of such customers.

And if looking at the future revealed the most attractive opportunities in the building arena then KAM in that segment will be vital.

With segmentation, and the close identification of needs and attitudes within each segment, the selection of key accounts can be made on a broader basis. Apples are now being compared to apples and each segment will have its own key accounts.

Let's just return to those bewildered colleagues in the support functions that we left at the start of this chapter and see if segmentation has helped them. If everyone in the business understands that the market is divided into segments that have different needs then they will understand why different customers, and sales people, might express different requirements. More than this, they will be able to develop their own plans and strategies to maximize their added value impact on those segments.

Every customer their own segment?

In theory a segment could be as small as an individual customer, with their own unique needs, attitudes, and behaviours. In practice this may indeed become possible through key account management. Whether this is so or not will depend greatly on the type of industry and market.

In fast moving consumer goods (FMCG) markets, while the e-revolution and concepts such as customer relationship management (CRM) suggest the prospect of every _consumer_ their own segment, in practice it is still very helpful (and practical) to aggregate customers together under some general definitions. In some B2B markets it may indeed be possible to view a _customer_ as a segment, provided that there are not so many customers that the supplier will be pulled apart at the seams.

The _'Lead Key Account'_?

Here's a thought. If a segment is a group of customers with the same needs attitudes and behaviours, and if you do your segmentation properly, would there be a need for more than one key account in any segment?

Only one Key Account per segment?

The idea here is that by devoting energies to one customer, and learning the right solutions for them, these solutions should also be appropriate to all other customers in the segment.

There is much to recommend such a view, provided you really do your segmentation properly. Consider a supplier to the medical industry, with customers ranging from hospitals to universities, to pharmaceutical companies. Those three groups may have been identified as the segments. Now, can you honestly say that the needs, attitudes and behaviours of all hospitals are the same, or all universities or all pharmaceutical companies?

BENEFITS OF SEGMENTATION FOR KAM

- Segmentation will allow you to select key accounts because of their importance within particular segments, not just because they are the business's largest customers.
- Segmentation will enable you to identify the 'winners' within each segment with greater certainty.
- Segmentation will allow you to focus your efforts as a total business (sales, marketing and support functions) on to clearly identified sets of needs.

- Where customer needs can be expressed as 'segment needs' there are enhanced chances of achieving economies of scale or efficiencies in operation.
- Segmentation will allow a clearer definition of standards, providing focus for support functions.
- Segmentation will allow you to identify and support a wider number of customers as long-term business partners.
- Segmentation will increase your chances of being able to work with competing customers through differentiated support packages.
- Segmentation will allow KAM to drive business processes without descending into the chaos of 'anything goes'.
- Segmentation will help to align the business behind the KAM concept.

The next chapter goes into more detail on how to identify key accounts with the assumption that we are now making these judgements within specific segments.

A NEW TYPE OF MARKETING PLAN? KAM AND RELATIONSHIP MARKETING

We have shown KA plans to be subsets of segment plans that are in turn subsets of the marketing plan, but it should be emphasized that this will be a new kind of marketing plan. Traditional marketing, the management of the four Ps, has been criticized as too short term, too tactical and too 'transactional'.

In its place, many argue we should put relationship marketing. Definitions of this new breed of marketing abound in countless books and articles, but in essence it is the attempt to align the whole business towards its customers through a focus on the relationship between supplier and customer. This is, of course, very similar to the aims of KAM.

Similarities include:

- A move away from transactional selling to relationship management.
- Relationships based on trust and value.
- The maximization of the lifetime value of customers and market segments.
- Focus on developing customer loyalty and retention.
- A concern to change internal organization and attitudes to align towards the customer.
- The need for cross-business processes.

So what is the difference? For practical purposes, not a great deal. KAM is principally concerned with the management of customer relationships – it is the delivery of the theory that relationship marketing propounds.

Christian Gronroos calls relationship marketing 'the mutual exchange and fulfilment of promises'. Grand words, but not a bad basis for partnership KAM.

21

Identifying your key accounts

This chapter deals with steps four through to nine of the 10 step process introduced in Chapter 19.

(The CD ROM attached to this book contains a software package designed to help with the process described in this chapter.)

There is a dangerous self-fulfilling prophecy in sales: 'They're our key accounts because they're key...' If today's largest customers are your key accounts then it is very easy for them to stay that way, even as they start to decline, as they inevitably colour all your thoughts about the future. We might call it the 'trapped by our own history' syndrome. Examine almost any 'once great' business now in terminal decline and you will find evidence of this syndrome.

Sometimes you get lucky and your largest customers take you where you want to be, but you wouldn't want to rely on it. At its worst, the syndrome can lead businesses into decline simply because they follow their customer's decline. They cannot escape the vicious circle; seeking alternative customers would be an abandonment of their key accounts...

So, we need to select our key accounts on some better basis than today's (or yesterday's) largest.

I once had a lengthy debate with a customer as to whether 'select' was the right word. 'You have obviously been very lucky in your sales career,' he said to me. 'I have never selected a customer in my life, they've always selected me.'

He was right of course; as far as today's customers go, the selection process is largely in their hands. What KAM gives you is an opportunity to start doing a bit of the thinking for yourself.

'Perhaps "identifying" would be a better word?' I suggested. He agreed and I went away happy, only to find the word 'select' burrowing its way back into my head.

In the end, KAM must involve both activities – identifying and selecting. KAM is about analysis and it is also about choices. One of the toughest decisions in KAM is the final choice, who's in and who isn't (note I don't say 'out'; there is a place for non-key accounts, as we will see later in this chapter), made simpler by the realization that it is a two-way process. You chase the ones that will take you where you want to go and they chase you if you meet their needs. Marry the two thoughts in the same customer and you have a key account and they have a key supplier. The 'diamond' relationship of partnership KAM is the result of mutual strategic intent (see Chapter 5).

Two nagging thoughts

So, what about all those very attractive customers that don't chase *you*. Are they key accounts?

And what about all those customers that *do* chase you, but you don't really see *them* as your future? Are they key accounts?

Take a moment to consider these two questions – you doubtless have customers, or potential customers, that fit both descriptions. What would you call them?

AN IDENTIFICATION AND SELECTION PROCESS

You can't call everyone 'key'. Customers are not equal – some are definitely more equal than others. Call them all 'key' and the term will fast become meaningless.

KAISM: The key account identification and selection matrix

If we remember that the purpose of identifying key accounts is to help us deploy our business resources, and commit ourselves to action, then we will see the value in the following matrix (Figure 21.1).

The matrix considers two sets of factors, the two sides of the identification and selection process: yours (do you like them?) and theirs (do they like you?):

- Customer attractiveness – what is it that makes customers, or potential customers, attractive to you?
- Relative strength – what is it that makes you attractive to your customers, in comparison to your competitors?

Figure 21.1 *Identification and selection matrix*

Having answered these questions, you might end up with four 'categories' of customer:

- key account;
- key development account;
- maintenance account;
- opportunistic account.

Key account

This is it; you want them and they like you, but don't relax. These customers are critical to your future and they deserve energetic attention from a KA team devoted to keeping on top of change. Remember the cliché, 'nothing recedes like success'.

Key development account

This is where it *could* be, if only you could improve your performance in their eyes. The KA team must focus on finding out what makes the customers tick, what they want, and committing the business to providing it. Such customers could be hard work, with all the 'chicken and egg' problems imaginable, but success will be well rewarded. Only remember; you have limited resources, so don't spread them too thinly. How many key development accounts could your business chase simultaneously?

Some businesses appoint their most junior sales people to look after these customers, or attach them to the responsibilities of account managers already burdened by too many top-right key accounts. Where this is done because the business doesn't see much prospect of progress, they are usually right – they make no progress! Another common approach is to make such customers the responsibility of the tele-sales team, an almost impossible task, to develop relationships that will enhance the customer's view of you – by telephone.

Success with such customers will come from applied effort, not from starving them of resource or expertise. If these are the 'jam tomorrow' customers then there should not be so many that progress is made with none, nor so few that there *is* no tomorrow – a fine judgement indeed, but one that will mark the winners from the losers.

There will often be more customers in this category than can actually be developed into key accounts, either through lack of resource or lack of opportunity. This is perhaps natural if you operate in a market with a wealth of attractive prospects. This will present you with choices – increase your resources or 'pick them off' as specific customer opportunities arise. Be prepared to experiment, to trial and to allocate resources as 'test cases', aiming to learn from each experience. Be prepared to put some on hold on the famous 'back burner', and finally, know when to admit defeat as an unconvertible customer can hardly be called 'attractive'.

Maintenance account

In many ways this is the hardest category. These are good customers, perhaps they have been loyal for years. Almost certainly they are personal favourites of plenty of your team. The tough decision, but the right one, is to pull resource and energy back from such customers – it is needed elsewhere. The answer lies in the category's name, 'maintenance'.

Some people (and very often the rep responsible for such a customer) might say you were abandoning them. Sales people don't like the idea of 'dropping' customers, not after all the work that has gone into winning them, and who would blame them? But this category is not about abandonment, it is about finding ways of looking after customers that won't trap you and your team into time-consuming commitments. The objective here is to reduce costs and maximize sustained earnings. Perhaps visits can be made less often and an efficient telephone ordering service or EDI system can be laid on. The customer might even prefer such arrangements, especially if they seemed more appropriate to their needs.

That is just one of many actions that might be required. Others might be harder, like withdrawing R&D resources, but if you are to practise proper KAM, you must find solutions to such problems and solutions that don't lose your customer's high regard.

Often, the success or failure of dealing with newly identified maintenance accounts lies in how the transition is handled. Let's say your solution is to

This is where you 'win' your time and your resource to invest in key and key development accounts

take an account, currently supplied directly from your own distribution depot, and place them in the care of local distributors. Compare two alternative approaches to such a transition:

Approach one

Apologies are sent to the customer, including a letter from the MD thanking them for their loyal support and hoping that it will continue, despite the need to reorganize business operations. The distributor is given the account to work with how they see fit. Once the handover is decided on, and the necessary meetings concluded, the previous sales contact has no further contact with the customer.

Approach two

The supplier and the distributor make a joint presentation on the advantages to the customer of moving to a local distributor, including shorter lead times, more frequent delivery, flexible terms, product variants to suit local circumstances and more personal attention. The distributor is helped to understand their new customer by the previous sales contact that stays in touch over a managed handover period.

Whatever your solution, the task is to free your time, and your team's time, and to sell the changes to your maintenance customers, *positively*.

Opportunistic account

These are customers that you will service willingly as and when it suits your priorities. You should not make wild promises that you cannot keep, nor should you treat them like nuisances. Be pleased with their custom, but recognize it for what it is – income that helps you develop your key and key development accounts.

IS ALL THIS REALLY NECESSARY?

I have been asked this many times by people reluctant to categorize or label their customers. It is a healthy reluctance if labelling means carving in stone. But if it helps you do the right things, when there are tough decisions, then it will be seen to have been more than necessary.

An international supplier to the oil industry once put at stake a number of their key contracts because they were over-eager to secure a large, but one-off, deal with Russia. They had a system of customer categorization that put the Russian customer in the opportunistic box, but it was only given lip service and not all functions agreed with the definitions. The order was large and tempting and the production people put in a superhuman effort to meet the deadlines. They made it and they felt pretty good about it, until the complaints started to flow from their *real* key accounts. They had all taken their eye off the ball.

Identification and selection of customers into these kinds of categories do not necessarily imply abandonment of some for the sake of the rest. It implies planned allocation of resources.

For some businesses, the people resources required for KA teams would be a big call and they must identify the real candidates for such support with care. Other businesses may have the people and perhaps many customers could enjoy the 'diamond' of partnership KAM, but the production resources would not cope with the variety of commitments that ensue. Remember the need to balance your objectives with the market opportunity and with your own business resources (Chapter 2).

The 'bow tie' relationship is perfect for many customer relationships, representing the right match of supplier and customer strategic intent.

In the end, judgements, not four-box matrixes, must make your decisions. Use the matrix as a tool, a focus for discussion and a guide, no more. Perhaps your business will be able to play variations on the theme – a relatively large number of KA teams with 'diamond' relationships in the making, but a recognition that at any one time only a few of these will be able to commit the business's resources. Or a large pool of development key accounts with 'skeleton' or 'virtual' teams waiting for the opportunity to form and take action with a much smaller number of active KA teams, or…

Avoiding shooting yourself in the foot

I have seen a supplier chase and win a major customer (in this case it was Coca-Cola), only to see it almost wreck their good work by then chasing that customer's competitor (in this case Pepsi). Does KAM mean that you cannot serve both? In some industries, large customers, and particularly those with dominant market positions, may try to keep their key suppliers out of their competition. This is done through suggestion, influence and pressure, not by contract. The reasons are clear – if a close relationship is to form, where sensitive information will be exchanged, then there must be some security. For the supplier, there may be a need to make choices – one or the other – and the KA selection process is one of the tools for aiding such decisions.

The key is in defining the attractiveness factors and comparing potential customers against those factors in the long term.

In many cases there will not be a need to make such a stark choice, but there *will* be a need to recognize the sensitivities of customers. The common solution is to ensure that the KA teams serving such competitors are not composed of the same people. In this instance (and perhaps the only justifiable occasion), the building of some *walls* within the supplier's own organization may be of benefit rather than a barrier.

Important health warning

This process is about getting you and your team to think. It should *not* be done as guesswork, or in five minutes on the back of an envelope. It is about understanding how and why you should deal with customers and how that might change over time. It is not about labelling them forever. And yes, of course you can break the rules and the definitions – provided you can explain why.

The identification and selection matrix is designed to help our thinking, not to replace our brains...

My own business, a training and consultancy firm, regularly conducts this identification and selection process and for many years our chosen criteria for the two axes always found a particular customer down in the bottom-left box. The reason was that this customer had their own in-house training organization, never an attractive proposition for a supplier of training and a hard act to be compared favourably against. But we all knew that this was a key development account, so were we doing something wrong in our analysis?

Not at all. We always had to remember that times change and that we should always be asking, 'What if the company should close its in-house training organization?' Then it would be catapulted into the top-right box. But, rather than wait until that happened, shouldn't we be treating it as a key account now, in preparation – perhaps even to encourage them in their decision to close their own operation?

In the event, the company began to wind down their own training operation and our key account attentions began to pay dividends. For a number of years we had a higher strategic intent about the company than they had about us, a position that we saw in Chapter 6 (The ugly story), and wondered if this mismatch was a problem. Sometimes it is, if there is no likely realignment of intent in the future, but sometimes you just have to wait, and prepare – and manufacture your own luck.

THE PERFECT INVESTMENT PORTFOLIO?

Any successful business will require a mix of customers: key accounts, key development accounts, maintenance and opportunistic, a balance across all four boxes of the matrix.

If all customers were key accounts then, even if the term didn't become meaningless, the effort involved to manage them properly could quite conceivably create greater costs than the income enjoyed. If all were key development accounts then the likelihood would be all the greater.

A business with too many maintenance accounts, while enjoying a handsome income, might have cause to worry about their future; might the bulk of their customers actually hold them back? And a business with too many 'opportunistic accounts', while they may be very profitable, is a business heading nowhere in particular. It is all a question of investment and return.

Customers are not equal, nor do they all serve the same purpose

Figure 21.2 shows the expectations you might have of where the resources will be invested and where the returns will come from. The customer portfolio should be seen in these terms, as a managed flow of time, energy, resources, and money, around the business. Time and energy saved by more efficient means of handling maintenance and opportunistic accounts can be invested in future development, as can the revenue and profit from those customers.

Like any managed investment, KAM must concern itself not just with the 'star' earners, but with managing a portfolio of customers, balancing short and long term income, and balancing the resources and the returns. Seen in this light we can see another capability that the KAM approach demands – an appreciation of the dynamics of investment and return.

Figure 21.2 *Investments and Returns from the Customer Portfolio*

THE SELECTION FACTORS AND THE SELECTION PROCESS

To recap, the two axes of the identification and selection matrix are:

- Customer attractiveness – what is it that makes customers, or potential customers, attractive to you?
- Relative strength – what is it that makes you attractive to your customers, in comparison to your competitors?

Each of these is made up of a range of individual factors, quantitative and qualitative, unique to your own business situation. The importance of defining these factors, and then using them as measures, cannot be over-stated. If the matrix is to be any kind of guide to allocating resources, deciding priorities, or determining customer relationships, then a great deal of thought should go into this exercise.

It is almost certainly true to say that the most value to be gained from this matrix is not in the final outcome, but in the thinking and the discussions that went into its origination. The matrix provides an ideal opportunity for cross-functional teams to meet and discuss, sharing the viewpoints of their different perspectives. As such, this exercise is a key part of gaining cross-business alignment and is of huge value even if the outcome tells you nothing particularly new or startling.

Customer attractiveness factors

What makes *you* want *them*?

These are factors that should relate to your longer-term goals as a business. If your competitive advantage is to come from some unique added value element in your offer then you might regard customers that valued that element as attractive. If high-tech solutions to customers' problems is your pitch then you might expect your most attractive accounts to be those that value such solutions and are prepared to pay the price.

These are also factors that take account of the market opportunity. Let's say you see your future in providing services that are currently provided in-house by most businesses. Your most attractive accounts may be those that have a positive attitude towards outsourcing such services. And there are factors that will recognize the limits to your own business resources. An attractive customer may be one that is easy to gain access to, perhaps because of geography or existing relationships.

In short, the factors for customer attractiveness go back to our thoughts on managing the future in Chapter 2, seeking a balance of objectives, opportunity and resources.

The examples given are perhaps rather simplistic; it is the balance of a *range* of factors that will determine the ranking of attractiveness.

The range of factors might include any of the following:

- Size – volume; value; profit opportunity.
- Growth potential – volume; value; profit opportunity.
- Financial stability – will they be there in the future and will they pay their bills?
- Ease of access – geography; openness.
- Closeness of existing relationships.
- Strategic fit – do they see the world the same way as you? Will they take you where you wish to be?
- Are they 'early adopters' – do they pick up on new ideas and products, or do they wait until the market has tested them?
- Do they value your offer? Is it relevant to their needs?
- Level of competition – low being attractive.
- Their market standing – industry leader, credibility, prestige and so on.

Your own business circumstances must determine your selection and the *weighting* you might give to individual factors. Working with a client in Russia, we spent a great deal of time identifying a list of six factors, but there was one that stood head and shoulders above the others: will they pay their bills? It was a crucial aspect of their market circumstance and without it there was little point proceeding – some factors are absolute 'must haves'.

If you are offering new ideas, solutions and products then customers with a tendency to buy into new ideas will clearly be attractive – we might call them 'innovators' or 'early adopters'.

Whatever your final choice, you must be able to apply these factors to each of your customers, measuring them against each other. It will become apparent at this stage how important it was to segment your market (Chapter 20), as this is the only way to make these comparisons on any kind of equal basis. The choice of attractiveness factors will almost certainly be different for different market segments, and so will your ultimate identification of key accounts.

Dulux Paints in the UK supplies to both the DIY market and the professional decorator market, two distinct segments of the decorative paint market. If we just take one factor that might determine customer attractiveness, we will immediately see the importance of segmentation in key account identification and selection. Let's consider scale.

In the DIY market, the goal of brand leadership makes the large DIY superstores very attractive customers. In the professional decorator market, a large firm means large-scale contracts, which means pressure on price, so not so attractive. The real key accounts might be identified as the distributors that give access to the small and medium-sized decorating firms. Different segments, different objectives, different attractiveness factors.

Remember the golden rule: segments first, key accounts second

Relative strength factors

This is where you must view things through your customers' eyes. What are *their* critical success factors in dealing with suppliers? What are they looking for and what causes them to prefer one supplier above another? Some customers publish explicit lists of vendor ratings, others are more secretive. This is no easy task, however explicit the lists, as you are dealing not only with measurable 'facts', but also with perceptions – something much harder to judge.

Identifying these factors will require great honesty. It is tempting to select all those things that you just happen to be good at, and you will feel very pleased with the outcome, only it will be worthless. The perceptions of different functions within your own business will be of great value to the debate – each will have their own awareness of what goes down well and what causes complaints.

The more you know, of course, the better. If you find this part of the exercise particularly difficult then it will at least have highlighted a priority action for your KAM implementation programme – find out.

Given the propensity for most of us to either pat ourselves on the back or whip ourselves unreasonably it may be valuable to gain some kind of independent insight as a route to the truth in this matter. Consider formal and independent market research into customers' views, needs and levels of satisfaction.

Using research as a way of talking to customers will be a good antidote to one of many a supplier's greatest failings – talking to themselves.

There are many companies with tools for identifying and measuring customer requirements and customer satisfaction, from surveys to interviews and beyond. Making use of such expertise may well prove to be one of those early investments that pays handsome dividends in the long run.

The range of factors (seen from your customers' perspective) might include:

- price;
- service – on time in full measures, just-in-time requirements, etc;
- quality;
- speed of response;
- relationships and attitudes;
- technical innovation;
- investment in the industry;
- value in use – value in the supply chain, total acquisition cost, etc;
- attitude to exclusivity arrangements;
- long-term sustainability;
- trust and confidence – ethical standards and behaviour.

These factors will, of course, be individual to each customer and it is against these factors that you have an opportunity to improve your own performance, turning a development account into a key account and achieving key supplier status into the bargain.

THE SELECTION PROCESS

The CD ROM attached to this book has a software package that will help take you through the process described in this chapter. However, it is no bad idea to commence with a paper exercise, however rough, for several reasons: it quickly identifies the black holes in your knowledge of your customers; it makes a team-wide analysis easier to facilitate; and most importantly, it engages the brain rather than your typing fingers.

The following tables are designed to help you identify where your customers sit in your portfolio. They will provide a 'first cut' analysis, but you may wish to go further than this. Weighting of individual factors is the obvious next step and it may be that at this point you should turn to the CD ROM for help – the mathematics start to get quite involved!

The portfolio represents the relative positions of customers within a specific market segment and you should have completed such a segmentation exercise (Chapter 20) before moving to this stage.

In Table 21.1, you will be rating and comparing customers against *your* chosen list of customer attractiveness factors. In Table 21.2, you will be assessing your relative strength, using *their* measures to see how they rate you in comparison to your competitors. The outcomes will be plotted in the identification and selection matrix.

Table 21.1 *Customer attractiveness factors – CAFs*

	Weight	Customers										
Attractiveness Factor												
1												
2												
3												
4												
5												
6												
Total												

Average Score:
(Total of all scores divided by number of customers rated)

- Enter your chosen customers across the top of the table.
- It is advisable to select a list of about six factors – of course, more will exist, but this will help to focus the analysis.
- Enter a score from 1 to 10 for each customer, against each attractiveness factor. The higher the score, the better your customer meets that aspiration. Try to set a benchmark of what is 'good and bad' before starting to score and try to stick to it! (It is all too easy to uprate your 'favourite' customers.)
- Calculate the average score. This will be used once you have completed table 21.2.

Table 21.2 *Relative strength versus the competition*

Customer:	Weight	Suppliers											
Critical Success Factor		**You**											
1													
2													
3													
4													
5													
6													
Total													

- For each customer under consideration, identify six critical success factors (CSFs) that represent their principal needs from their suppliers and by which they would judge you in comparison with others.
- Complete one table for each of the customers selected in table one – it is quite likely, of course, that each customer will have their own distinct set of CSFs.
- Place you and your competitors across the top of the table and enter a score from 1 to 10 for each supplier, against each factor. This is how the customer views you and your competitors, fact and perception – so be honest! The higher the score, the better the supplier meets the customer's needs.

Completing the matrix

Using the information from these two tables, you can place each customer on the identification and selection matrix, shown again at figure 21.3.

From Table 21.1, if a customer scores higher than the average score then they will be in one of the two upper boxes; if lower than average, they will be in one of the two lower boxes.

Figure 21.3 *Identification and selection matrix*

To identify which of the two, use the results from Table 21.2. Where you score better than your *best* competitor, you will occupy the right-hand box and the left-hand box if you score worse.

HOW MUCH EFFORT AND HOW MUCH DETAIL?

As has been said before, it is probably the thinking behind this exercise, rather than the outcome, that is important. The main effort should be put into identifying the measurement factors and then in seeking to make good assessments. Calculations to two decimal places that shift customers a few millimetres on the matrix are unlikely to add much to anybody's understanding.

Where you simply do not know the answers, most likely in looking at your relative strength, make a note to find out. A supreme benefit of this exercise is the demonstration of what you don't *and must* know. Seek professional advice on how to do market research into customers' needs and current satisfaction – it takes more than the salesperson asking the buyer's opinion.

Top tips:
– **use as a spur to what you must now find out**
– **involve the team**

This is an exercise that should be done repeatedly, each time seeking for more completeness and greater certainty in your assessments. Over time, you and your team will build up a substantially better appreciation of how you view your customers and how they view you.

This exercise is far from easy and that is why sometimes it doesn't get done at all. Involve a good cross-section of people from your business to discuss and debate around this exercise – you will discover just how different functions see your customers in different lights:

- Folk in distribution like customers who order regularly, with lots of notice, and preferably the same each time.
- Folk in credit control like those customers who pay on time, and the few that pay early are *very* special.
- R&D probably like those customers that share ideas and let you use them as a test bed.
- Sales managers like the ones that will help meet their sales targets, especially those that will give large orders just before the end of accounting periods.

Which of these views should predominate in determining customer attractiveness?

Try to relate perceptions to the overall business circumstances; if you are in a low-margin high-turnover kind of trade, where cash flow is crucial, then your friends in credit control may have a point. The exercise will certainly help to clarify what you really *do* want.

If it is possible, involve the customer, but take care not to build expectations beyond what can be delivered.

Should we tell the customer?

KAM has been described as an outward-facing process, but there is one aspect that should perhaps remain internal – these labels of customer categories. Telling a key account they are such is one thing, but how about being told you are in maintenance, or are viewed opportunistically?

KEY ACCOUNTS AND MULTIPLE BUSINESS UNIT SUPPLIERS

An interesting challenge for KAM is the situation where the supplier is formed into a number of business units, working independently of each other and selling to common customers. Let's say a packaging company, divided into business units focused on different packaging solutions and materials, has common customers that use a variety of these solutions and materials.

Who is a key account here, and who has responsibility for them?

Business Unit Alpha makes high-tech plastic film and its No. 1 key account – let's call them 'X' – is designated so because its business is developing fast in the pre-packed, pre-cooked food industry where such high-tech films are going to be of increasing importance.

Business Unit Beta makes corrugated cardboard boxes and it also sells to customer 'X', but not in particularly large quantities.

Is customer 'X' defined as a key account for Business Unit Beta? Probably not. Is there scope for 'difficulty' here? Absolutely.

What if Business Unit Beta, having defined customer 'X' as one of its opportunistic accounts, decides to let go a piece of business with 'X'? Perhaps, worse than that, it has to let 'X' down in order to meet the demands of one of its own key accounts? How does Business Unit Alpha feel about this?

Well, maybe it is so separate from Business Unit Beta that it doesn't even realize what has happened. So no problem? What if customer 'X', frustrated by the poor regard the supplier holds it in, chooses to take out its frustration on Business Unit Alpha? *Plenty* of scope for difficulties.

One 'solution' is to insist that any one business unit's KA must be regarded as the same by all other units. Seems logical, but just wait for the fights to start.

There is a larger question: does the supplier have anything to gain by acting more in concert? The answer to this will come primarily from the customer's perspective. Does the customer buy film and corrugated card, or do they buy packaging solutions? (See 'The good story', Chapter 6, for another angle on this situation.)

Some businesses try to solve this using hierarchies of key accounts. They consist of:

- the global key accounts that cross all business and regional boundaries;
- the regional key accounts;
- the business unit key accounts;
- the national key accounts;
- sometimes even the sales representatives' key accounts.

There are two dangers in such hierarchies: confusing yourself and confusing the customer, which is quite enough confusion for anyone!

If such designations also come with clear definitions of responsibilities and accountabilities then they may yet succeed. Who will get first call on the resources available? Where will we aim to forge diamond relationships? How far will we allow the account to drive business decisions? Where does the ultimate responsibility for this customer lie? What is expected from support functions?

Should companies with multiple business units act in concert in front of shared customers?

245

22

Customer distinction

Having gone to all the effort of classifying your customers you now need to move to the all important step, Step 10 in the process outlined in the previous chapter – doing something that makes a difference!

Three sins... at least...

If you don't determine to manage each type of customer differently – I am calling this differentiation *customer distinction* – then there are at least three particular dangers awaiting you.

An academic exercise with no buy in

It is all too easy for the KAISM exercise to become an academic one, taking large amounts of management time, building up expectations across the organization that something big is about to happen, and then there is nothing. The process easily becomes discredited and it will take some time before people will be convinced to revisit such ideas.

Service Creep

Key Accounts get the top level attention, and as a result they get the best of everything – best ideas, best services, best everything. In time, the sales people servicing the other categories of customer want the best for their own. It is like allowing sales reps to give discounts, sooner or later everyone gets them. The problem with this is that all these extra things cost money, and the chances are that the returns you got from key accounts, which justified them in the first place, are not forthcoming from the other customers.

No energy for the Key Account Challenge

It will not be unusual for the majority of your customers to be in the bottom right hand box of the KAISM (see figure 21.1) – maintenance accounts. It is here then that the majority of the sales team's time is taken up.

...and by far the worst sin...

We have seen that the task of KAM is a time consuming one, and so where is all this new time and energy to come from? It must come by freeing up energy from the non key accounts, as indicated in figure 22.1.

Figure 22.1 *Freeing up the energy for KAM*

Without new ways of servicing maintenance accounts, this just isn't going to happen. Indeed, for many the real challenge of KAM is not managing the key accounts, but finding ways to look after the other classifications of customer!

DETERMINING DISTINCT STRATEGIES

For KAM to be effective energy and resources must be liberated from the non key accounts. Distinct sales and service strategies must be developed for each customer type that allow for that reallocation of resources.

Figure 22.1 suggests a possible broad brush approach by using the terms we discussed in Chapter 5 – the milk round, the hunters and the farmers.

Key Development Accounts require an approach that can see the opportunities fast, and can pounce on them and make something happen – some quick wins, a very typical 'hunter' approach.

Key Accounts will not thrive with such an approach however, and at some point in the journey it may be necessary to hand over responsibility to a more farmer orientated key account manager. Or, by developing the KA team, the team itself provides that longer term 'farmer' approach.

Maintenance Accounts just need to be maintained, and often a milk round approach can do this very well. This may be through a traditional sales force, or perhaps through an outsourced team, or increasingly it is achieved by other means – inside sales staff, customer service staff, call centres, electronic trading, etc.

The Steps Towards Customer Distinction

Identify the possible 'bases' for distinction – the things by which you will distinguish your offer, your services, your proposition, to each customer type.

Figure 22.2 lists some of the most common bases:

Sales and service strategies must be designed for each customer type, distinguishing across a number of bases, perhaps including the following:

- Profitability and the time horizon
- Frequency of contact
- Level and depth of contacts
- Nature of commitment to the customer
- Contracts – *long or short, or none at all*
- Allocation of resources
- Nature and number of projects
- Provision of services
- Charging for services, or part of the package?
- Terms and Pricing
- Use of distributors

Figure 22.2 *Customer Distinction Bases*

1. For each possible base, how would this be applied to a key account – can you identify a minimum and a maximum range of application. For example – if the base in question is frequency of contact, for a key account you may decide that this should never be less than once a month, with a maximum of once a week.

    Similarly, for level and depth of contact, you should always aim to know and meet with, let's say, the CEO, with as a minimum the functional directors or vice-presidents.

2. Repeat this exercise for each of the other customer classifications. If we repeat the example from above but this time with an opportunistic account, we might decide that against frequency of contact this will be nil for the sales professional but maintained by a telesales call once a month (just as an example), and that there is no need for you to know or contact senior staff in such an account – the one who places the order will do.

3. Steps 2 and 3 will result in a table, an example of which is shown in Table 21.1. You can now use this table as the basis for preparing specific sales and service plans by customer (in the case of key and key development accounts) or for preparing generic plans for the maintenance and opportunistic categories.

SOME COMMENTS AND ADVICE

Removing resources

Chances are that history has brought you to a point where you already do too many things for too many customers. In such a case the impact of a Customer Distinction strategy is more to do with removing than adding – never easy.

There are two bits of advice. First, take it slowly, pilot, experiment, discuss with customers before doing anything dramatic – don't abandon your customers overnight. Second, use the practice of KAM, to improve your understanding of what customers really want and value, and how that differs from the things that they take but perhaps couldn't care less about! Figure 22.3 shows what I mean by this.

Don't give people unwanted Christmas presents

Most suppliers are guilty of giving customers things they don't want or value. This is usually because they did once want them, but no more – they just never got around to telling you. There are at least three big problems with this:

1. These things cost you money.
2. These things sap your strength.
3. The customer doesn't value you more for these things, they value you less! What do you think of people who give you unwanted Christmas presents? That's what they think of you.

All members of the KA team should be charged with keeping their ears and eyes open for any indications that help you determine what is north, and what is south of the line in Figure 22.3.

Charging for services

History again…. Chances are you give services for free that you really should be charging for. There is perhaps not much you can do about this for those things already committed to, but you should be doubly determined to get it right for all new services.

Table 22.1 Customer Distinction by base

	Key Account	Key Development Account	Maintenance Account	Opportunistic Account
Profitability and the time horizon	• Measured over a minimum 2–3 year period • 'Life Time Value'	• Be prepared to invest up front • Have a clear timetable for anticipated returns • Regular reviews	• Constant attention to enhancing profitability • Take an 'accountants' viewpoint on costs	• The prime measure of success • Returns must be instant
Nature of our commitment to 'understanding the customer'	• Fully understand the customer's business strategy – their vision, drivers, market position, USPs, attitude to risk, attitude to costs, competition • Fully understand their view of our competitors • Know their vendor ratings	• Make full use of analytical tools to assess and anticipate the customer's business strategy – Ansoff Matrix, PLC, Porter, Weirsema's Value Drivers	• Continually monitor for changes in their business strategy that might cause us to reclassify the account	• Understand their market position • Understand their competitors
Nature of our contractual commitment	• Full contract designed to promote trust and confidence, as a platform for developing full partnership	• 'Letter of intent' approach, outlining aspirations and expectations • No financial penalties	• Full contract designed to protect current business and build barriers to exit	• No contracts
Relationship and level of contacts	• Full diamond relationship • Formal KA team • Full contact matrix for each DMU • Formal GROWs for all KA team members	• Targeting a diamond relationship • Building the KA team • Focus on the key sponsors and influencers in the DMU • Aim to understand their organizational structure at the earliest opportunity • High level of senior contact up front	• Seek increasing efficiency of contacts • Use of virtual and automated communication methods • Make greater use of support staff • Reducing the account team while maintaining DMU contacts • Focus on the key sponsors and influencers in the DMU	• Bow-tie relationship
Account plan	• Full written KA plan • Focus on long term growth and long term profitability	• Full written plan • Focus on long term growth and long term profitability	• Full written account plan • Focus on improving profitability and building barriers to exit	• No written plan • Standard budget/forecast
Customer's perception of us	• 'Their No. 1 'helper' • A strategic supplier • Supplier of >60% share	• A bringer of specific and targeted improvements • A key supplier	• Steady and reliable supplier • Eager to keep our business	• Commercially astute • 'We can do a deal with these guys'
Allocation of resource	• Resources formally agreed with providers on an annual basis (minimum) • Agreed and provided as part of a clear written KA plan	• Allocated against clear and realistic targets • Clear timetable of returns • Regular review of progress • Be prepared to withdraw	• Adopt a 'common-sense liberation' of resources over time • Aim to regulate the offer on clearly defined levels • Appoint a techno/commercial account manager?	• Limited commercial effort • Occasional short term bursts of commercial activity – sales drives • No technical resource unless paid for (and even then, take care not to stretch our resource)

Table 22.1 continued

	Key Account	Key Development Account	Maintenance Account	Opportunistic Account
Provision of services	• Formally agreed levels of service • Full briefing of the internal • Formalized access to R&T • Technical openness • Priority technical feedback • 24 hour hotline • Enhanced Portal • 'Belt and braces' logistics process • Consignment stock • FOC samples	• Superior R&T access • Full briefing of the internal providers on 'expectations' • Technical openness • Priority technical feedback • 'Belt and braces' logistics process • FOC samples	• Standard TS • Standard CS • Standard Portal • Consignments stock where paid for	• Minimum TS (charged) • Standard CS • Full use of e-commerce • Samples charged for
Delivery	• Meet OTIF • Provide an interface with logistics	• Meet OTIF	• Meet OTIF • Charge for additional costs	• No extra costs • Lowest priority
Nature and number of projects	• Projects formally agreed by the account team • Financial investment where required	• Small list of highly targeted projects (mainly tech) • Clear criteria for success • Clear timetable for returns • Ensure we learn from the process	• Provide 'copy/paste' projects	• Only short term projects • No financial support
Availability of technology	• Provide latest technology developments in close partnership • High speed of delivery • Long term development	• The No.1 Priority • Tailored 'new' technology • Top speed of delivery	• 'Spray' of existing technology • Limited support on 'modifications' • Medium speed of delivery	• Existing 'off the shelf' technology • No development work
Pricing	• Market Based • Benchmarked to the key selective competition • Aiming to help them 'win' in their market	• Value based • Aligned with our technical performance	• Cost plus • Based on attributes	• Tactical penetration • Based on capacity available
Knowledge Sharing	• Technical – Full sharing • Commercial – High level • Provided on the basis of 'partnership'	• Technical – High level • Commercial – High level	• Technical – High level • Commercial – High level • Used as a deliberate 'barrier to exit'	• Technical – None • Commercial – Low level
Telling them their classification?	• Yes, when benefits are tangible	• Not until benefits come on stream	• No	• Yes, as a piece of negotiation 'positioning'
Overall Sales Strategy	• Farmer • Long term focus	• Penetration (breaking down immediate barriers to entry)	• Seeking 'Lock in' • Raising barriers to exit	• Hunter • Short term focus
Outcomes to avoid...	• Higher than justified cost to serve • KA Bureaucracy	• Getting locked into commitments with little or no return	• Becoming complacent • Treating the customer as 2nd class citizen	• Destabilising the market • Irresponsible reputation

Figure 22.3 *Avoiding unwanted Christmas presents*

The Customer Distinction process forces you to consider this each time you introduce anything new – who will pay, who will not?

Using Key Accounts to develop solutions for the rest

This may sound in direct contradiction of the point about 'service creep' made earlier in this chapter, and perhaps it is, but there are some circumstances where you can see your key accounts as a kind of test bed for the rest. Develop new ideas with those customers, and then let them filter down to the others.

I think that this avoids the criticism of service creep if it is done in a planned way – if it was in fact the intention from the start.

Outcomes to avoid

You will see from table 22.1 that the last line shows 'outcomes to avoid'. This is particularly valuable in such an exercise as there are some potentially dangerous tendencies.

First, the tendency to overdo the reduction of resources or the toughening up of the stance against maintenance and opportunistic accounts. Remember, maintenance means just that – these are not customers anyone wishes to lose.

Second, the tendency to 'over-egg' the package for key and key development accounts. We may well be in unwanted Christmas present territory here. Remember, the whole purpose of this is to improve profitability, not just increase costs.

Part V

Entry Strategies

Part V

Entry Strategies

Yes there is life
beyond the
buyer...

The customer's decision-making process

We have done our homework; we know what we are trying to achieve and we know that we are chasing the right customer, but they're not buying. Why?

Is our offer going to have a positive impact on their business? An important question, addressed in Part VI, but let's suppose for the moment that it will and they're *still* not buying. Why?

Do we have the right *entry strategy*?

ENTRY STRATEGY

Remember Ken Reilly from the opening pages? He was calling on a key account and he had a good story to tell, but he was telling it to the wrong person. His entry strategy consisted of 'sweet talking' secretaries.

The salesperson, when confronted by a new customer, has a daunting task: who to talk to in an organization that positively blossoms with departments, functions, sites and all the rest. The path to the real decision makers can seem like a maze, only most customers will not allow you the luxury of exploration – no second chances if you take the wrong turning.

23

**Yes there is life
beyond the
buyer...**

It may seem one of life's blessings that customers try to make things easy for the salesperson – they supply someone called a buyer. And, who knows, perhaps salesperson and buyer get on like a house on fire – same hobbies, common backgrounds and the salesperson relaxes into the comfort of familiar surroundings.

Warning bells should already be ringing – the buyer may suggest that they are all-powerful and may promise the prospect of a trial, a big order and a glowing future, but is it *really* in the buyer's hands? In the real world, especially in the days of supply chain managers, the buyer is only one part of a much larger jigsaw.

The buyer may only be the 'front man', held hostage by a variety of people with a variety of interests and influences. Perhaps the production department has clear views on what materials they need and the buyer's teasing promises that they might consider a change of supplier are little more than warm air.

The buyer may be the puppet of those other interests, a rubber stamp, but how many would admit to so much? Here is the seller's quandary – is the buyer the real focus of power, or should that be sought elsewhere, and how, without antagonizing the buyer?

There are two fundamental questions when trying to sell to a new customer, or trying to penetrate further into an existing one: How does the company make its buying decisions? Who is the right person to talk to? As the answer to the second will depend entirely on the answer to the first, we had best start by understanding how a customer makes its decision to buy.

THE BUYING DECISION PROCESS

Most buying decisions go through three stages:

- Realizing that there is a need.
- Looking at the options.
- Clearing up concerns and making a choice.

Of course, not all customers realize they have a need and here lies fertile ground for sales people able to develop such a realization, but without it, the prospect of a sale does not even glimmer.

Most sales are made on three levels:

- By meeting the business needs.
- By meeting the personal needs.
- By understanding how the organization operates and makes their buying decisions.

This is represented in Table 23.1.

Table 23.1   *Sales/buying process*

	Business Needs	**Personal Needs**	**Organizational Decision-Making**
Need exists	What are they?	Understanding style and values	Who has the need? Who makes the decision?
Options are considered	Presenting benefits	Matching style and values	Influencing the DMU*
Concerns are resolved	Negotiation	Rapport	Giving the DMU* a means to decide

*DMU – Decision-making unit (see Chapter 24)

Finding the right level

New and enthusiastic, but inexperienced sales people, particularly those from a technical or scientific background, often make a basic mistake – they forget that customers are human. They can so easily lose the sale by rattling on about the features and benefits of their product while irritating the customer with their arrogance. By only considering one of the three selling levels, they lose the sale.

Older, more experienced sales people, often have the personal side of the job sewn up – they know their customers better than their own families (and they probably see them more often!). Yet, they too can lose the sale by thinking that *this* is all that matters. They have been immersed in the customer for so long that they might even have 'gone native', forgetting to sell on the other levels. Some sales people can even fall into the syndrome of thinking they are a nuisance to their customers by suggesting change – time for a change themselves.

The key account manager must work on all three levels. Most importantly, with complex accounts, they must be able to work on the level ignored by so many, new or old: the customer's *organizational decision-making process.*

Think back to the key account management model and the idea of moving from the 'bow tie' relationship to the 'diamond' or beyond. This implies a more complex set of relationships and it recognizes that the buying decision is made in a more complex way than many buyers might lead you to suppose. They might try to impress you that the decision is all theirs, this being a combination of their own ego and conditioning you for the negotiation. In reality, you know that it lies elsewhere, probably in the hands of a strange entity – the DMU.

24

Selling to the organization – the DMU

DMU – THE DECISION-MAKING UNIT

Most decisions, or at least the important ones, are made by decision-making units. In some companies, these may be quite formal – project teams, sourcing teams or the procurement committee. In others, they may be so informal as to be unidentifiable; but they are there all the same, working by inference, by nods of the head and the raising of eyebrows.

To simplify things a little, it is helpful to think of three types of DMU and the implications of each on the seller:

- Authoritarian DMUs.
- Consensus DMUs.
- Consultative DMUs.

The authoritarian DMU

This is where there is a key individual that makes the decision – perhaps the boss, very often the owner of a smaller business. The decision is imposed on colleagues and staff, sometimes even against their better judgement.

For the seller, this is in some senses the easiest DMU to influence; you simply have to identify that individual and go for them, with the right message and taking pains to ensure you meet their personal needs. Of course, this may upset other people in the organization, particularly if you are seen to ignore their views and simply 'kow-tow' to the boss. For the unwary, short-term success may be followed by a concerted campaign against the supplier. The wise salesperson will target the key decision maker, but be sure to keep the rest involved.

The consensus DMU

This is where the decision is made by some process of 'democracy'. Ideally, all members of the DMU agree or, if that cannot be achieved, the majority vote has it. Typically, consensus DMUs might be found in cooperative organizations, institutions, government bodies, voluntary groups and so on.

For the seller this is harder work, having to influence at least a majority of members, if not all. Such decisions are usually taken in private, with no access to the 'committee' for suppliers. The problem with this is that you don't always know *why* the decision was taken. Even when successful, not knowing *why* is a handicap. Even more importantly, when you have been unsuccessful, knowing why is invaluable. The temptation is to forget it and move on to the next opportunity, but the wise salesperson will spend some time looking for the reasons and learning from them.

The consultative DMU

This is where an appointed decision maker – very often the commercial buyer (or supply side manager) – will make the decision based on the views of the key influencers in the DMU. They will consult with those people and decide accordingly. This might result in a minority view prevailing, in terms of head count, but a minority that has the clearest reason to be consulted, perhaps because they are the final users of the product or have particular expertise.

For the seller, the key to success is identifying those issues that carry most weight and identifying the interested parties to whom these things matter most – and then influencing them towards your viewpoint. Simple to say…

INTERESTS AND INFLUENCES – ENTRY STRATEGIES

In each of these DMU types, but most challengingly in the consensus and consultative, it is important to consider:

1.   What is the buyer's role?
2.   Who else is in the DMU and what are their interests and influences?
3.   Levels of seniority.

The importance of getting this right cannot be overstated. To sell to a complex organization you will need to plan and develop your entry strategy:

●   who to see?
●   who should see them?
●   in what order will they be seen?
●   what will you be saying to them?

THE BUYER'S ROLE

They may suggest they are the kingpin and, of course, they might just be. Even if they are not, but simply a 'gatekeeper', then great care must be taken not to ignore them, or be seen to ignore them. Of course, you *must* get past them to make contact with the *real* decision makers, but you must not be seen to go around them. This is not a job for the insensitive, brash, 'bull in a china shop' salesperson. The buyer may not be the one to decide *for* you, but upset them, and don't be surprised when they present a very strong lobby to decide *against* you.

First establish the buyer's role in relationship to the rest of the DMU

The key account manager needs to identify what role the buyer actually plays and, based on that, they can determine what further actions should be taken.

Figure 24.1 indicates some of those roles, based on a combination of the level of interest demonstrated by the buyer and their level of involvement in the buying process.

Lead – Within this area, buyers play a key role. The decision probably impacts on their own performance measures – stay close.
Specifier – Buyers are interested enough to set some guidelines for the purchase and this sees their involvement early on. Perhaps it was only their professional expertise that led to their involvement, but having done their task, that involvement wanes. They have been asked to take part in a

Figure 24.1   *Roles of the buyer*

decision that is really to be made elsewhere. If so, then that is where you should be seeking more information. The interest of the specifier is worth maintaining as they may prove a useful ally and could give you valuable advice – keep them involved, ask their advice and report on progress.

Service – Buyers perform this role on behalf of someone else. The issues involved, and the outcomes, perhaps do not impact on their own personal performance measures, so you should not expect them to be unduly interested in discussing them. This makes it hard for the seller. The buyer is perhaps only concerned with price, whereas you suspect that the final user, the *real* client, is far more interested in quality. You have to go beyond this type of buyer, but only with their permission. This will not be granted if your reasons are self-interested. You must demonstrate that you can be trusted, and that you can help make the buyer's job easier by discussing 'nitty-gritty' issues directly with the user. If you are seen to perform a service for the buyer then access will be more forthcoming.

Gatekeeper? – It is not uncommon to find buyers put up as your principal contacts when they have no great interest or involvement themselves, yet they deny you access to those with more. The reason? Perhaps you are a minor supplier, or still a potential supplier, and the buyers act as gatekeepers, protecting their organization from the 'interference' or 'nuisance' of overzealous sales people. If this is the way they see it then you have much work to do:

- Rule one – recognize their reservations and don't go behind their back.
- Rule two – keep pressing to find other points of contact, but always with the relevant buyer's permission, perhaps utilizing other members of your own team.
- Rule three – patiently work on winning the buyers' trust and confidence; give them reasons to allow you in; reasons that mean something *to them*.

It is also possible that they may be acting perfectly responsibly. If responsible and professional buyers realize that their involvement in a transaction can add no value then they will probably remove themselves. Allowing individuals in a company to authorize their own purchases through the use of company purchase cards is an example of such an approach.

Lead role responsibilities and sourcing teams

As the purchasing role becomes more sophisticated, and as you deal with more complex organizations, you might expect to encounter more complex purchasing 'solutions' – buyers with 'lead role responsibilities', or perhaps 'sourcing teams'.

The purchasing revolution has also brought changes to roles and responsibilities

Where, for instance, the purchasing operation extends over more than one site, business or country, you might expect to find either of these circumstances – lead roles or teams of buyers. It is now doubly important to understand who pulls what strings and where.

The following matrix, Table 24.1, outlines some of the variations and trends when looking at what buying mechanism and what breadth of responsibility.

The table only seeks to indicate current trends in many larger purchasing organizations. Purchasing groups are trying to increase their buying power and the value they bring to the business by extending their activities beyond individual sites, territories or businesses. If we think back to the risk/spend supplier positioning model from Chapter 9, with the spend axis representing

Table 24.1 *Responsibilities and mechanisms of the buying function*

Responsibility	Local Responsibility	Regional Responsibility	Global
Individual Site or Territory	Standard role		
Individual Business	Standard role	Increasing role	Possible role
Lead Business, Site or Territory		Target role	Possible role
Sourcing Team		Target role	Possible role
Shared Service	*Option*	*Option*	*Option*
Outsource	*Option*	*Option*	*Option*

the power of the buyer, then we can see how (at least in theory) aggregating a number of local purchasing decisions into one regional decision will increase spend under a particular buyer's control, and hence their purchasing power.

Where the attempt is made to purchase on a wider front, the change is often made through a 'lead role' or 'sourcing team' approach.

A lead role is where one site, business or territory takes on the main responsibility for purchasing for a wider group. The chosen lead may be selected for a number of reasons: particular expertise, largest share of purchase value, particular supplier relationship and so on. The other sites, businesses or territories will be expected to fall into line with the lead.

A sourcing team is where a group of interested parties gathers to pool their expertise, buying power and resources. Decisions will be taken by consensus, probably with greater allowance for local variation than the lead approach.

The shared service is a purchasing arrangement where a unit is set up, independent of all businesses, sites or territories, to provide a service to all. This might be for all purchasing or, more usually, for some particular aspect of purchasing – perhaps one requiring special expertise or additional after-purchase service, such as IT. This is an attractive option to large, widely spread organizations where a number of the smaller entities are too small to support their own purchasing unit or to have the necessary expertise in all areas.

The outsource option is where the organization employs an external body to perform its purchasing, perhaps in order to gain some particular expertise. A typical example in many larger companies is the purchase of travel services through 'in-house' agencies like AMEX or Hogg Robinson, specialists in business travel.

Supplier implications

The implications for the suppliers are enormous.

As the organization of purchasing shifts from local to global (and possibly back again), so must entry strategies change

It is imperative that you understand what purchasing roles and responsibilities exist and how the customer hopes to see them develop in the future. If your relationship is based on an individual site or business and the responsibility for purchasing is removed to a wider body, perhaps a global office in another territory, then you will have to start from scratch. You will almost certainly find yourself up against a competitor already 'well in' with that global office, even though on a local basis. They may well be given first option to bid for the global business, perhaps for no greater reason than a common language between buyer and seller.

If you wish to have influence on specifications, product listings and so on then you will have to establish relationships with the lead sites or businesses, or with the sourcing teams. In some cases, this may involve you moving, not only outside your territory, but also outside your industry.

Let's say you sell a chemical product to the paint industry. Your customer is a major manufacturer based in the UK, which is part of a larger chemical company. The larger company has discovered that it buys huge quantities of this particular chemical around the world, not only for its paints business, but also for a number of its other businesses. It decides to establish a lead business responsibility and selects the largest purchaser – its resins business, based in Germany. If you want to stay in business (and of course, if you want to expand your business, too) then you must establish a relationship with your customer, in Germany, in the resins business.

There are major challenges here, but also huge opportunities. Perhaps the new buyers have never purchased on behalf of the paint industry before – perhaps you can help them? Perhaps you have never sold outside the paint industry before, but your product is fully suited to wider uses – perhaps they can help you?

Regional buying might increase purchasing power, but there are attendant problems. In practice, the difficulties of buying 'at a distance' from the point of use can often lead to *less* value added by the purchasing function. The wise suppliers will be aware of this possibility and will act to avoid it. They can often be more effective providers of local information – needs and issues – than the buyer's own organization.

The trend towards lead roles and sourcing teams is not a disaster scenario for suppliers, provided you observe its coming and act accordingly. It could even herald a new lease of life for your business.

In theory, the move towards regional or global purchasing is to give the buyers more control and more leverage. While this may be the theory, the practice is not always so straightforward. Plenty of things conspire against the buyers in their attempts to take a more global view. Global suppliers are not so easy to come by. BOC is one of the companies seeking to establish more regional and global purchasing activities, but they have expressed concern recently that they cannot find UK suppliers able to give a seamless global service. This is fair warning for all 'national'-minded suppliers – there is an increasing need to think globally. Perhaps the worst thing you can do, worse than ignoring the trend, is to fight against it.

If your customers go global, appoint lead responsibilities or set up sourcing teams then you must follow. Trying to ignore central edicts and carry on as normal on a local basis will be frustrating and, in the longer run, terminal. The more you can do to facilitate the shifting responsibility to help them with their goals, the greater your reward – though there will be discomforts. Your local contacts, trusty and loyal for so long, may well resent the shift in power and try to persuade you to stick with *them*. Out will pour the stories of favours done and the good old times. Suppliers will need to steer a middle course through such transitions, meeting the head office requirement while providing local support. Once again, *think global and*, as the cliché continues, *act local*.

OTHER INTERESTS AND INFLUENCES

As well as the buyers, there are plenty of other members of this DMU, formal or informal. The formal members may include people from other departments. The informal members, as important influences on any decision, may include people from outside the customer's own company – *their* customers, government bodies, regulators, local communities, etc.

It is helpful here to remember that there are many different types of interested party, each playing their own role in the DMU, each bringing their own particular influence to bear, each requiring their own kind of attention.

The following sections look at four different tools for identifying and defining those influences in order to determine your entry strategy. These are complementary tools, overlapping and enforcing each other:

- Influence through involvement.
- Influence through interest.
- Influence through acceptance.
- Levels of seniority.

As an illustration of the tools in use, I will use an example of someone wishing to sell sales training, let's make it KAM training, to a sales team in a large multinational company.

Influence through involvement

Why are they involved?

We might identify four principal 'types' of involvement common to most sales situations – the 'user', the 'specifier', the 'economic' influence and the 'sponsor', as illustrated in Figure 24.2.

These involvement 'types' might exist as different people, or an individual might have more than one reason for their involvement – whichever the case, it is important to identify the different motivations that result.

The specifier

This is where things get down to brass tacks – drawing up standards to be met. Obviously a crucial stage of any decision process and, if you can influence the design of that specification, then you are in with a strong chance. The problem is that this activity is often far removed from your

Figure 24.2 *Principal types of involvement*
(Adapted from Miller, Heiman and Teleja, 1988)

normal contact and might be happening well before you are called in to 'quote for the job'.

In our example of selling KAM training, this could be a professional buyer; a person with the expertise to draw up selection criteria for comparing rival suppliers; or it may be the training manager, brought in to define some standards of learning and post-event application. The specifier's role is sometimes almost that of a neutral. They will not be making the final decision, but can set the ground rules for how the decision *will* be made. In this role, the specifier will effectively 'select out' non-conforming suppliers.

The economic

This is the one that thinks in money terms – how much and can we afford it? An important influence, but one that can take a rather narrow view, often to the detriment of a supplier wishing to argue value in use rather than absolute price.

In my example, this might be the business manager, who controls the training budget. In this case, the final decision *will* be made there, but it will be made based on the options put before them. If one supplier can argue better 'value in use' than another then they may win the day, despite being more expensive. The economic influence is one that can often be heavily influenced itself by the arguments of others within the same company.

The user

Users are the people who will receive your product or service and will have to do something with it. It is very likely that they will have strong views on what they want to get from it. These people obviously represent a key influence, but they are not always easy for the seller to contact.

In my example, the users are the sales manager and the potential delegates on the training event. As well as their particular reasons for wanting or needing KAM training, they may also have specification requirements that will influence the decision, like a desire to run the event in a particular location, to specific timings or alongside a sales meeting, to save costs of travel and time. The supplier that understands these needs, and responds, will be in with a better chance than the one that speaks only to the person with the money.

The sponsor

Sponsors are people who, for all sorts of reasons, will ease your path through the complexity of the buying organization, perhaps even pointing you in the direction of the specifier, the user and the economic involvement. Why might they do this? Perhaps they sit at a level above the day-to-day operations. Perhaps they have a more strategic vision. Perhaps they like you and your company. Perhaps they want to see something done.

In my example, the sponsors could be one of the customer's own customers. Perhaps they have received poor treatment at the hands of their supplier, now your potential customer. Perhaps they know that you are able to help their supplier – you did the same for them only last year when they were having difficulties with KAM and now they are suggesting to you that you might be able to help *their* supplier. (It happens!)

What a sponsor! They have a reason to want something done. They point you in the right direction, they provide support and endorsement and, above all, they are listened to.

Influence through interest

Are they receptive, do they have problems, do they have power?

The 'involvement' model looked at influencers by their function in the decision. The 'interest' model can be used to overlay that analysis, seeking to identify broader and perhaps more fundamental reasons for the person's likely attitude and subsequent influence.

In this model, we look for three broad reasons for people's interest in the decision:

- Those that are receptive to the supplier's ideas or approach.
- Those that have problems with their own current situation.
- Those that have power regarding the final decision.

Those that are *receptive*, are people who will listen to you, perhaps already like your offer and agree with your proposal, but may have little to do with the decision to buy. A typical example might be store managers in a large retail multiple. Buying decisions are taken centrally, but these store managers have opinions and they will certainly point you in the right direction, armed with valuable information, if they like your ideas.

In our example of selling KAM training, there might be a particularly receptive salesperson in the team, perhaps someone who attended one of your events when working for a different company. This sort of person can be very valuable in helping you to build your case, pointing out the hurdles to jump and the hot spots to hit. They may well introduce you to those that have *problems*.

Being introduced to the people with *problems* is of course the key, for this is where the needs lie that your offer will meet. As we know in selling, the needs might not always be explicit. The clients have a problem, but do not see a potential solution, and so are not armed with a specification; nor are they out looking for a supplier. This is where your *receptive* contacts came in – they put you in touch.

In our KAM training example, this might be a definition of the customer's customer, or perhaps the hard-pressed sales manager on the receiving end of their dissatisfaction. Solve these people's problems and you may have no need to go any further, for they will do their own selling to those that have *power*.

Those with *power* are the ones with the authority to act, perhaps through seniority, perhaps through holding the purse strings. They are often hard people to meet and your sales proposition may rely on getting those with *problems* to sell to them for you.

The business manager is in the position of power in our example, but I would be very careful about approaching them first. I would much rather do my homework by understanding the issues and difficulties that this manager's staff are facing. That way, I am far more likely to be able to argue a convincing case when I do find myself in front of them.

Influence through acceptance

People take up new ideas at different rates. Some people like anything that's new – we might call them 'innovators'. Others might be last in line for change – we might call them 'laggards'. We might in fact identify a spectrum of attitudes between these two extremes and consider the number of people in a typical audience who might be considered as representing each attitude. This spectrum is shown in Figure 24.3, a model that we have seen before, in chapter 20 when looking at segmentation, but is equally useful here.

Why might they think it a good idea?

This model is much used in marketing as a means of ensuring the right message and approach is made to customers that express these attitudes. It is equally applicable to our purpose of who to talk to, and how.

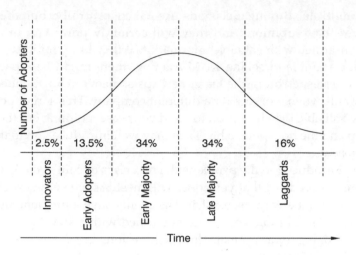

Figure 24.3 *The adopters curve*
From Everett Rogers (1962)

Innovators and *early adopters* are relatively easy to sell to. They like novelty and the words risk, experiment, trial and leading edge are music to their ears.

The *late majority* and the *laggards* are much harder. They want evidence and proof. They want to see a track record of success; to know that somebody else has ironed out all the problems.

The *early majority* represent the people who come knocking on your door in floods once the idea or product is fairly well established.

In our customer's DMU we might be able to identify these types: the sales manager who will leap at any new idea (innovator); the training manager who sees no problem with the training that has been used for years (laggard); the man in R&D who has been reading about a success story involving a competitor that has been implementing a KAM strategy (early adopter).

How might this help? The idea is to use acceptance of your ideas, where you can find it, first as a point of entry and then as a base for approaching the next stage in the curve. Don't start with the laggards – you need to build a case first. If you have to start with laggards then at least be realistic about the obstacles ahead and act to meet their particular needs for proof, evidence or whatever.

Having determined the order of contact, the model indicates the type of approach you might need to take. When you do get to the laggards, don't talk about risk and excitement but show them the proof, show them their colleagues' comments and affirmations. With the innovators, don't bore them with case study after case study – they just want to hear what's new.

One word of warning. Innovators like new things, your competitor's new things as well as yours. In this sense, they may not be loyal or 'reliable'. Worse, they might be regarded as 'suckers for anything new' by their more 'early' or 'late majority' colleagues and they might not be regarded at all by the laggards! Selling your ideas to innovators may be easy, but it can sometimes hold you back with the rest of your audience.

LEVELS OF SENIORITY

Understanding the different attitudes that come with different levels of seniority can be very valuable in weaving through the DMU. The junior contacts have targets to meet, rules to conform to and a dozen other people to see. Their boss, who set the targets and made the rules, may feel more inclined to ignore them or break them – it demonstrates their seniority.

Don't get stuck at too junior a level, but also don't cause resentment in the ranks by only attending to the bosses

The junior contacts may be focused on tomorrow. Their boss may have the luxury of considering next week.

A useful exercise can be to note down some comparisons of the wants and needs of these different levels ('wants' are desires, 'needs' are necessities). What do the junior contacts need, what might they want and perhaps even what do they dream of? Do the same for their boss and compare notes. Do they correspond? Do they conflict? What does this tell you? Does your offer suit one more than the other?

The regional sales manager in my example of selling KAM training may not be all that keen on the idea, seeing it as a potential threat to their position, while the national sales director is all too aware of the challenge of managing global accounts and is a very much more receptive audience.

There are conflicting opinions on the value of making contacts at senior levels. Many sales people will resist involving their own boss and positively refuse to allow their MD anywhere near the customer (perhaps experiences like the tale of the CEO in Chapter 5 have had an impact!). Such attitudes could be a major weakness in a KA strategy as involving your own senior management is often the best, sometimes the only way to establish contacts at the customer's senior levels.

It is very often the case that the strongest relationships and the longest-running partnerships have, as a common theme, contacts at senior level in both supplier and customer. Seeking such contacts should be a goal of a managed entry strategy. It is the key account manager's job to ensure that they work without mishap.

Each level of seniority in the customer's organization has its own role to play in the relationship and successful KAM will recognize this and act accordingly at *all* levels (see Figure 24.4).

Figure 24.4   *Levels of seniority*

Junior levels of contact are what make the machine run, meeting expectations. Middle management contacts manage the relationship, ensuring satisfaction. Senior management contacts can forge loyalty and commitment, the key to long-term security.

ENTRY STRATEGIES

Breaking down the DMU, by any of the tools described, will be of great importance when deciding your entry strategy.

The questions to resolve, as raised at the start of this chapter, are:

- who to see?
- who should see them?
- in what order will they be seen?
- what will you be saying to them?

There is a natural urge among sales people to head straight for the people with power: the budget holders, the actual decision takers, the boss – but take care. Once thrown out, it is hard to get back through the door. Use the analytical tools to plan your contacts.

Start with friends, the receptive ones in the organization, the ones who will tell you things.

Try to identify a sponsor. Make sure you are involved with the specifiers. Move on to those with problems, perhaps the users. Try to identify the level of acceptance for your ideas. Use the adopters' curve to tailor your approach and build support by stages. Remember that the buyer's boss may be working to a different agenda.

If you do all of this well, you will have gone a long way to getting the customer's DMU to do your job for you – selling to the people with power. Indeed, with a disciplined entry strategy, you will have the DMU *demanding* to be given your solutions!

THE CONTACT MATRIX & GROWs

In Chapter 5 we noted two tools, the contact matrix and GROWs that provided the simplest way to ensure the success of a diamond team. They are in fact the tools that will help you to manage your entry strategy.

In any key account plan this is perhaps the most important element of all – who sees who, and for what purpose

The Contact Matrix

Things can get complicated once more than the sales professional is involved in front of the customer. It is what we should regard as 'good complication' because of what it brings us, and the job of the Key Account Manager is to manage that complication. They must direct, and co-ordinate their team as it is used against the customer's team – they are managing a matrix of contacts.

The Key Account Manager should prepare a contact matrix, as shown at Figure 24.5.

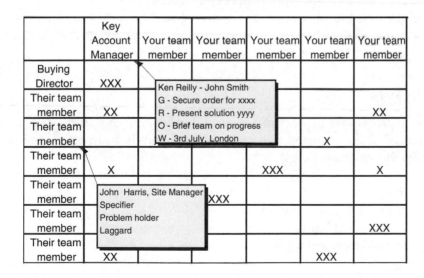

	Key Account Manager	Your team member	Your team member	Your team member	Your team member	Your team member
Buying Director	XXX					
Their team member	XX					XX
Their team member					X	
Their team member	X		XXX			X
Their team member		XXX				
Their team member						XXX
Their team member	XX			XXX		

Ken Reilly - John Smith
G - Secure order for xxxx
R - Present solution yyyy
O - Brief team on progress
W - 3rd July, London

John Harris, Site Manager
Specifier
Problem holder
Laggard

Figure 24.5 *The Contact Matrix*

This matrix lays out clearly each team member's contacts, and enables us to indicate the purpose of those contacts. If an Excel spread sheet (or similar) is used for this tool it is relatively easy, using the 'comment' facility, to add all sorts of information to the matrix – details about the customer, their influencer type, their personality, their interests, and whatever else is useful to you to know. The same can be done for the supplier's team, showing their all-important GROWs (see below)

The ever changing scene...

The matrix is not a static tool, people come and go, and it needs to recognize these changes. One way is to indicate who is involved at the different stages of the buying decision, by splitting the left-hand column into the four stages we noted in Chapter 23:

- Awareness of needs.
- Comparing alternatives.
- Selection.
- Post purchase concerns.

The customer contacts will change as you move from one stage to the next, and the team members used, listed along the top, will also change to reflect that. Of course, in a complex relationship where there may be several buying processes going on at once, each at different stages, it may become too complex to try to capture this all on one matrix. You may then choose to have a matrix for each DMU, or perhaps a matrix for each sales project. Above all else, use this tool to suit your own circumstances.

Keeping on track...

Every time the team meets the matrix should be reviewed. This simple discipline will probably do more than any other to ensure that your diamond team keeps on track.

GROWs

The matrix shows the fact of a contact, but what of the purpose of those contacts? There are many purposes of course, but they can be summarised under four main headings:

- To get information.
- To promote your solutions.
- To build credibility.
- To build trust and rapport.

Of all the tools suggested for KAM, this is perhaps the simplest and yet the most vital

It is vital that everybody involved with the customer knows their purpose, and their boundaries. Without that definition of role and purpose all the potential perils and pitfalls of the diamond relationship (as highlighted in Chapter 5 and 6) can, and probably will, befall you.

I recommend a simple acronym, GROW, (borrowed from a project management process) to ensure that the necessary elements are captured.

- G – Goal
- R – Role
- O – Obligation
- W – Work Plan

Goal – the overall purpose of this contact – the ambition.
Role – the nature of the activities undertaken to achieve the goal.
Obligation – the responsibilities, in particular to the rest of the team.
Work Plan – the nitty-gritty details of dates and actions.
Each contact should have an attached GROW, either written on a separate page in the plan, or perhaps using the 'comment' facility within something like Excel.

How many contacts?

Preparing the matrix will raise another important question: how many people can you justify putting in contact with the customer?

Common sense should prevail, but here are some guidelines:

- Do nothing that causes the customer to see you as a nuisance, a time waster, or a burden. Try to avoid the mismatch of strategic intent seen in Chapter 6. By all means create your KA team but, until the customer matches your strategic intent, be wary of putting them in front of the customer too often.
- Consider the decision style of the DMU – how many people do you need to see?
- Use the tools for identifying the influencer types to focus your attentions rather than seeking a blanket coverage.
- Go as far as the customer will let you and no further – often they will invite you in, if they see you as a key supplier.
- If your main need is information then throw your net wide.
- If your main need is to influence views then focus your contacts on the key influencers.
- Remember that people are human – don't force contacts where there is bad chemistry. It is the key account manager's responsibility to coach team members that encounter difficulties, regardless of their seniority.
- Never go behind your main contact's back – always let them know who is seeing whom and ask permission before initiating new contacts.
- Make sure that the information from these contacts is communicated within your team and back to the customer.

- Consider your own organization's resources and remember that the members of your team may also be involved with other customers.
- Don't put your own team in the position of making promises they cannot keep or committing time that they do not have.

CONTACTS OVER TIME

Every contact counts – never abandon them

The right contacts will, of course, change over time. At the early stages of the sale, while the customer is still identifying a need, the contacts might tend to be sponsors and users, those that are receptive, and innovators and early adopters.

As the sale progresses and options are considered, expect to meet with the specifier and economic interests, people with problems, and perhaps some of the early majority or beyond.

Once the sale is complete, *don't disappear!* This is the stage where continued contact is most important of all, to help things bed in and to handle the teething problems. The stage of post-purchase concerns is as important as the initial contact. Demonstrating that you can handle early problems well will lead to repeat business and a long-term relationship. Like a marriage, it is how the bad times are handled that defines the success or failure of the relationship.

Figure 24.6 *Pre- and post-sale levels of contact – the wrong approach!*

Many successful sales are tarnished (sometimes even reversed) by a tendency to move on to the next project once the sale is made, as illustrated in Figure 24.6.

The gap, post-sale, is a chasm when viewed from the harassed and disappointed customer's perspective. Above all else, remember that the customer's need for contacts is not the same as yours:

1. Respect this at the early stage and try to avoid being a burden.
2. Don't disappear when they need you most – post-purchase concerns.
3. Have a contact plan for *all* stages of the sale, before, during *and after*.

AVECIA – A LIVE APPLICATION

Avecia LifeScience Molecules (LSM) has seen significant business development, both through winning new customers and by retaining existing ones, by adopting a new method of DMU analysis and managing the resultant interactions between contacts.

A significant part of the Avecia LSM business is with major pharmaceutical companies, selling customized organic chemicals for use in new drug development. The customer DMU is huge, and by any standards, complex.

This complexity is due to a series of overlapping circumstances. Lead times are long, but there are always important and impending milestones to be met. New drug development budgets may appear large and flexible, but there are stringent controls on every stage, and some of the decision points involve very significant commitments of both time and money. The science involved is complex, involving overlapping project teams, very often with supplier involvement. Internal debate within the client team can be long and torturous; rarely is there only one option for consideration, and suppliers can find their contacts on a broad spectrum of pro and anti views on grounds of science, technology, relationships and commercial considerations. Significant stages of development might be outsourced to key suppliers, while other aspects of the project might remain uncertain, for reasons of security, for lengthy periods of time. Add to all this the fact that most of this work is charting new territory, with few guarantees of success for client or supplier, and it can readily be seen why the DMU might be complex.

Avecia LSM has moved away from the traditional sales approach of developing contacts through a sales-led team, finding new contacts and building relationships as the sale advances. The problem with such an approach is too little information, too late, and a limited ability to influence the key decisions in the process.

Their approach requires a broad team effort with a variety of contacts and relationships being nurtured at once. Such a team approach begins with a serious assessment of all client DMU members against two main criteria, represented by the following matrix (Figure 24.7).

Strategic agreement indicates the extent to which the DMU member supports the supplier approach. Do their strategic intentions match? In Avecia's business, *agreement* involves more than price, or service package, or an approved quality level; it encompasses much broader issues such as determining the outsourcing policy and approach, working practices, risk sharing, or preferring one technology platform to another. A true strategic agreement is where the outsourcing service fits the outsourcing need.

277

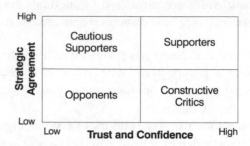

Figure 24.7 *Strategic agreement/trust and confidence in the supplier*

Trust and confidence is a more subjective measure that may result from past history, track record, or relatively short-term experiences of the client/supplier relationship, and can of course be very individualistic.

In placing DMU members on this matrix, it is hugely valuable to have inputs from the whole KA team. The issues are rarely black and white, judgements will differ, and attitudes are not static. The team, by discussing these placements, will not only achieve a more accurate picture of the client's views, corporate and individual, but will also reach a far more significant understanding of the customer.

Each box in the matrix describes a particular attitude, and a range of expected behaviours:

- The lower left, disagreement with the supplier strategy and low trust in their ability or approach, is clearly the home of the opponent, finding views of every hue from quiet disregard to active opposition.
- The upper-left box finds those in agreement with the strategy but having low trust and confidence – the cautious supporters, as Avecia call them. They are largely unwilling, often there through limited choice, and ever on the lookout for new alternatives. Though they may be supporters, they are far from loyal.
- The upper right is occupied by the supporters, people that agree with the supplier strategy and have trust and confidence in their ability. They will range from passive supporters to active advocates for the supplier within their own organization.
- The bottom-right box, high trust but no strategic agreement finds one of the most valuable of DMU member types – the constructive critic.

One of the interesting things about this analysis is the way in which DMU members that might otherwise have been disregarded become important. The constructive critic is such a person. Their lack of agreement might simply see them put in the opponents' camp, but their level of trust in the supplier shows them in a different light. They are invaluable contacts, advising you on how to improve, willing you to change, and speaking well of you when you do. These contacts can often lead you towards success more speedily and effectively than either the staunch opponents or the avid supporters.

Another interesting observation can be made about the people that are placed on the horizontal line of the matrix, undecided on their view of the supplier's strategic approach. Those that have high levels of trust in the supplier will be significantly easier to move upwards than will those who sit between *opponent* and *cautious supporter*. *Constructive critics* will see and applaud your efforts to meet their needs, while *oppo-*

nents can find many ways to ignore or devalue your efforts. This thought brings us to the next stage in Avecia's process of relationship management.

This analysis is only the beginning, simply the initial layout of the field. Avecia now seeks to identify the activities required to shift the placement of DMU members. These activities may include everything from advocacy and relationship-building to a modification of the supplier's capabilities and approach.

The successful sale rarely requires that all DMU members are shifted into the top-right box. We have seen from the various tools used to analyse influence and interests that different players have different significance as the situation unfolds. Such an analysis will help identify the starring roles, as distinct from the walk-on parts.

With this additional analysis, Avecia will apply one last analysis, assessing the importance of shifting a member's position, and their ability to affect that shift (Figure 24.8).

Figure 24.8 *Importance/ease of shifting views*

Those that are both important to move, and the actions required are relatively simple, must represent the first priority. Others may be harder work, but as client *supporters* increase, the effort is increasingly tackled on your behalf. It is important not to fall victim to the easy option of tackling only those that can be made *friendly* with ease but whose views are of minor importance. It is surprising how often a supplier can believe it is making great progress by such an approach, only to find an uncomfortable rebuff around the corner.

Avecia's approach has gone a long way to avoiding such a scenario, reducing surprises and increasing the ability to forecast so allowing for longer-term planning of their own resources. In this way, management of the customer relationship has a significant impact on the ability of the business to respond, and to do so effectively, efficiently, and profitably.

Of course, when it comes to shifting views, the role of trust becomes very significant. Converting an *opponent* into a *cautious supporter* is no easy process, and even if achieved, the result will be vulnerable to further shifts backwards. Trust must be won first; changing *opponents* into *constructive critics* and thence into *supporters* is a more likely and sustainable journey to plan.

Part VI

Meeting The Customer's Needs

25

Meeting the business needs – beyond benefits

Not only are we with the right customer, but we also have the right contacts in front of us and we have the right team member beside us. Now all that remains is to ask the right questions, talk the right language, make sure they respect you and make a successful proposal.

This is more than fancy presentations with slick PC-assisted slide shows. This must have substance, getting right to the heart of the customer's needs, going beyond mere benefits, giving them solutions, perhaps even satisfying their *total business experience*.

We are getting into some fancy words here, let alone fancy presentations, so what do they mean? Remember that first sales training event you ever went on, the one about *features* and *benefits*? Well, we need to start back there, and then make a little progress besides.

There are four stages that a company's sales approach might go through. This is not a pre-ordained progression; the development over time will be the result of nurture, not nature. It is a development that takes time, patience and an understanding of where you are and where you are going. Of course, you may already be well beyond stage one or two, but take time here just to be sure by checking against Table 25.1.

KAM takes us beyond benefits to solutions, and beyond that to the 'total business experience'

Table 25.1 *Stages of a sales approach*

	Stage 1	Stage 2	Stage 3	Stage 4
The Offer	Features	Benefits	Solutions	Total Business Experience
Customers	All	Segmentation	Key accounts by type	Individual key accounts
Sales Approach	Traditional 1:1	Enhanced 1:1	Partnership KAM The team sell	Synergistic KAM Team collaboration
Competitive Advantage	Perhaps none	Specific benefits	Quality of solutions	Quality of relationships & key supplier status
Supplier Organization & Focus	Sales focus	Marketing focus	Customer focus	Total Business Experience focus
Typical Skills	Journey planning	Questioning Selling benefits	KAM Project management	Business management, strategic influencing

WHERE ARE YOU WITH YOUR CUSTOMERS?

Lets take as an example a company that sells fertilizer to farmers and, at the first stage, that means all farmers.

Stage 1 – Take it, because that's what I'm offering and I know you want it...

You regard your customers as essentially the same and you deliver a standard product or service – you probably talk 'features'.

Your product is fertilizer, in three bag sizes, and it contains the magic ingredient, 'Oomph'.

Stage 2 – It's all in the presentation...

You uncover customer needs that allow you to present those features as relevant 'benefits'. The product or service may remain much the same, perhaps some minor cosmetic changes, but you are starting to recognize your customers as being different from each other, often expressed through some kind of customer segmentation.

You have segmented your market, perhaps by crop types, and so now you have to address yourself to wheat farmers. The magic ingredient 'Oomph' is still there, but a reformulation has made it particularly beneficial to wheat growers – 'Oomph Plus'.

Stage 3 – Tailored just for you...

You uncover a deeper set of needs that forces you to make more substantial changes to your product or service, recognizing the increasing individuality of the customer. This allows you to present your offer as a tailored solution. This is usually done only for a small group of customers – your key accounts, perhaps even types of key account.

You have identified a trend towards minimal use of chemicals and have developed some low-application formulations of your product, still containing 'Oomph', but the real trick now is the application rate. Based on this trend and your ability to meet the need, you have identified a key account 'type' – large farm, keen to minimize chemical use, wheat production for human consumption, likes high-tech solutions, 'early adopter'.

Stage 4 – Managing the customer's total business experience

You uncover a breadth of needs that allows you to understand the customer's values and aspirations in full. This is not just with regard to your offer – you understand their Total Business Experience (TBE). Your tailored solutions are now designed to have a positive impact at all levels of this business experience, before, during and after the use of your particular product or service. Indeed, your customer regards you as more than a simple supplier of a product or service; you now add value at many (why not all?) points of their business experience – you have achieved the status of key supplier.

Many of your farmers, you discover, regard fertilizer application as a very low-grade task in the great scheme of things. It takes a lot of time, time that they could use for doing other things, but all these new high-tech fertilizers make it difficult to pass the job on to a jobbing contractor. Your offer has now been transformed. You no longer talk about 'Oomph' or 'Oomph Plus', indeed, you rarely mention the product at all, for now your business is in providing a managed fertilizer application service for key farmers. You charge by results (a percentage of farm profits), not by volume of material and you are continually developing formulations to reduce the volumes required. Indeed, your *joint* aspiration is to move to a stage where you can use more environmentally friendly alternatives and be rid of 'Oomph' for good. Less, truly, is more.

The key to success here, in moving from stage to stage, is the ever-improving understanding of what your customer wants. Features tend to be supplier focused; benefits begin to consider the customer; solutions are about meeting requirements. But addressing the total business experience requires you to go beyond this, beyond expectations to anticipating the customer's needs.

At its best, you understand their aspirations, not just with regard to your products as a supplier, but also with regard to their total business and so you have an opportunity to enhance their total business experience. For the farmer in our example, the TBE is being able to forget about the fertilizer issue altogether and spend time on more profitable, more challenging or perhaps just more interesting activities – it all depends on the farmer.

TBE in the oil supply industry

Another example of a supplier going beyond benefits and enhancing the customer's TBE is found in the oil supply industry. BP, among others, has identified that they have a certain expertise in managing fluid supplies on a customer's site. For key accounts, BP will offer to manage the customer's total 'fluid requirements'. This will almost certainly involve taking responsibility for the supply of products outside their own portfolio, perhaps in some cases even working with a competitor's products. As with the fertilizer example, the focus moves to reducing the volumes of product required and improving efficiencies of use. The focus is squarely on providing value rather than lowest prices. Indeed, the price of the product becomes almost irrelevant as the services are charged for in more creative, more *holistic* ways.

TBE and value

We are looking here at the difference between price and value, an idea introduced in Chapter 10 in discussing what the customer's supply chain managers and supply side managers are looking for. Providing solutions and enhancements to the customer's TBE are excellent ways of moving the relationship away from price and squarely on to value. The debate over open-book trading (also Chapter 10) becomes less pressing, or at least it is no longer a threat to the good supplier.

Solutions for all?

How many customers you can do this for will depend on your business and market, but rarely will it be the majority. The importance of identifying true key accounts becomes even more apparent. Many of these TBE solutions will be giving customers competitive advantage, that is, compared to other of your customers. Can you therefore do it for all? Is there any point? Would the customer let you?

Remember the chain

Chapter 3 introduced the idea of the market chain, taking account of suppliers' suppliers and customers' customers, right through to the end-consumer. As your sales offer moves towards solutions and beyond, the significance of the chain will increase. From the example in Chapter 3, an agrochemical supplier, it was at the supermarket/ consumer interface that most market *noise* was generated and solutions for farmers must take account of that noise.

Don't be surprised if customers start looking back up the chain, beyond you, for solutions. Rather than being surprised, anticipate it and act in concert with them.

The tale of the frustrated customer

A major UK supermarket was concerned that stocking major brand food products did nothing for their competitive advantage – everyone else had them. They tried to get suppliers to offer variants, but failed. Their next move was to approach their supplier's suppliers, manufacturers of additives and flavours, asking them to create unique products that would only be used in that supermarket chain's products, but sold through the food manufacturers for use in their brands. The supermarket people were not asking for their own label: they wanted their own versions of branded products and this was the only way they could see to get them.

Everyone was uncomfortable about this – the additive supplier feared upsetting their customer, the food manufacturer felt squeezed and the retailer remained frustrated.

Moral of the story? If there are solutions to be found in the chain then suppliers and customers need to act in concert to find them.

THE CUSTOMER'S TOTAL BUSINESS EXPERIENCE

In the bad old days, sometimes we would tell our customers what they needed and sometimes we were lucky and we got it right. Then, *sometimes* wasn't enough and we realized that we had to learn to ask – and some of us are still learning. But now we hit on some problems:

- What if our customers don't know what they need?
- What if things are changing around them so fast that they can't see a clear way forward?

- What if the things they keep telling us they want are just, well, what they think they *should* be saying? After all, everyone wants a lower price, a better product and slicker service.

When Alexander Graham Bell invented the telephone, he toured the USA, showing it off to what he hoped would be interested businessmen. After one such session, he was approached by an apparent enthusiast: 'Mr Bell, I really like your new toy. It's my daughter's birthday party tomorrow and I would be very grateful if you would come along to show it.'

Well, the great man was incensed: 'It is not a toy!' he exploded. 'Don't you realize that this will revolutionize communications and your business? Just think, with one of these you can talk to a customer 300 miles away.'

The businessman thought for a moment and then answered: 'But, Mr Bell, I don't have any customers 300 miles away…'

Telling them isn't enough. But sometimes, even asking your customer is not enough. Who knew that they needed 'Post-It' notes before they were invented, or the Internet, or a telephone?

The job of the KA teams is to try to identify and understand what the customers might want (based on their latent needs) and then aim to provide it and to sell them the vision.

And how do you gain this new insight?

Benchmarking?

Useful, but why should we think that everyone else has seen the light? And anyway, we want competitive advantage, not a 'me too' solution.

Market research?

Of course, but asking traditional questions will get traditional answers. Yes, of course they want a lower price, a better product and slicker service: hardly an *insight*.

And, in any case, asking rational questions about needs that might be irrational has its limitations. Suppose you were in the car business and were thinking of launching an 'off road' vehicle. You commission an agency to find out how many people need to drive 'off road' and how often. The answers come back – almost none, and hardly at all (which happens to be the truth of the matter). So, you abandon your idea and miss one of the biggest growth sectors of the car market in recent years.

In the early years of the 20th century, Benz conducted one of the first market research studies into the potential car market in the UK. They concluded that total sales of all cars would never exceed 1,000. The reason? A shortage of chauffeurs.

My company once commissioned a piece of research to see why training managers chose particular training suppliers. The answers seemed very worthy – value for money, value for time, leading edge and all the rest, only we knew that wasn't the truth, at least not the truth that went to the root of their desired experience. The truth of the matter was that many training managers chose the supplier least likely to make them look foolish. See it from their standpoint: they arrange an event, they commit people's time – it is their reputation that is on the line if the trainer turns out to be an embarrassment.

How did we know that? Because we focused on what the training manager wanted from the *total experience* of doing business with us – their TBE. We got customer-intimate and it helped that we had all seen life from our customer's side of the desk. This is what you must do for your customers if you are to match their total business experience. Ask yourself the following of your customers:

- Are they seeking to improve the product they sell to their customers? *And why*? (Not, do they want a specific product enhancement?)
- Are they seeking to reduce costs by improving their production process? *And why*? (Not, are they after a cheaper product?)
- Do they want to break into new markets? *And why*? (Not, are they looking to place a larger order?)
- Do they need to improve their service to their own customers? *And why*? (Not, do they want a price cut because their customers are pressuring them?)

Answer these sorts of questions and you are well on the way to uncovering what they *really* need and, from there, you are staring competitive advantage in the face.

So, don't do market research?

None of this is arguing against market research. Research is vital if we are to understand our customers and their needs. What this argues for is the *kind* of research required. In the KAM environment, when dealing with sophisticated purchasing organizations that talk of supply chains and value, and when you seek to go beyond benefits to solutions and enhancements to TBE, you need to research into the customer's motivations, aspirations and values. And beyond that, you need to uncover the things that they didn't even know themselves.

Remember, customers are lazy. This is not a prejudiced remark – suppliers are probably even lazier. That is, they seek the simplest solution to a problem. For a customer, the simplest solution to many a problem is to ask the supplier.

'The supplier,' said one of my customers once, 'is the soft under-belly of the market; they'll do anything to get the order.'

Certainly the buyer might assume that, and their requests and demands are often made in that light. Does the buyer demanding that you provide consignment stock really want consignment stock? Perhaps they want to reduce their working capital and consignment stock seems a much easier option than installing EDI and efficient response ordering (see Chapter 27). Easier for them, but not for the supplier and, in the end, it is not the optimal solution for either.

The customer may find it difficult to articulate their desired total business experience; they may even lie to save themselves time, money or effort. It is the supplier's responsibility to understand their customers well enough to be able to articulate that experience for them and to argue for the appropriate activities to meet it, not just the simplest.

The following chapter looks at one way of doing this and one way of structuring your market research – *positive impact analysis*.

Positive impact analysis (PIA)

The purpose of this tool is to link a deeper understanding of customer needs and sense of value with a move to action. It aims to answer the following question: what set of activities within your own organization will result in a *positive impact* being made on the customer's *total business experience*?

Let's consider an example. You travel by air, in business class, from London to New York. Why do you travel business class? Is it because of the champagne? Unlikely. Is it because of the wider seat? Perhaps, but surely that's not the whole story. Perhaps you are doing it because you believe that doing so will help you arrive in better shape to do your job. You are a sales-person and you want to do the deal. Flying business class increases your chances.

This is important to realize (if you are in the airline business) for two reasons:

1. If people are paying for an increased likelihood of 'doing the deal', not just for a wider seat, they will probably be prepared to pay more – they perceive greater value.
2. If your customers want to 'do the deal' then enhancing their TBE will take more than a good flight. It will involve getting them to the airport, checking them in with ease, speeding them through security, speeding them through immigration in the United States, collecting their luggage, having them met, getting them to their next destination and,

Making a positive impact on the customer's total business experience should be a top priority for the key account team

making sure that they don't come down with a cold the next day (one they are convinced they caught on your plane).

We know the experience being sought and we have some clues already as to how we might be able to make a positive impact on it.

Yes, I know what you are thinking – what about status and ego, isn't that why people travel business class? For many, yes, but they are a different segment of the airline business that will require different activities to meet their needs. For this example our target segment is 'serious-minded business people'.

One of the continuing marvels of the air travel business is that they continue to market themselves to widely differing customers through well-segmented offers with huge price differentials – and they do this within the confines of an aircraft that gets everyone off the ground at the same time and puts them down in just the same way. The explanation, of course, lies in TBE and positive impact analysis (PIA).

THE VALUE CHAIN

Having identified the customer's TBE (in this case 'to do the deal'), the next thing to do is list all the activities that your customer currently has to go through to do business with you and to achieve their TBE. This can be called a process chain or a *value chain*.

Table 26.1 charts the typical activities of a flight from initial route enquiry through to the return trip.

So far so good: we know what our customer is up against.

Table 26.1   *The customer's value chain*

Customer activity

Route enquiry	Boarding	Passport and
Ticket purchase	Safety procedures	immigration
Receive tickets	Take off	Luggage
Drive to airport	Watch a movie, play	Customs
Park in long stay	games	Into the terminal
Shuttle bus to	Read, talk, work	Find taxi
terminal	Meals and drinks	Check in to hotel
Check in and luggage	Sleep	Business meetings
Security	Meals and drinks	Reconfirm flights
Passport	Landing	Recommence the
Waiting	Disembark	process

The next stage is to try to understand all the things that can go wrong at each stage, such as what it is that could make each stage a burden or a frustration. After that we aim to identify the range of activities that could have a positive impact on the customer's TBE, which we can call 'doing the deal'.

Table 26.2 suggests such a list of potential problems, and some possible actions for positive impact.

Table 26.2 *Value chain analysis – problems and potential solutions*

Customer activity	Problems	Positive impact
Route enquiry	Confusing alternatives, no personal incentive	Corporate client service, 'air miles' packages
Ticket purchase	Frustrating administration	Electronic commerce
Receive tickets	Worry of not receiving	No ticket – electronic ticketing
Drive to airport	Time, getting lost	Limo door to door
Park in long stay	Time and hassle	No need, given the above
Shuttle bus to terminal	Time and more hassle	No need, given the above
Check in and luggage	Queue, debates over cabin baggage	Completed in limo
Security	Time	Fast track
Passport	Time	Fast track
Waiting	Time, lack of business facilities	Deliver direct to business lounge, with IT and secretarial services
Boarding	A rush for locker space	Larger lockers, wardrobes
Safety procedures	Fine, but you didn't listen – heard it all before	Cartoon video, personalized briefings?
Take off	Long waits on the tarmac	Fast track arrangement with air traffic control
Watch a movie, play games	Great, but caught a cold from the guy next to you	New air conditioning
Read, talk, work	Couldn't because of noisy neighbours	Design seating so that it can be 'closed' off from neighbours
Meals and drinks	OK, but the choice and timing is so limiting	Offer a buffet rather than a served meal
Sleep	Couldn't because the seat was too small	Put beds in business class
Meals and drinks	You usually have an earlier breakfast	Have a buffet option
Landing	Never-ending circling and circling	Fast track arrangement with air traffic control?
Disembark	A tedious wait – so close but yet so far	Psychology…
Passport and immigration	Big delays	Fast track arrangement, schedule to arrive at less busy times
Luggage collection	Worry of non-arrival	On arrival limo service handles
Customs	Time	Check on departure, not arrival?
Into the terminal	Tired, can't send your e-mails	Arrival lounges with showers, business services
Find taxi	Huge hassle	On arrival limo
Check in to hotel	Tired and emotional	Check in handled by limo
Business meetings	Lots of admin, no support	Associate hotels provide support
Reconfirm flights	Plain nuisance	Not required
Start over	Etc	Etc

293

Of course, not all of the ideas for positive impact will work, nor should we seek to attempt them all. We will come to a screening and selection process later in the chapter, but for now we should remember that this stage of the process is a brainstorming one, expanding our horizons before narrowing in on our choice of activities.

Enhancing the total business experience

Staying with our airline example and the search for added value ideas, a particular favourite of mine is a service from Virgin Atlantic, where visitors to Walt Disney World in Orlando can check in their luggage at the park to allow them a proper last day to their holiday rather than the traditional slog to the airport and check in three hours before the flight.

Why this particular service? Because Virgin has identified the desired total experience sought by a particular segment of the market – the family on holiday. This group wants to squeeze the most holiday time out of their week or fortnight.

For the business traveller, a different segment of the market, there is a different total business experience sought. This traveller may be focused on completing a business deal, and anything the flight does to assist them – reduced waiting times, space to work or office space on arrival – will be regarded as adding value.

Always try to map out the value chain in the customer's process from as early as possible to as late as possible. In many cases, it will be both convenient and illuminating to divide the value chain into three sections: the before, the during and the after (see Figure 26.1). Portraying the chain as a circle rather than as a linear table is perhaps more helpful, as it reminds us that we are not in a one-deal operation; we want customers to return and go around the cycle again and again.

Figure 26.1   *The value chain 'before, during and after'*

'Before' relates to all the activities that occur before the customer is directly involved with purchasing and using your product or service. This will include their generation of ideas, identification of needs, selection process, vendor ratings, trials, supplier negotiations and purchase.

'During' includes all the activities from purchase through to use, whether that is the final consumption or an intermediate use.

The 'after' section of the value chain includes all those activities for the customer in their own market, ie the customer's customers.

The purpose of this split will become clear as you enter the steps in the customer's chain around the circle, and then enter those activities that you already carry out to add value to the customer's experience. There is a good chance that you will have a very full picture of the 'late before' (they are talking to you and thinking of placing an order) through to the 'mid during' (they have taken your product and started to use it). You probably have a much hazier picture of the 'early before', the 'late during', and most likely of all, the 'after'. It is in this white space that many of the opportunities for competitive advantage lie.

Dividing the value chain into 'before', 'during' and 'after' reveals where the opportunities for further added value lie

Very often a supplier will have exhausted most of the value-creating ideas in the 'during' stage, this is after all where they have most contact with and knowledge of their customers. Using our example, perhaps the flight is as good as it can get. Exploration of the 'before' and the 'after' can often pay dividends in such circumstances.

The before–during–after split reminds us of two more important issues, the market chain and the opportunity snail (see Chapter 3).

Products or solutions?

Where the supplier has a poor understanding of the steps around the customer's value chain, or perhaps only knows about a small portion of the chain, then the chances are that they are selling products, and only that. This situation is shown in Figure 26.2.

If however the supplier has a much wider understanding, and has found the means to make an impact on that chain at multiple points, then the chances are that this supplier is selling solutions, as indicated in Figure 26.3.

Or at least they should be selling solutions if they realized the breadth of their impact. Often the left hand of a complex supplier will not know what its right hand is doing, and there are in fact many positive impacts but nobody is joining them up in one coherent proposition.

Selling solutions takes joined up thinking...

Figure 26.2 *Limited impact on the value chain*

Figure 26.3 *Multiple impact on the value chain*

Value chain analysis and the market chain

Chapter 3 introduced the idea of the market chain, taking account of supplier's suppliers and customer's customers, right through to the end consumer. As your sales approach moves towards solutions and beyond, the significance of the chain will increase. From the example in Chapter 3, an agrochemical supplier to farmers, it was at the supermarket/consumer interface that most market *noise* was generated, and solutions for farmers must take account of that noise. In pursuit of value, each part of the chain will be looking for the impact it can have on solutions for the final consumer – the greater the impact, the greater the share of the reward in the chain. For a supplier some way back in the chain to the final consumer, the more they can understand the experiences sought by each step in the chain, the more chance they will have of securing a greater share of the value in the chain.

Figure 26.4 shows how you might need to consider a series of value chains, each starting off in the after stage of the one before. As you get further from your own customer so the circles may become hazier, and that spells an opportunity to gain competitive advantage, provided you have the capabilities.

Figure 26.4 *Value chain analysis in the market chain*

Category management

Suppliers to the retail industry talk of *category management*, the idea that they should base their propositions on a combination of the retailer's and the consumer's perceptions of value received, all of which is considered on the broad canvas of the market, not simply the supplier's own product. This calls for an understanding of at least two separate value chains plus the dynamics of the market.

How Kraft makes a positive impact throughout the chain

A food supplier like Kraft combines their knowledge of the consumer with their knowledge of the retailer to deliver a high-value proposition to both. In the United States, Kraft has segmented their consumers into six broad types based on their shopping behaviour. They have then designed specific ranges of products to appeal to these six types in different ways. Working with the retailer, they assess what balance of these six types shop in each of the retailer's stores, and plan the store's range and layout accordingly. By looking beyond their immediate customer (the retailer), Kraft is able to add value to that customer, *and* to the final consumer offer.

Value chain analysis and the opportunity snail

We also looked at the idea of the opportunity snail in Chapter 3, a representation of how an idea develops in a business and how the practice of KAM seeks to penetrate into that process. Our example of a food flavours supplier selling to an FMCG company placed marketing at the centre, moving out through R&D, manufacturing, purchasing and sales. We observed that if the supplier could gain access to the marketing people, they would enhance their opportunities to add value, to gain competitive advantage, and to be regarded as a strategic supplier. The problem was gaining access. Why should marketing people want to see a raw materials supplier?

If we turn to the idea of the value chain we may see an answer to this question. Perhaps the best way to gain access to the marketing people at the *early before* stage is to demonstrate your value to them at the *late after* stage – after all, this is a circle.

If the flavour supplier gains an understanding of the consumer's preferences by focusing on the after stage of their customer's chain, and if they can demonstrate this expertise for example through research reports, then they might be invited into a dialogue to discuss future trends – the beginning of the opportunity snail.

Screening and selecting positive impact activities

We now have a range of *possible* activities that *might* make a positive impact on the customer's TBE. Of course, no supplier could work on all these at once, and in any case, no customer is likely to want them all at once. The next step is to screen these possibilities, selecting the priority actions. Table 26.3 gives a suggested checklist to be applied to each possible action.

Screening helps you to focus your limited resources

Table 26.3 *Positive impact analysis – screening questions*

- Does it add value to the total business experience sought?
- Does it remove the problem?
- Does it reduce the problem?
- What value does the customer put on this?
- Does it impact on their core values (for example, Weirsema's value drivers)?
- What does it cost them – time, money, other?
- Would they pay for it as part of a service?
- What will it cost you to provide?
- Can you charge enough to cover cost, or make a premium?
- Can you secure your fair share of the value added to the market?
- Do you have the capability?
- Can you work with a partner to provide the capability?
- Does it give you sustainable competitive advantage?
- Does it enhance your service to other customer groups, segments, markets?
- Does it help you avoid competitive disadvantage? (see below)
- Does it give you 'lock in', in other words, is this something that will tie your customer to you, and is difficult for your competitors to replicate?

As a more general test of an idea, we might look for those that provide the best win–win outcome, which means that there is something in it for both sides. This is, after all, one of the tenets of working in partnership.

Using a selection matrix for screening activities and projects

If the number of potential activities is large or complex, you may want to go one step further than asking the screening questions as a means of identifying the runners. You could use a modified version of the key account identification and selection matrix shown in Figure 21.1 in Chapter 21 (and included as a software package on the CD ROM attached to this book). The vertical axis will now be the attractiveness to *us* of the project or activity, and the horizontal axis will measure the attractiveness of the activity or the project to the *customer*.

As with the key account identification and selection matrix, each axis of this new matrix is made up of a number of factors. These factors could include the checklist questions used in the screening process and any additional factors that might apply in your own circumstances.

Attractiveness to *us* might include:

- Will revenue earned (or protected) outweigh the costs to us?
- Do we have the capability?
- Can we develop the capability – is there a partner to provide the capability?
- Does it give us competitive advantage?
- Does it enhance our service to other customers or markets?
- Does it give us lock in?

Attractiveness to the *customer* might include:

- Does it reduce or remove a known problem?
- Does it impact on our (the customer's) core value drivers?
- Does it reduce risk?
- Is it of high value (using the customer's definition of value received)?
- Is it of low cost to us?

Use a similar weighting and rating system as described in Chapter 21 to complete the matrix. You can, of course, use the software package included in the CD ROM attached to this book.

Projects that fall into the top right-hand box are the most likely to be progressed and those that fall into the bottom left are those most likely to be dropped.

When a project falls into the top left-hand box, the next question to ask is: could this be made more attractive to the customer? It is very important not to invent attractions that are not there; it is very easy to justify any action if you lie hard enough. The point of the question is to simply double check.

Similarly, question those projects that fall into the bottom right: are they really so unattractive to you? If they benefit the customer so highly, can this also be turned to your advantage? It's not another excuse to lie to yourself, it's simply a double check.

'Lock in'

Make an impact – then get them coming back for more, and more, and more...

This is a matter of huge importance. Any supplier can do things that are of value to the customer, but whether they bring sustainable competitive advantage is another matter. Extended credit is certainly of value to a customer, but it is very easy for a competitor to match or even offer more. Such added value is short-lived, the competitive advantage is not sustainable, and worst of all, it can start a process that will spiral out of control as competing suppliers vie to improve the last offer.

Sustainable competitive advantage comes from activities that encourage loyalty and that competitors are not able to match without costly effort. *Buying* loyalty rarely works. Frequent-flyer miles are said to be about loyalty, but they are very often false loyalty; the customer goes elsewhere as soon as the scheme is stopped. Worse, everyone can do them.

The secret of lock in is to find an activity or service that customers value and would rather not perform themselves, that the competitor doesn't offer, and that doesn't involve handing the supplier too much power. It is a delicate balance – 'lock in' implies supplier power, and suppliers should tread carefully. The airline that offers to manage their corporate clients full business travel arrangements must take great care not to abuse their position, for example, London to Moscow via New York (the airline has no direct flight) is not value, it is an outrage!

Perhaps the most famous example of a misplaced attempt at lock in was that of Apple. Apple had a truly splendid operating system but they wanted to hang on to it and use its strength to sell their own machines, in other words you could only have it if you bought an Apple computer. This effectively restricted the value that consumers could receive and when Microsoft allowed MS DOS to be put on any machine you liked, they won the day.

The lock in that got them locked out

Lock in can be unpopular if it is used for obviously selfish ends. Much of the complaint against the development of genetically modified seeds is that they are designed to resist the effects of the suppliers own pesticides, a clear attempt to lock in the customer to the purchase of those pesticides. Somewhere along the line, the intention to help the farmer improve their yield becomes confused with other more selfish intentions if the marketing is not handled well. The notorious 'terminator gene' that would prevent the crop from producing new seeds was a step too far, particularly when considering the sale to Third World countries, and that particular attempt at lock in was withdrawn.

Gaining a share of the value

You do a thorough PIA, select an activity and come up with an innovation. Will you be able to get your fair share of the added value in the market? Of course, one of the PIA questions was just this, but how to judge? If you supply to the 'owners' of the market, then it is certainly true that your definition of *fair* will have to be modified. 'Owners' tend to get the lion's share. However, that doesn't make it a bad move because it secures your position with that 'owner' and you might consider that very good value.

Your best chance of gaining a fair share is by doing the analysis ahead of customer demands. By waiting for them to ask, immediately the potential reward of your activity has diminished. By being pro-active and by offering solutions to problems they are only just becoming aware of, you increase your chances of *fair* reward.

Companies with an excellent track record of gaining a fair share of the value put into a chain, despite their position some way from the end consumer, include DuPont with materials such as 'Teflon' and 'Lycra', and perhaps the most notable, Intel, with their ubiquitous 'Intel Inside' stickers.

Sometimes, a supplier will choose to allow the chain a greater share of the value because they stand to gain something in return, which is not a bad definition of 'fair share'.

How Toyota manage the value in the chain

When Toyota launched the Lexus car in the United States, they wanted dealers to offer levels of customer service that would leave competitors standing. They knew this would mean dealers having to invest in new systems, people, training and so on. Their solution was to allow dealers a substantially higher margin on selling the Lexus than was the industry norm, with the proviso that this margin went towards customer service improvements – a fair share of the value created by the whole Lexus package.

Gaining advantage or avoiding disadvantage?

The PIA process will help to identify those activities that will add most value to your customer's business. Some of these things may be unique to you, called *differentiators*, and they provide a real source of competitive advantage.

However, don't fall into the trap of thinking that added value ideas have to be big and bold, and that small, nitty-gritty activities are too mundane to be worth anything.

While the big ideas may well gain you advantage, it is equally important to avoid suffering disadvantage by failing to attend to the smaller, everyday things. Here we might identify another class of activities called the *givens*. These are the things that must be in place for business to be carried out.

Avoiding disadvantage is as important as gaining advantage, and may well involve attention to a more mundane list of activities; just the sort that might be discounted as administrative, clerical or even, if we're honest, dull. Making sure, for instance, that invoices are raised in a way that corresponds to the customer's requirements will rarely win you the account, but it may well help secure your position, and failing to do it will certainly lead to your disadvantage against those who can. It is surprising, and worrying, just how much of the already short time available between seller and buyer can be occupied by the discussion of such shortcomings.

More than this, a customer will be loathe to listen to your ideas for adding value if they feel that you are letting them down on the everyday front. Failure to attend to givens leads to a perpetual round of catch up and fire-fighting that can quickly sap a supplier's energy and dull a customer's enthusiasm.

By understanding the customer's *total business experience*, and by looking at the options for making *positive impact* on that experience, you will also be able to distinguish those activities that will gain you advantage (the differentiators), and those that will help you avoid disadvantage (the givens). It may be useful to list them separately and perhaps give particular attention to the givens, if you think they might be ignored in all the excitement!

Research carried out by Cranfield University School of Management uncovered the following:

> If there is one supplier strategy that can move a supplier/customer relationship into partnership, it is to install quality processes which will make it easier for customers to do business with the company. Purchasing decision makers hold suppliers who make it easy to do business with them in very high regard.
>
> Cranfield University School of Management (1996) *Key Account Management: Learning from supplier and customer perspectives*

Such a strategy will need to combine both givens and differentiators – the result will be a very powerful package indeed.

Adding value by *removing* features

It is easy to get into a mindset that says, 'To add value you must always do more', but sometimes less really *is* more.

Understanding the customer's value chain allows us to ask the vital question: what elements of their experience with us are valued most (some perhaps hugely so) and what parts are valued least (perhaps not at all)? If elements of the experience are not valued at all, they can only represent unnecessary costs in the customer's eyes, so why not remove them? The result is a stripped-down offer that truly meets the customer's value perceptions, and one with lower costs to boot. If those lower costs are then passed on to the customer through a lower price, their perception of value received will be even greater – people might even talk about 'bargains'!

SOME HINTS ON USING POSITIVE IMPACT ANALYSIS

- Involve a cross-functional team so that each member will see a different aspect of the customer relationship, the value chain, and thus the different opportunities.
- Establish PIA as a focal part of team membership, with a responsibility on each member to 'fill in the gaps'.
- Use PIA as a means of uncovering gaps in your knowledge and as a spur to further research.
- If possible, involve the customer (but take care not to build unrealistic expectations).
- Examine the value chain from the customers' perspective, from before they are involved with you (as supplier), during their involvement, and beyond that involvement. Very often the most value can be added at the before and after stages, the 'during' is usually fine, so real competitive advantage lies in stretching the boundaries of your relationship.
- Don't stop at considering the customer's value chain, include the customer's customer, and beyond, all the way to the consumer. Go beyond your customer.
- Identify activities that are 'givens' as distinct from 'differentiators'.
- Ensure the 'givens' are in place.
- Seek out options for competitive advantage through the 'differentiators'.
- Be open-minded about the need to work with partners.
- For each screening question, set parameters for good, OK and bad.
- Use it to establish priorities: A, B, C activities.
- Use it to determine project teams.
- Repeat the exercise regularly, backed up by market research, customer surveys and customer involvement.
- Once the PIA is complete, you will be in a much better position to select the package of activities required, thus moving from analysis to action:

  – identify the projects;
  – create the project teams.

27

Key account management and the e-revolution

It should be of concern to any key account manager or salesperson that the majority of e-commerce initiatives nowadays are coming from the purchasing department and not the sales department.

The purchasing department has often seized more eagerly than sales and marketing on the potential of this revolution and has often derived much greater immediate value. The opportunity to trade more efficiently at much reduced transactional costs is clear, and also to trade more effectively through access to a much wider pool of suppliers. This ability may well lead to a reverse in the trend of the late-20th century for downsizing of the supplier base.

The arrival of the Internet *online auction* places the buyer squarely in the driving seat for a range of basic purchases, and the new *B2B marketplace* phenomenon sees the emergence of new middlemen. In both cases, the initiative is being taken away from the seller. As customers increasingly call the tunes, suppliers gain less and less kudos from using the technology, they simply suffer if they don't!

There are some rational explanations for this:

● It is hard for a supplier to impose a system on a customer – customers have their own unique requirements. Much easier for a customer to lay down the law on what must be used.

- It is usually easier for a purchasing organization to gain approval for an investment in their e-capability based on clear and tangible returns, such as reduced purchasing costs or improved prices. It is much harder for a sales organization to do the same with as much certainty.

These are the rational reasons. Then there is the less rational – fear of the unknown. Good suppliers – those that understand their customers' needs and deliver genuine value – have very little to fear, it is the cowboy suppliers and the price merchants that have most to lose.

Fear has led many suppliers to underrate the value of this new medium. Too many marketing people see the e-revolution principally as enhancing their ability to promote, while too many sales people see it mainly as a means to receive orders automatically. This is a dangerously limited view.

The e-revolution has driven the purchasing revolution…

The e-revolution is at the heart of the purchasing revolution, as discussed in Chapter 8. Improved IT has given buyers the information to build spend maps and initiate supplier positioning exercises. EDI, the Internet and other forms of e-commerce have allowed them to reduce transactional noise from the lower two quadrants of the positioning matrix and so helped them to concentrate their time and efforts on strategic suppliers. These new tools have helped them to reduce the costs of purchasing and to improve their prices. No wonder they are so bullish about the technology!

… will it now drive a sales revolution?

The e-revolution is also at the heart of the KAM revolution. Without e-mail, it would be difficult to imagine how the communications that result from dealing with complex global accounts could be managed. Building on this, there is the range of software systems that facilitate the management of customer contacts, make customer information available to global teams, and analyse that information to identify patterns, opportunities or to help measure customer profitability. We shouldn't forget the role of call centres, fuelled by customer information, using e-commerce and CRM systems to sell to customers where only five years ago a physical call was required. Without these new tools, suppliers would never have been able to devote so much of their attentions to their key accounts.

There are as many tales of woe cited by the denigrators as there are tales of success cited by the promoters, and it is not the purpose of this chapter to take sides. The aim is to help you consider how the varied aspects of the e-revolution could be harnessed in support of your key account management strategy.

Most of the problems experienced by 'sellers' in seizing the opportunities have not resulted from the technology, nor from their sales proposition, but rather from the lack of attention to basic stuff, such as do we have the stock, will our logistics system cope, do we have enough cash?

Boo.com was created by two fresh-faced entrepreneurs to retail clothes over the Internet, a simple enough idea that grew to a business valued at £250 million. The business crashed in May 2000 for the simplest of reasons: 'we didn't attend to costs and we ran out of money', the two founders admitted with what seemed like almost total innocence.

Why dotcoms crash...

A recent advert from Bull, one of the big players in the e-revolution, promoted the need for their system networks with the following 'sad tale': *'The success of John's virtual store exceeded all his expectations. It also exceeded the capabilities of his company.'*

SOME USEFUL TERMS

B2B marketplaces: (also known as supply chain backbones, vertical portals or trading exchanges) these provide an Internet-based meeting place for suppliers and customers in a specific industry or market, allowing suppliers to provide information, tender for business and participate in online auctions, and customers to seek out new suppliers, check credentials and practise electronic procurement.

CRM (customer relationship management): techniques for harvesting information about customers that can be used to provide sales and customer service and to design new propositions.

E-business: a much broader canvas, which uses the information gathered from customer transactions to drive other business systems, including fore-casting and production planning, distribution, promotional planning, product development, etc.

E-commerce: computer-to-computer transactions between supplier and customer, whether providing information, placing orders, invoicing or giving after-sales support, etc. The range of options expands almost daily, and doubtless this chapter will already be out of date before the ink has dried on the page!

Intranets and extranets: an intranet uses Internet technology but is quite independent of the Web, providing an electronic database for everyone in the company. An extranet is an intranet that allows access for external users.

STEPS TOWARDS THE REVOLUTION

How to seize the new opportunities? As ever, the actual use will depend on the customer. How far do they want to use the medium: simply to find information, to source new suppliers and materials, to trade, to drive costs out, to beat prices down, to work collaboratively? There are so many 'it depends' that each supplier's strategy for using the e-revolution must necessarily be unique.

At the risk of being supplier- rather than customer-focused, we might identify five generic stages through which a supplier can make use of the e-revolution:

1. As an opportunity for promotion.
2. As an opportunity for trade – *e-commerce*.
3. As an opportunity for locking the customer into your supply chain – *e-business*.
4. As an opportunity for information and knowledge – *CRM*.
5. As an opportunity for customization or individualization.

The stages are not necessarily in any chronological order, nor are they independent of each other. Our concern in looking at each is not to explore the technology but, more importantly, to examine how the customer might wish to proceed and how this opportunity might impact on your key account strategy.

Opportunities for promotion

Providing information to your customer has never been easier. Indeed, they should no longer need to ask but simply be able to visit your web site to gain access to the sort of things that previously would have been the subject of lengthy conversations. This should be seen as far more than promotion on your part – this is an opportunity for dialogue. Indeed, the customer will not thank you for subjecting them to a promotional barrage when all they want is access to information. Company web sites should be designed so that the customer can find what they want readily and is then encouraged (because it will be to their benefit) to enter into some kind of dialogue with the supplier. Denying them the full information so they have to ask is one way to do this but it is rather clumsy, transparent in its self-interest, and ultimately very damaging!

Given the potential for a valuable conversation, it is sad to see how poorly so many companies use the medium. Constructing the web site is too often a job for the most junior member of the team or the IT department whose grasp of HTML and the like might be fine but who has little experience in the business of customer relations.

Frighteningly, only about 40 per cent of enquiries through UK company web sites are answered at present. Remember that this is potentially a dialogue so it's the same as putting the phone down on a customer halfway through the conversation, 6 times out of 10!

For a key account you may well go beyond a simple web site, allowing them direct access to your own systems. If you provide an extranet (see above), they can access a range of information that would be too sensitive (or valuable) for open public access. This might include details on contacts within the key account team, visit reports that can be shared with the customer, specifications, information on new product development, stock availability, or access to training programmes. Access to an extranet will go much further than promotion or the provision of information – it will encourage a dialogue that brings the customer much closer to the supplier's supply chain, with all the potential for lock in.

Opportunities for trade – e-commerce

Let's recall a statement from Chapter 26 that emerged from research done by Cranfield University School of Management: '*Purchasing decision makers hold suppliers who make it easy to do business with them in very high regard.*'

E-commerce provides one of the main highways for achieving this good reputation, so it is stranger still that so many suppliers remain reluctant to engage.

One of the main aims of any professional purchasing organization will be to make the business of *doing* business with suppliers easier. This might take the customer down many different routes, such as bullying large but inefficient suppliers, helping small but equally inefficient suppliers, or looking into their own purchasing systems for undue red tape and bottlenecks. Whatever route is pursued – bullying, assistance or self-help – the effort should ultimately work to both parties advantage. Supplier's costs will be reduced, and so their offer should be more competitive, and the customer's purchasing costs will be reduced, gaining them more value from the transaction. Moreover, easier transactions will free up time for the more important issues.

If e-commerce will help in this process do you imagine that it will be valued? The full answer to that depends on what sort of supplier you are.

E-COMMERCE AND SUPPLIER POSITIONING

If we review the supplier positioning matrix introduced in Chapter 9, we can consider how e-commerce may be regarded by the customer in each

Assessing what form of e-commerce the customer may want

supplier circumstance. Figure 27.1 reproduces the matrix with the addition of a typical purchasing organization's intentions from e-commerce in each case. It also shows the likely development over time of e-commerce solutions, starting with suppliers in the bottom-left box and finishing with the strategic partners. What this represents is the relative cost/benefit in each case , with the lowest investment and fastest returns seen in the bottom left, building to the highest investment and slowest (but potentially largest) returns in the top right. The easy wins are in reducing transactional noise (bottom left), then comes the pursuit of price and cost reductions, and only then does it move on to conquer the heights of collaborative partnership. We can see e-commerce progressing in this way from a means of making business easy to a means of adding value.

Tactical make easy

If you occupy the *tactical make easy* box, then e-commerce can offer the perfect solution. Relatively simple *EDI* systems, *telemetry* or *catalogue purchasing*, can remove paperwork, eliminate invoices, and dramatically reduce the need for expensive and time-consuming personal intervention by buyers or sales people. Ironically, there are circumstances where you can enhance your chances of being perceived as a *key supplier* by allowing the customer to spend more of their valuable time *not* speaking to you! E-commerce in this case is an exercise in making it easy to do business and removing costs. From the customer's perspective, this is where the quickest gains can be had for the lowest investment, particularly if suppliers can be made to bear the costs, and so it is no surprise that this is where we saw most activity in the closing years of the 20th century.

Figure 27.1 *Supplier positioning and e-commerce*

Tactical profit

The opening years of the 21st century have seen the attention move to the bottom-right box – *tactical profit*. By using the Internet, customers can open up their offers for tender to suppliers as yet unknown. As well as reducing their own purchasing costs, this injection of new competition can have a dramatic effect on prevailing prices. For the supplier, trading using the Internet can reduce the costs of supply and these savings can be passed on to the customer. There is potential for win–win, even in this highly competitive arena.

Access to suppliers by this means of e-commerce allows customers to look for the best offers, and access to customers gives suppliers an outlet for those offers. A supplier seeking economies of scale from a big jump in volume might find it difficult to 'turn on the taps' through traditional means of selling: too small a sales force, too small a home market, etc. The Internet could open up a whole new range of customers, from the unvisited to the unknown, even to the 'unthought of'.

It is largely in this quadrant that we see the increasing use of the Internet *online auction*. Unlike traditional auctions where the seller sets the scene and the highest bidder wins, here the buyer is in the driving seat and calls for the sellers to bid. Sellers who do not learn the rules of this new medium will soon find themselves excluded.

It is also here that we are seeing the development of the *B2B marketplace*, which is covered in more detail below.

Strategic partner or strategic security

If you occupy the *strategic partner* or *strategic security* boxes, then the more advanced forms of e-commerce (perhaps in the form of access to extranets) provide the means to achieving far more intimate systems of supplier/customer communication. E-commerce in this case is very much more about adding value through collaborative relationships (see the example of BP and virtual team working in Chapter 16), though the challenge to make it work is great, requiring as it does both technical *and* cultural convergence between customer and supplier.

SOME MORE TERMS...

EDI (Electronic Data Interchange): supplier and customer computer systems are designed to talk directly to each other. Orders can be sent down the line, acknowledgements returned, invoices raised, payments made, and not so much as a business breakfast is needed. Buyers talk of *efficient response* ordering systems linked to targets for *just in time* (JIT) deliveries. Indeed, for some suppliers it is only through the efficiency of EDI that JIT becomes feasible. EDI can bring win–win because the customer gets their efficient response and the efficient supplier gets lock in through an automated system that requires human intervention to alter.

Telemetry: the customer's stock levels are monitored automatically and remotely. A typical example would be fluids held in tanks with electronic sensors that monitor the level at any time. With such systems, re-ordering can be completely automatic. The humble barcode has provided a hugely successful telemetry system, where the process of scanning a product through the supermarket cash-out starts the whole process of re-ordering by remote and automatic means. Wal*Mart has used this process par excellence to drive out the costs of purchasing and become one of the world's most efficient retailers.

This is another element of an *efficient response* ordering system, shortening the supply chain and reducing the customer's working capital. Beyond this, suppliers can be given the task of managing stock levels (particularly attractive in either the *tactical make easy* or the *strategic security* boxes), perhaps even on a consignment basis, where stock is held on the customer's premises but owned by the supplier until the point of use, with obvious benefits to security of supply, cash flow and working capital reduction.

Suppliers can achieve a significant lock in and will enjoy significant security provided they ensure the system never fails. This raises an important requirement for telemetry systems to work, which is mutual trust. The customer is increasing their reliance on a supplier, so increasing their risk. They will expect something in return. A supplier that pursues telemetry purely for their own security is likely to find a reluctance on the buyer's part to give them full control of the system.

Not all products are suited to telemetry but the innovative supplier that finds an effective means of remote and automatic ordering for such items will certainly stand to establish this form of e-commerce as a differentiator, rather than a given.

What means are available in your business?

Catalogue purchasing: this is a purchasing system where standard items, regularly bought, can be listed on an electronic catalogue, available to all buyers in the company. Suppliers will agree such things as price, lead times, delivery terms, etc, and all buyers are able to take advantage of this without the need for separate negotiations. The catalogue can contain specifications, data sheets, health and safety information, supplier data, almost whatever the customer wishes. This is clearly a powerful tool for standardizing purchasing across a large company, perhaps one with multiple sites or multi-national operations.

For the supplier, once listed, the world might appear to be their oyster, but the challenge is to ensure listing. Purchasing departments see this tool in particular as a means of limiting supplier numbers, even ensuring a single supplier is used, whatever the local buyer's views! Intimate knowledge of the customer's decision-making processes and the DMUs responsible for setting up such catalogues will be invaluable. Access to the specifiers in those DMUs will often be the key to success.

Online auctions: suppliers are asked to bid for business within a short time frame and in immediate competition with other suppliers. This is an excellent medium for trading in what are called 'near commodities' – easily defined products with broadly similar specifications across competing suppliers. Sometimes they will be given the results of the first round of bidding and asked to resubmit. This calls for new skills for the supplier and unfortunately many of them will be gained the hard way.

An evangelist for the technique is United Technologies (Otis elevators and Sikorsky helicopters among others) who regularly determine contracts worth millions through online auctions. Suppliers to UT are virtually obliged to use e-commerce one way or another. The head of purchasing at UT, Kent Brittan, has argued strongly that e-commerce has huge benefits for large industrial companies in what might be regarded as the 'old economy', just as much if not more than in the 'new economy'. He also sounds a warning: 'Some of our suppliers didn't think we could do it. They are no longer with us.'

Applying 'new economy' tools in the 'old economy'

There is a danger that online auctions that only focus on price will drive down the quality of products and services. Since the price of the product is only a part of the story for most buyers (there are then the costs in use), this could lead to problems and so a decline in the use of the medium. This is a case where experience will lead to the medium reaching its appropriate level, but doubtless many fingers will be burnt in the interim.

The B2B marketplace: one of the predictions made in the early days of the e-revolution was the death of the distributor – all business could now be direct. In fact, we are seeing quite the reverse. Traditional distribution channels are still required to move products, but they must take on board the systems required to link them into the suppliers' e-business network. And we are seeing the emergence of a new kind of middleman, the B2B marketplace.

Most prevalent in fragmented markets where there are literally hundreds or even thousands of participants, these electronic trading exchanges provide a place for suppliers and customers to meet and do business. They seek to improve the efficiency of the supply chain through the kind of processes hitherto only possible in highly integrated markets.

A marketplace can be established by an individual buyer in search of efficiency from an inefficient supply chain. These might in time become larger but still industry-specific (*vertical marketplace* is the jargon) if other buyers, sometimes even competitors, join the exchange. Covisint is such an example in the automobile market, made up of Nissan, Renault, Daimler-Chrysler, General Motors and Ford, having been set up by the last three of these companies. If such an exchange can force its suppliers to use it then it can quickly gain the level of transactional volume required for sustainability. The most significant advantage for the buyer is a one-stop shop for a huge range of items in a complex industry.

Vendor-led marketplaces also exist, an example being Softgoods Matrix.com, an exchange that targets the clothing market and includes Lee, Wrangler and Ralph Lauren in its list of participants. The challenge of such an exchange is to have a sufficient range of participants to attract buyers – very much like the challenge for an out-of-town shopping centre.

The customer-led marketplace is currently set to take the lead over vendor-led equivalents – they promise to deliver more value to both parties in the exchange.

Still in their infancy, such enterprises are most likely to succeed in markets where the costs of buying and selling are high and such middlemen can add value through their efficient systems.

GETTING INTO E-COMMERCE...

As with any new technology, system or process, there are shark-infested waters ahead. Many people within a supplier organization will think of a dozen reasons to avoid it, such as it's too complex, removes the human element, too expensive, the customer doesn't want it, or even 'it's just a passing fad' (yes, I've heard it!). Most predictions for its future impact probably hit wide of the mark one way or another. Some say sales forces are already a thing of the past, while others say it will be a decade before suppliers see the benefits. I am reminded of the comment by a small-town mayor in the American Midwest who, when he got to hear of that new-fangled contraption, the telephone, said: 'One day, **every** town in America will have a telephone,' doubtless feeling very radical.

Those advocating e-commerce as an added value business solution, or those realizing that they must become involved simply to stay in business, need to address four questions:

1. What does each form of e-commerce bring to the supplier/ customer relationship?
2. What are the relative cost/benefits and where should we start?
3. Who's responsibility is this, supplier or customer, and who should bear the costs?
4. Given the pace of change, when should we jump on board?

We have addressed the first two questions, lets now turn to the third and fourth.

Who should pay?

The benefits to both supplier and customer are clear, yet when it comes to footing the bill, the mists can suddenly descend! E-commerce interventions are certainly not cheap, though they can provide excellent value in terms of their payback in short spaces of time.

Some customers will make e-commerce a standard for a supplier wishing to do business: a vendor rating. By doing this, they clearly imply that any costs of development and implementation should be borne by the supplier. In a competitive market, customers can impose their will in this way.

Where the customer is more reliant on the supplier, they may have to take a different attitude. Some customers might even go as far as saying that they should bear the costs themselves, and perhaps even those of their supplier, _in order to reduce the supplier's costs of doing business with them_. Not all is rosy, however, for if the above was indeed the case, then the supplier might expect a demand for lower prices, based on having their costs of supply reduced.

In the end, this is an issue that may go beyond who pays. Suppliers that can provide advice on implementing e-commerce, evidence of success elsewhere, a willingness to trial, train and give support post-implementation, will enhance their chances of being regarded as key suppliers. If that status is already achieved or if the relationship is already one of partnership KAM, then perhaps a sharing of costs is the most equitable outcome.

With many e-commerce mechanisms, telemetry being a good example, the customer is locked in to the supplier. In such cases, the partnership may consider it fair and reasonable for the supplier to pay a substantial share of the costs in return for that not-insignificant benefit. The advantage to suppliers of food and materials to the hotel industry is clear (the opportunity to secure sole supplier status) so that many wholesalers will provide EDI ordering terminals to hotels free of charge, as part of their service.

When to start?

The answer has to be 'as soon as possible'. 'Possible' meaning as soon as both parties are confident that they understand the objectives, the potential benefits, the costs, the risks, and the technology involved. Quite a lot to take on, and working through expert consultants has to be good advice in this rapidly changing arena.

Perhaps you are tempted to wait and see how others get on with this new technology? Only you can weigh the risks of this caution, the risk of losing competitive advantage, versus the risks of implementation. Seek professional advice and try to steer a course between those two business 'philosophies' discussed in Chapter 2: the *'Viking'* approach that might land you high and dry, and the *'gently does it'* attitude that could leave you standing at the starting line.

One last warning: don't plunge into e-commerce without ensuring that your existing operational systems can cope. Tesco was caught out by the massive response to their home shopping service, leading to long lead times (often a week ahead) for deliveries. What this highlights is the need to have the supply chain infrastructure in place ready to cope with this new channel. At present, the logistical constraints of the old systems and channels are restricting the growth of the new, slowing down further the development of new capabilities. This gives an opportunity to new entrants who can benefit from the learning experience of the trailblazers. The winners in the electronic trading contest will not be the suppliers with the fanciest web sites (important though this 'front end' is), but the ones with the best supply chain – the best expediters.

E-COMMERCE, THREAT OR SOLUTION?

If e-commerce, in whatever form, eases your customer's task of doing business with you, then it is not only a solution, but also a top priority

By now the answer to this should be clear. We can see how e-commerce can be regarded either as a *given* or as a *differentiator* (these terms were described in Chapter 26) depending on the circumstances. Which one it becomes will depend on several factors:

- How advanced are your competitors in using such methods?
- How advanced is the customer in using such methods?
- Where are you positioned in the customer's supplier positioning matrix?

If all your competitors can do business through EDI, if the customer is able to take advantage of this, and if your area of supply is perceived in the tactical make easy box, then e-commerce is without doubt already a given. If you lack the capability in such a circumstance then you will suffer significant competitive disadvantage, perhaps even finding yourself unable to trade. Meeting the standards will carry no particular kudos, it will simply be a licence to trade. Those suppliers without this capability will certainly see e-commerce as a threat, but burying heads even further into the sand will be of no great help.

As a potential differentiator there are perhaps four important opportunities:

1. Reducing the costs of getting products and services to the customer.
2. Differentiating the offer through the ease of purchase for the customer.
3. Differentiating the offer through the customer's ability to access your supply chain.
4. Differentiating the offer through the ability to customize.

The first two have perhaps already become givens in many markets so it is to the third and fourth of these opportunities that we must turn for the pursuit of competitive advantage.

Opportunities for locking in the customer into your supply chain

We have seen how an extranet can allow a customer access to a supplier's data banks. This is but a step (if you wish it) to giving them access to your internal operating systems.

Purchasing organizations have already opened the doors in the other direction – suppliers who have an office on a customer's site, an implant on their production line, or access to the customer's systems in order to provide paperless invoicing or to police OTIF. Traditional seller/buyer bottlenecks are avoided, and collaborative tasks such as designing new plant, testing new products, or installing new systems can be carried out with much greater ease. In effect, customers are outsourcing aspects of their own supply chain to key suppliers, with huge benefits to costs and time.

Such developments will only happen where trust has been well-established, but for suppliers, the benefits of winning this trust are huge. Allowing the customer into the supplier's supply chain will also require trust, perhaps even more than allowing supplier's into the customer's supply chain. The benefits of such partnership strategies can be great, promising long-term security through *lock in*.

By understanding the way that the customer makes their purchases, the supplier can design their supply chain to maximize the customer's ease of access – direct to the factory, direct to the distribution depot, and direct to the service providers. Once inside, and if the experience is good, the customer will find it very easy to stay doing business that way – the supplier will have achieved lock in.

It is at this point in the e-revolution that the supplier's capabilities will have to change most dramatically. So many of the operational systems in place in traditional businesses are designed to keep the customer out, relying on internal data to drive them, and craving uniformity, not the variations of individual customer demands. The supplier of a highly standardized product with low costs does not have to become a supplier of complex menu choices, but perhaps they do need to be able to deal with the different purchasing behaviours of their customers – a standardized, lowest-cost product but a flexible, differentiated supply chain?

Opportunities for information and knowledge – CRM

Time after time with the e-revolution we find ourselves saying that the concept is not new but the application is revolutionary. Nowhere is this more true than in the area of customer information. Knowledge about customers has been stored from time immemorial in everything from card index files to the salesperson's head. Some of these formats are more reliable than others, but all suffer from two particular problems: how to get the information back out, and how to do anything constructive with it.

CRM (customer relationship management) has become synonymous with this activity: capturing information, analysing it, and using it to help construct better customer propositions. It has come to be regarded as an electronic activity as so many supplier/customer interactions are through the electronic medium, but it is just as applicable to the more old-fashioned forms of information capture such as face-to-face meetings. Having said that, there is no doubt that the e-revolution has provided a hugely improved means of managing this knowledge in order to enhance the customer relationship.

A simple example of how such a system can work to both parties' advantage is the sale of books through the Internet. The customer's search activity and final order can be analysed for patterns. What were they interested in? What were they bothered about? Using this information, several enhancements to the service could be built in — perhaps the customer could be informed by e-mail when new books in their area of interest are published, or perhaps they could be helped through parts of the search and order process that were causing them problems.

Once it is realized that every interaction with the customer has the potential to provide information about their needs, their buying behaviour, their perceptions, their concerns and their frustrations, then it becomes possible to take action to improve.

Chapter 16 outlined a number of emerging new techniques to facilitate this process. The analysis of the customer's *clickstreams* as they work their way around your site and into your system can reveal how they go about making their choices:do they look for information first or do they check for alternatives?

Virtual sales assistants allow customers to ask questions, and in so doing reveal much about their interests, their certainties, their doubts and their priorities. *Virtual customers* can be quizzed for references or even for complaints. And, of course, as customers make more use of such interactivity, so the ability to analyse their behaviours, interests and concerns increases.

The information is kept in a *data warehouse* and is *mined* by increasingly sophisticated techniques searching for patterns. Signalling, for instance, is a technique for analysing the customer's purchasing behaviour, looking for clues to their intentions. Not so much what *did* they buy, as, what did they *want* to buy, and how much might they have spent?

Analysis of the information opens up a raft of possibilities, from redesigning your supply chain to allowing customers to design their own offer to their own specification. But there is in all of this a potential danger lurking for the unwary supplier. As the complexity and sophistication of such data capture and the accompanying analytical techniques increases, so the task of customer care can easily find itself shifted towards the IT experts. CRM is a facilitator, potentially excellent, but its own systems and processes should never be allowed to become the master.

Customer care is a business-wide issue, not the sole preserve of IT experts or software vendors

Call centres, by their 'one-stop shop' nature, are seen by many as excellent places to gather such information and to have access to it from one point, on behalf of the customer. The real test of such centres will be: in whose interests have they been set up? Customers who want a 'one stop shop' will approve them, but those wanting a more complex and searching dialogue may not be so enthusiastic.

How does this impact on key account management? Starting with those customers categorized as maintenance or opportunistic (see Chapter 21), CRM techniques offer new ways of servicing with significantly reduced human resources. This resource can be invested more effectively in the key accounts. For the key accounts themselves, the potential for increased understanding is huge, not least the question of measuring customer profitability. The true value, however, will be seen in the ability to customize and even individualize the offer.

Opportunities for customization or individualization

Perhaps the most exciting application of new technology for the key account manager is in using it to drive the design of the offer itself. The relative efficiency of e-commerce and the information won through CRM bring on to the horizon the realistic prospect of a customer forming their own market segment. A market segment deserves its own marketing mix – product, price, promotion, place – that is indeed a definition of a segment. The practice of segmentation is to customize the offer to a specific group of people – and why not to a particular customer?

The problems with making such a notion reality are of course many and complex, but the challenge is on. Two obstacles are: first, current manufacturing systems will stand in the way of such 'interference' from customers, and second, the supply chain logistics could easily be frozen solid by such 'infinite variety'. Of course, once customers wake up to what they can get from a supplier, and once the demand starts to build, then manufacturing and supply chain systems that cannot oblige will leave their owners looking like dinosaurs. Competitors that *can* oblige will start to siphon off the customers prepared to pay for such close attention, most likely the high-margin end of the business, and the dinosaurs will find themselves in a potentially vicious circle of decline.

The supplier that best understands their customer will be best placed to develop the appropriate systems to offer such customization. If customer knowledge is used to drive better value propositions, we will enter the rising curve of a virtuous circle of growth.

This, of course, is precisely the challenge and purpose of KAM.

28

Making the proposal

Proposals are opportunities to show you have listened

At all stages of the key account relationship there will be a need for presenting proposals. At the early stages of the relationship these presentations will be about demonstrating the supplier's understanding of the customer's needs and their suitability as providers of assistance.

The tendency is for presentations to be boasts about the supplier's scale, abilities or ambitions – almost always a mistake.

It is to be hoped that as the relationship develops towards the partnership and synergistic stages, those presentations will become less formal – the customer's need to 'test' you against the competition will decline and the focus will be on specific projects. However, this should not lead to any complacency on the supplier's part. Nowhere is the cliché 'familiarity breeds contempt' better demonstrated than here. However close the relationship, always remember that the customer can break it at a moment's notice – particularly if there is an attractive competitor in the wings.

Each time you need to make a proposal – a new product launch, a pitch for a greater share of the business or whatever – the following thought process will be helpful:

1. Is the customer open to change?
2. How does your proposal stack up against the alternatives?
3. How should you put the case?

OPEN TO CHANGE?

In Chapter 18 we looked at the change equation (see Figure 28.1) as a tool for assessing how we might influence and manage change within our own organization. This is an extremely versatile tool, equally applicable to dealings with the customer. Let's say we wish our customers to replace an existing product line, purchased from us, with a new, higher-grade version at a higher price.

Figure 28.1   *The change equation*

Do they have any dissatisfaction with the status quo?

If so, who has it and where? Perhaps the buyer is entirely happy with existing arrangements and certainly does not want to entertain price increases.

You must look elsewhere, perhaps to the users, who have been finding some problems with the existing product. You may need to prepare a summary of recent complaints or an estimate of the costs of recent problems in the customer's process. (This is, of course, a delicate affair; you are detailing a catalogue of problems with your own product – only a good idea if you have a solution!)

Perhaps everyone is happy? Then the future is your only hope – might the existing product have problems in the future? Perhaps it contains an ingredient that will have to be phased out, or maybe your customer's competitors will be starting to use higher-grade alternatives?

Do they share your vision for the potential future?

Don't be too sure about this and remember the problems Alexander Graham Bell (Chapter 25) had with his telephone. Find out how your customers are thinking before making any big assertions about how things will be in the future. Perhaps you believe that the whole market will move to using similar high-grade materials as a means of trading up. Perhaps they believe that the whole product line will be defunct in three years' time anyway, so why the bother? This is the sort of thing that can be embarrassing!

Do they see some first practical steps?

Can you make the transition painless? Perhaps you can provide assistance on the customer's site – getting the new formulation worked into their process, or maybe you can offer to swap current stock for new at no premium?

Is all of this greater than the cost of change?

For the buyer, maybe not. For the other members of the DMU, it may be very compelling. This, of course, calls on the art of selling to the organization (Chapters 22 and 23).

PROPOSAL ANALYSIS

The change equation will help you assess how your proposal may be received, compared to the buyer's simplest choice – doing nothing. We now need to look at how it might stack up against a potentially tougher proposition – a competitive offer.

The proposal analysis provides a simple means of making this comparison and then judging where your relative strengths and weaknesses lie. This will be vital when you come to presenting your case or defending yourself against competitors' claims.

Do you have a competitive advantage, in the customer's eyes?

The following example assumes that you are trying to sell a flip chart stand to a training company. The training company's staff are comparing your offer to the purchase of an overhead projector.

To ensure that you consider all the customer's needs (and not just the ones that we think our proposal stacks up well against), I have categorized needs into performance, financial, other, and the total business experience.

Once the needs are determined, you must score your proposal in comparison to the competitor's, with a score of two meaning the proposal meets the need well, a score of one means it is OK and zero means it is poor or doesn't meet the need at all.

You also want to consider the members of the DMU. Might there be differences of need or opinion? Can you find a proposal that suits all requirements? Note a particular interest with X or XX for *very* significant.

In this example (see Table 28.1), the buyer is one of the trainers in the company, but they will also need to consider the needs of their customers – delegates on an event. You know a little about the buyer: they are eager to please and like to put on a good show for the delegates.

Table 28.1 *Proposal rating*

Customer's Needs	Your Proposal	Comp's Proposal	DMU Member	DMU Member
	Flip Chart	OHP	Trainer	Delegate
Performance				
Clarity for a room of 20 people	1	2		X
Use in a variety of environments	2	1	X	XX
Easy to prepare	1	2	X	
Portable	0	2		
Financial				
Purchase <£200	2	1		
Low running costs	1	2		
Other				
N/A				
Total Business Experience				
Want to be seen as professional	1	2	XX	X
Total Score	8	12		

So far, it isn't looking too good for the flip chart business. If the buyer were a computer, you would have lost on points. Fortunately, the buyer is human.

You have some choices:

1. Argue with the customer's assessment – 'But you're wrong, it's very easy to prepare!' Rarely a good idea.
2. Downgrade the competitor's offer – 'But have you seen the price of bulbs?' An even worse idea – this just gets the customer defending the competitor.
3. Raise the importance of those needs where your offer shows a clear strength. The best plan by far.

There are many ways to do this, but let's consider two.

Consider the DMU

Are there any issues or needs where your offer can satisfy all, or most, of the important members of the DMU? Are there points in your offer that provide a compromise for different members of that DMU?

In our example, the issue of being able to use the presentation tool in a variety of environments might just be the answer. Delegates on an event don't want to be victims of a one-way lecture from someone armed with a folder full of slides. Still less do they want to be trapped in a darkened room with the blinds drawn and the sun shining outside. And what if the weather was so clement that they wanted to take the course outside?

Your proposal would allow the trainer greater flexibility and the delegates a more enjoyable experience – grounds for a good compromise of needs.

Questioning strategy

Prepare questions and statements that will help you raise the importance, in the customer's view, of those needs where your proposal makes the strongest case. This is a four-part questioning strategy:

1. Identify the customer's current circumstances. Where and when do they need to use this tool? In what circumstances?
2. Uncover potential or existing problems and issues. What problems are there with running events? What can you do when attention is flagging? How do delegates feel about sitting inside all day?
3. Expand the concerns about those problems or issues. How would it be if it were a very hot day? How would it be if they all wanted to get outside? How might your delegates feel if you kept them trapped inside?
4. Suggest possible solutions. Might a flip chart presentation actually make you very popular?

The best propositions are rarely lectures. Questions lie at the heart of persuasion and are key to building partnerships

This is, of course, a huge simplification of a questioning process that might take some time. Increase the complexity of the sale and this is a process that might extend over several meetings.

Proposal analysis and the subsequent questioning strategies are perhaps best regarded as tools for planning. In front of the customer, great care must be taken not to be seen as laying traps. Moreover, in the heat of debate, questions are never answered as you hoped; the conversation never runs to script. Such planning and preparation will help point you in the right direction, help you to see the customer's perspective, help you to consider alternatives and help you to be fast on your feet – not inconsiderable advantages for a salesperson.

29

Selling to the individual

In the last chapter, we considered selling a flip chart to a customer, comparing our offer to an overhead projector. On a rational assessment, giving points for performance against identified needs, we lost – and yet we still made the sale.

This was in part due to sales technique, but perhaps even more due to a single recognition – we sell to human beings, not computers.

Our drive towards KAM, the customer's drive towards supply chain management, the complexity of the customer's DMU, the importance of the sale – these are just some of the things that can take our eye off one truth about selling, a truth that has not changed since selling began: the customer is human.

What do we conclude from this? That we can bamboozle them? Perhaps, but rarely a good sales strategy. That we can pressure them? Ditto.

Let's recall some of the purposes of KAM: to develop more intimate relationships, to increase trust between seller and buyer, to enhance long-term security. Let's add to that one of the bases for the customer's positioning (Chapter 9) of suppliers – trust and confidence. What we are highlighting is one of the key factors for a successful relationship – rapport between selling and buying companies.

This chapter will not attempt a full treatment of the vast subject of how to develop rapport between individuals. The next few pages aim to raise the importance of the issue and introduce some basic concepts – fuller coverage is available in a number of excellent books or, best of all, through training events

focused on the interpersonal skills of selling (see Chapter 32 for further suggestions). When you come to consider the training needs of KA team members,
expect to find 'improve interpersonal skills' high on the list of priorities. If the
team is composed of members with little previous direct customer contact, and
add to that a background in a function based on 'logical process flows' (R&D,
production, distribution, etc), then expect the priority to be number one.

Perhaps the hardest lesson for non-sales people to learn (and, for that
matter, a few sales people as well) is that the customer does not always make
their decisions for logical, let alone rational, reasons.

LOGIC OR EMOTION?

Consider a buyer looking to buy a steel-making plant. This is a massive task.
The decision will run over months, maybe years. The decision will involve
large teams of people from the buyer's own organization and from various
potential suppliers. Even once a decision is made, there will be a lengthy
process of determining specific needs and tailoring the supplier's offer. All
in all, the buyer might expect to be dealing with the chosen supplier over a
number of years. In such a circumstance, how far will the buyer proceed
with a potential supplier that they cannot trust, feel uncomfortable with, or
just don't like?

'80% of decisions taken in business are taken for "emotional" reasons' (Harvard Business School)

Research has shown that when customers change suppliers, while it
might be expected that the key reasons were better products or prices elsewhere, the real reasons lie in more human issues. The biggest killer, it would
seem, is a supplier that demonstrates indifference to their customer's needs,
problems, or complaints. Think of your own purchasing decisions as a
consumer – do you return to shops that don't seem to know you are there?

Purchasing decisions, and so making the sale, result from activity on a
number of levels, as we discussed in Part V:

- by meeting the business needs;
- by meeting the personal needs;
- by understanding how the organization operates and makes their
  buying decisions.

Many experienced sales people would argue that it is the second of these,
the personal needs, that makes all the difference and that non-sales people
find this impossible to accept.

Consider a buying decision. Two companies are offering the same
product, a commodity. The specification is identical, the price the same and
the service offered matches. How does the customer decide? A series of
factors will come into play:

- Previous experience of either supplier – good or bad.
- Treatment received from the suppliers during the sale.
- Who does the customer trust?
- Who does the customer like?

Deep down in each of these factors it is the personal rapport between supplier and buyer that will make the difference.

Consider another buying decision. Two companies are offering high-tech solutions to a complex problem. To find the real solution, the suppliers will need to understand the customer in depth. They will need to identify with a series of needs, across different departments and functions. Which supplier is more likely to identify these needs, the arrogant supplier or the supplier that strikes up a personal rapport during a series of contacts?

ENSURING RAPPORT

So, how do you ensure that contacts with your customer are enhanced by personal rapport?

Rule number one – make sure that all members of your KA team recognize the importance of rapport and actually *believe* in its value. No book will do this for you, hence the limited aims of this chapter. This is a job for training. A major international player in the biotechnology industry, recognizing the importance of customer intimacy and so of 'one-to-one' rapport, devoted the majority of their training effort not to matters of science and technology, but to matters of interpersonal relationships.

The training of all team members in interpersonal skills will be a top priority

The following themes are all important in developing attitudes and behaviours that will ensure rapport. As written words, they may not be all that convincing. Given that, don't expect to convince your team by merely asserting these points – which brings us back to training:

- Persuasion skills are much less about objectives and logic and much more about personal feelings.
- The best persuaders recognize three key needs: to focus on the personal needs of others; to persuade through involvement; to earn the right to proceed.
- Earning the right to proceed comes as much from being liked and trusted as it does from being regarded as an expert.
- Sellers with great skills of 'projection' come to little without corresponding skills of 'empathy' with their customers.
- The best sellers speak as little as possible and when they do, it is to ask a question.
- The best sellers listen to the answers.

- The customers' perceptions are at least of equal importance to the facts of the matter and usually of more importance.
- Understanding what makes your customers tick, that is, what motivates them personally, is the key to rapport, giving you the opportunity to mould your style to meet their perceptions.

There are a huge variety of tools for analysing buyer behaviour, personal motivation and the like. The best are those that can be used in practice. They may not be perfect from the standpoint of the professional psychoanalyst, but they provide a KA team with a shorthand for discussing the customer, the members of the DMU and the best way to approach individuals.

Chemistry

Getting the chemistry right is very important. At the 'bow tie' phase of KAM, the relationship is largely between two individuals and the supplier puts forward their trained chameleon, the salesperson. Once we arrive at the partnership 'diamond' relationship, the contacts are numerous and you might not expect every individual to have the same interpersonal skills as that trained salesperson. Training these team members will be important, but so will planning for good personal chemistry. Choosing who should see whom might be as much about who will get on with whom as it might be about professional or functional expertise.

What is it that makes personal chemistry? Excepting all those marriages made up of complete opposites (the happy Mr and Mrs Jack Spratts of this world), the usual route to chemistry and rapport is a matching of outlooks and attitudes. People driven by ambition usually get along best with like-minded souls – those that just want to get through life might frustrate them or just leave them cold. Similarly, those that thrive in the company of others will seek out similarly sociable or affiliative animals.

One of the best tools is that developed by David McClelland, which is used to look at how people are motivated to interact with colleagues, particularly when making decisions. A model highlights six particular motivational drivers, present in all of us, of which three stand out – a motivation for power, for achievement and for affiliation.

With training, it is possible to learn how to observe these motivations in others, and so modify your behaviour in order to match their expectations from you, and thus gain rapport. I deliberately choose to go no further in the explanation here; this is not something that can be learnt from a book – it requires training, an understanding of your own motivations and a proper understanding of the limits of such tools. (Chapter 32 provides some advice on how to follow up this issue.)

A conscience prodder: **Key accounts are important, relationships are vital, and chemistry matters. So do you select your key account managers and teams based on geographical location?**

Part VII

Keeping On Track

30

Getting there – timetables and performance

We have seen over the last 29 chapters just how much effort will be required to make KAM work. And like any investment, we ought to know how it is doing. In the early days at least, you will face a stream of questions from all parts of the business, all on the same theme – was it all worthwhile?

How will you measure success?

It has often been said, 'If you can't measure it, you can't manage it', a regularly abused and misinterpreted bit of advice. Sure, measuring helps, but the advice has been taken by many to conclude that things that *cannot* be measured are by definition of no significance and so of no value. It is a great relief to many not to have to think about relationships, trust, communications and a whole host of other vital but hard to measure ingredients of good KAM practice. A relief perhaps, but a disaster looming.

It is debatable as to just how much effort should be put into trying to measure some of these less tangible elements: arguing *for* the effort will help focus minds on their importance; arguing *against* the effort – well, perhaps such energies would be better spent elsewhere. Fortunately, there is still room in business for an element of gut feel and faith.

The secret to measurement of progress is in laying out clear targets in the first place. These might include targets for:

- customer performance;
- business performance;
- KA team performance;
- project performance;
- relationship performance;
- customer satisfaction;
- KAM implementation.

There will doubtless be others that apply to your own business. For each of these, you will need to identify where you currently stand and where you wish to be. Only then can you hope to find any means of measuring progress.

Good investments result from clear objectives and regular tracking

Some of these measures lend themselves to quantifiable analysis. There are sophisticated tools, for instance, for measuring customer satisfaction and its movement over time, although professional expertise should be sought in this area. Tempting though it may be to send sales people out with home-grown customer questionnaires, a host of factors conspire to make such exercises next to useless (not least the salesperson's determination to get a good report!).

Having set the performance targets, they should be tracked over time with mechanisms for review and corrective action.

TIMETABLES FOR IMPLEMENTATION

You will want to measure progress on implementing KAM and to identify hold-ups and bottlenecks. This can only be done if you start out with a clear timetable for implementation.

Let's suppose that you are right at the start of your KAM journey, a traditional sales force with traditional selling strategies and a business run in functional 'silos'. Your goal is to establish KAM as a cross-business process with the whole business focused on identifying and satisfying the needs of a carefully identified group of customers.

How long do you give yourself? Different industries can change at differing speeds, and some markets will have customers more ready for KAM than others, but all of that aside, we are almost certainly talking timetables of years, not months and quarters.

Such long-term timetables will be necessarily general and simplified, detailing a series of phases of implementation. Each phase will require its own more detailed timetable. Of course, when it comes to going into action, you will find that the phases are not purely consecutive; they will overlap, some will run concurrently for months, even years, and some that you thought you were past will need returning to.

This does not invalidate the original timetable. Any plan that attempts to predict the many twists and turns of fate and fortune will take so long in the making that you will have long missed the bus by the time it sees the light of any day.

The following *sample* implementation timetable may seem rather simplistic, but it is a start. If starting out with such a plan seems to you like trying to walk the Pennine Way with the aid of a motorway map of Great Britain then good – you will certainly do a better job for yourself:

- *Phase 1* – Determine your expectations from KAM.
- *Phase 2* – Identify the obstacles.
- *Phase 3* – Ensure top management support and cross-business alignment.
- *Phase 4* – Market Segmentation.
- *Phase 5* – Customer Classification.
- *Phase 6* – Identify the KA managers and potential teams.
- *Phase 7* – Customer Distinction strategies.
- *Phase 8* – Ensure the appropriate support systems are in place.
- *Phase 9* – Develop the relevant skills and capabilities for each KA team.
- *Phase 10* – Prepare Key Account plans.
- *Phase 11* – Continuous review and improvement.

Many businesses think that KAM is simply about getting the sales force to behave differently, a training course should do it.... I know, my own company gets asked to do this all too often, and our response is always the same – are you ready?

It can't be stressed enough how important it is to have the 'infrastructure' in place. Following the timetable suggested in this chapter will help ensure that you don't rush too quickly into building capabilities and expectations in the sales team that can only be frustrated as they hit a brick wall of obstacles. The result of this is much worse than a temporary setback – people revert to previous behaviours and attitudes that will be all the harder to change at your next attempt.

It had become clear to one of BP's business units that its growth targets were not being met, and nor would they be without a radical new approach to their sales effort. Account Management was seen as the vital change, a change that would allow them to seize on opportunities beyond their normal reach. With such a clear vision it would have been so easy to plunge straight into changing the behaviours of the sales team, but BP took this step by step.

In implementing KAM, patience really is a virtue

- A segmentation study that resulted in the selection of one vitally important segment that could support their growth ambitions. (Phase 4, and see chapter 20)
- The classification of customers in that segment, using current and potential profitability as the lead attractiveness factor, moderated by other less tangible factors such as the customer's own market position, or the opportunity to build the brand or the knowledge base. (Phase 5, and see chapter 21)
- The creation of four distinct service packages designed to achieve the right balance between resources deployed and rewards received. The distinctions between customer type are made through factors such as the use of direct sales, telesales, or distributors, the use of 'diamond teams' or solo 'bow-tie' sales efforts, the depth of contacts, the frequency of contacts, provision of services, charging for services, or not, etc. (Phase 7, and see chapter 22)
- The creation of a knowledge management support system for use by the account managers and their teams. (Phase 8, and see chapter 16 *'oiling the wheels of KAM'*)
- Then, and only then, training of the account managers in the new skills and techniques required. (Phase 9, and see chapter 15)

Training at this point stands a much better chance of working when the trainees know where they are pointed, what is expected of them, and that they have the systems in place to support them.

TRAINING DEVELOPMENT TRACKS

Phase 9 of this sample timetable is concerned with training, a vital ingredient of KAM implementation given the changes involved. Training must be planned, like any other activity, against identified needs and with clear performance outcomes. The first thing is to identify the skills and capabilities required for KAM (see Chapter 15). Once this is understood, you are ready to audit the current level of performance and competency. This will uncover what we might call the 'skills gap' and so point us in the direction of training required. This should be done for prospective key account managers *and* for prospective KA team members.

A useful tool to consider is the *training development track*, an idealized training programme specifically designed for the implementation of KAM. The track lists the full range of training available, though in practice it will rarely be necessary to take any one individual through the whole programme.

It provides a means of relating current skills and abilities against an ideal, back to the 'skills gap' noted above.

Table 30.1 is an example of a possible training development track for a key account manager at the very start of a KAM implementation programme. Spread over a period of 12 to 18 months, such a programme would allow the key account manager to apply the learning to their job as it develops.

Table 30.1 *Example training development track for a key account manager*

Main Track	Key Skills Track	Related Skills Track
KAM I Strategy & Planning ↓		
	Marketing Awareness ↓	Influencing Skills ↓
KAM II Team Dynamics ↓	Financial Understanding ↓	Face-to-Face Skills – Review ↓
KAM III Project Management	Business Management	Creative Thinking

A similar track should be developed for team members, taking particular note of the needs of those from non-commercial backgrounds or with little experience of face-to-face customer contact.

How will you know when you get there?

Most journeys have an end, but not this one. There is no ultimate point of arrival, no perfect state of KAM – the whole thing just keeps turning. Someone once asked me why sales people have annual conferences in a way that engineers or accountants, for instance, don't. After thinking a while, I realized that it was the annual aspect that is so particular. The annual conference might be the only time in a year that a salesperson gets to feel that things have come to a conclusion, something has been completed and everyone can now gear up for a new start. It is an artificial full stop placed in a sentence that otherwise would have little punctuation at all; managing customers just isn't like that.

So, if there is no end-point, the best that can be done is to note where you are headed, keep a log of the journey and hold frequent reviews to see if course changes are required. Every now and again the whole purpose of the journey may change and new destinations appear. One of the arts of KAM is the ability to keep up with such changes, not to regard them as failure of the original plan.

REGULAR HEALTH CHECKS

Start a 'well key account' clinic...

Recent years have seen a boom in 'well man', 'well woman' and 'well baby' clinics. Their main purpose is prevention rather than cure, based on regular check-ups. Perhaps you should start a 'well KA' clinic in your organization.

A simple health check along the lines of Table 30.2 and Table 30.3 might go some way to keeping you on track. Choose your own questions, but perhaps the following categories, or characteristics, are universal:

- Internal support and capability.
- KA team dynamics.
- Customer relationship.
- Key supplier status.
- Customer intimacy (identification of value chains).
- Project management.
- Account profitability.

Table 30.2 _KAM health check 1_

Characteristic	OK	Could Improve	None	Action Plan
Internal Support and Capability				
Do you have senior management support?				
Is your KA team empowered to act?				
Do functional 'barons' present obstacles?				
Is KAM a recognized cross-business process?				
Are the right organization and resources in place?				
Are the right systems in place?				
Do people have the right skills?				
KA Team Dynamics				
Do team members have clear GROWs?				
Is communication clear and constructive?				
Customer Relationship				
Do you understand their DMUs?				
Do you have broad access to the customer?				
Do you have integrated processes?				
Are you part of their communication network?				
Does the customer want you to succeed?				
Do you have shared goals, planning and info?				

Table 30.3 *KAM health check 2*

Characteristic	OK	Could Improve	None	Action Plan
Key Supplier Status				
Are you regarded as a key supplier?				
Is your status improving?				
Do you know how they 'position' you?				
Are you acting appropriately?				
Customer Intimacy				
Is your business customer focused?				
Do you share their values and culture?				
Do you understand their value chain?				
Do you have a positive impact analysis?				
Project Management				
Have projects been identified?				
Do they proceed to schedule?				
Have they been implemented?				
Account Profitability				
Can you measure account profitability?				
Is it improving?				
Do you share the value in the chain?				

Writing the key account plan

Written key account plans are few and far between. It is as if there is a fear of consigning to paper any forecasts, predictions or promises that may come back to haunt the key account manager, customers being what they are. Sales people used to living by their wits seem to find it difficult to adhere to this kind of formal planning. Or is it simply that they don't know how, or more likely, they see no purpose in it?

No plan – no key account

THE PLAN'S PURPOSE

How big should the ideal key account plan be, that is to say, how many pages long?

The answer must have something to do with the purpose of the plan, so let's consider some possible uses:

- A repository for all the data and information on the account.
- Getting your own thoughts together.
- A means of communicating the importance of this customer to the business as a whole.
- A means of communicating objectives and actions to key account team members.
- The best way of tracking progress against targets and so determining the success of your efforts.

The first possible use – the grand repository – is not the purpose of a key account plan. Such a database record is essential, but it should not be confused with a document that is focused on action.

The same applies to the second possible use, which involves getting your own thoughts together. This is a hugely valuable exercise, but the plan is the refined outcome of that process, not the history of your thoughts.

A good plan should achieve the third objective, but there will also be other means of raising your customer's profile. The plan will form part of a wider influencing strategy and should be written so that it supports rather than hinders that strategy, but this is still not the core purpose of a key account plan.

It is the fourth and fifth uses that we should focus on. These are communicating objectives and actions, and providing a way to track progress.

If this is the purpose, then the answer to the question 'how long?' must be 'as short as is possible'. Plans that run to dozens of pages and overflow with analysis and background data are not very helpful in this respect. Such plans are probably written to communicate the importance and expertise of the key account manager (not on our list of uses) and few readers are fooled. That is if they read it at all!

The ideal plan should be focused on objectives, and the actions required to achieve those objectives. If this can be condensed on to three or four pages then all the better, but there is an issue here because the plan is more than a list of sales objectives and more than volumes and revenues. The key account plan will necessarily deal with objectives for the relationship, objectives for the team, objectives for the business as a whole and this may run to a few more pages than the much requested one side of A4.

A KEY ACCOUNT TEMPLATE?

The CD ROM attached to this book contains a key account planning document. Is this a recommended template? In short, no. There is no blueprint for a key account plan, nor should there be. Blueprints and pro formas tend to result in box-ticking, rather than thinking. Moreover, they are unlikely to meet the requirements of your own unique situation. The planning document (and the rest of this chapter) is simply an attempt to provide a framework for your planning activity.

The task of designing your own format will in fact be a part of the thinking and planning process, determining what is important to you and what less so. There can be nothing worse than agonizing over a piece of analysis, perhaps even commissioning research, simply to fill in the spaces of an academic model that will never be used. And there will be nothing better than getting everyone in the account team to agree on the things that matter in your business, and what should be included in the plan. Writing the plan should be a team effort, and as such, a source of team cohesion.

SOME 'MUST HAVES'

So, no blueprint, but there are perhaps a few things that just *must* be in the plan:

- Goals and targets.
- People.
- Projects and activities.
- Resources, risks and contingencies.

Goals and targets

Without these, there is no direction, no hope of a common approach and no way of judging success. There should be targets for a number of things and not just the obvious ones of sales revenue and profit. Targets for how the relationship should progress, targets for communications, targets for progress on key projects and targets for customer satisfaction ratings to name but a few. Just because some of these may be hard to quantify, that does not make them unimportant.

People

People are what will make KAM work, so don't forget them in the plan. Perhaps the most important part of the plan will be the identification of who is in the customer's DMU, what makes them tick and who in the KA team will be responsible for them (the contact matrix – see Chapter 24).

People are at the heart of key account management and so must be at the heart of the plan

As well as having a customer-contact role, team members will have other roles and obligations. Identifying these clearly in a written plan – who is on your team and what goals, roles, obligations and work plans (GROWs) they have – will be of enormous help.

GROWs are important, particularly when a team sets out on unclear waters. They should be set for each individual.

GROWs will help a team do just that

Goals speak for themselves – what is to be achieved for the customer and the team?

Roles are important, particularly in a cross-functional KA team. Individuals will already have functional roles (the chemist, the market researcher, the production planner), but they will also need to take on team roles. What do they bring to the team? Why are they there? How will they do what they have to do? The roles might indicate two separate things: What functional activities will they carry out in the team? What *team* role will they perform?

Dr Meredith Belbin has done a lot of work on this second kind of role, how people behave as team members, and the value that different styles of behaviour can bring. A KA team could do worse than going through the Belbin team-analysis process as a means of discovering their own team make-up and using it to advantage (see Chapter 32).

Obligation is a word that might unnerve a few. This is a means of agreeing 'who owes what to whom'. For a KA team to succeed, people will have to perform tasks for each other, communicate with each other and receive instructions from each other. At an early stage, when responsibilities between KA team and individual function are far from clear, it will be important to start to identify just what these obligations are and what they will imply.

Work plans are the nitty-gritty of the tasks and projects that team members will be working on. They can come in many forms – project plans, critical path analyses and more – but one ingredient is vital to them all – timing. Work plans without time deadlines are work plans that don't get completed.

Projects and activities

What is going to be done by the team, with clear plans for each project. There are some vital ingredients here: objectives, who is responsible, timetable, milestones of progress – *critical path analysis* and a means to measure success.

Critical path analysis is simply the practice of laying out the timetables of activities and noting the interrelationships between them – some activities will depend on others having been completed. As a result of this analysis, you can prioritize what must be done first in order for others to follow and so on – the critical path.

Projects will result from value chain and positive impact analysis (Part VI). They will also include activities designed to create the right environment for KAM, overcoming the sort of obstacles identified in Chapter 14: modifying structures, developing new systems, adding skills and finding the right resources.

Resources, risks and contingencies

One of the most important reasons for writing a KA plan is to identify the resource required and put up a case for winning it. Resource needs may appear in many guises: new people, additional skills, more access to IT support, greater R&D involvement, expansion of production capacity, investment in new technology and so on. It is only when we know the resources required to achieve objectives set that we can make a full judgement as to the value and priority of a particular key account.

Putting the case is only the start. Of course, the aggregate resources required by *all* the key account plans must be assessed before projects and activities can commence. We must go back to Chapter 2 and remember the balance between objectives, opportunity and resource: the KA plan is an action plan and must be rooted in the reality of the finite.

Beyond that, resources may be allocated, but will they bring success? Will the new plant be able to produce to the quality required by the customer, and in time? Will the investment in e-commerce be enough to satisfy the customer's demands for transactional efficiency?

Every expansion of resource carries an attendant risk, a risk of failure, of higher expense or of any other kind of shortfall and the KA plan must assess that risk and propose an appropriate contingency in the event of any such shortfall.

A FEW TIPS

- Don't write *War and Peace,* and avoid anything looking like a telephone directory. Six pages is good, four would be better.
- Keep it updateable (that means short and preferably in a medium that makes revisions easy).
- You don't have to write it in one sitting – the best plans will form over time, perhaps a *long* time.
- Start off with some strong comments on direction, goals and targets (but note the final tip in this list). People reading this will want to know where you are headed.
- Stress the *actions* resulting from the plan and who is responsible for them.
- Prepare it as a team effort (committees should not write novels, but the KA plan is a practical tool, not a work of art).
- Make it available to the whole business. Remember whom you are writing this for – the people who have to put it into action. The written KA plan is a key ingredient in ensuring that KAM becomes a cross-business process.
- Include an 'executive summary' of the key points – direction, benefits, actions and requirements.
- Make background information on the account available, perhaps as an appendix to the plan, otherwise pages of data start to obscure the direction and the actions.

- Include your analysis. For instance, the customer's value chain and your positive impact analysis, again as an appendix.
- Avoid unsupported hype. A good plan will go a long way to winning senior management support for change, new resource, investment and so on, but only if it is balanced and objective.

A SAMPLE RUNNING ORDER

Having said there are no blueprints, regard the following with care. It is no more than the headings of a 'typical' key account plan. The exact order and weight given to one section against another will depend to a great extent on what level the relationship is currently working at. If you are at the pre KAM stage then the plan will lean heavily towards exploration and information required. If you are already at the partnership stage then the focus will be more on projects and activities.

The sample running order given below might suit a supplier just entering the partnership stage with their customer. Let's suppose they have a history of writing plans heavy on long and worthy analysis with little practical application, so the focus here is very much on action.

- The Key Account Team – *core and full.*
- Executive Summary.
- The Profit Plan – *current profitability and future target.*
- Opportunities and Objectives.
- The Contact Matrix and GROWs.
- The Value Proposition – *Positive Impact on their Total Business Experience.*
- Projects – *Project teams and Milestones.*
- Resources required – *Actions required by management to commit resources.*
- Implementation timetable.
- Appendices – Analysis & Information.

Appendices – Analysis

At the early stages with a key account it may be important to show a good deal of the analysis that has been done in the body of the plan itself – the actions part. As the relationship develops and matures so such analysis might 'withdraw' by stages to an appendix.

In other words, the length of time you have been managing the account will determine to a very great extent what is analysis, and what is action.

Some typical pieces of analysis might include any of the following:

1. Market segmentation.
2. The KAISM analysis. (see chapter 21)
3. Historical account profitability analysis – life time value analysis.
4. The Market Chain.
5. The Competitive Position – Porter's analysis – SWOT.
6. Our source of competitive advantage in the market chain.
7. Customer's purchasing strategy – Organization, supplier positioning.
8. Customer's decision making process – DMU analysis.
9. Value Chain Analysis.
10. Positive Impact Analysis and screening.
11. Proposal Analysis.
12. Belbin team roles.
13. KAM Health Check.

Appendices – Information

Keeping these kinds of things in an appendix prevents the plan from becoming a glorified telephone directory, or a historical record.

1. Address Book.
2. Customer's organization charts and contact profiles.
3. Customer's strategy and market activities.
4. Customer's performance – sales, growth, shares, profitability, financial status.
5. Our sales performance – history, current, forecast – share of business.
6. Vendor Ratings.
7. Competitor profiles.

Some tips on writing key account plans

1. Keep the plan focused on people and actions, not data and history.
2. Keep detailed information in appendices.
3. Use PowerPoint (or something similar).
   Using Word leads to paragraphs of unreadable waffle.
   Using Excel leads to a mass of numbers and budgets.
   Using PowerPoint keeps you short, to the point, and makes your plan easy to present to others – a vital component.
4. Have as few pages/slides as possible – and then edit further!
5. Don't write this alone – get the team to contribute (especially their GROWs).
6. Could you present it to the customer? With a few subtle edits, this should be an objective (at least in theory), and being able to answer yes is a test of a good plan.

Key Account Plans are for making things happen not for recording history, and certainly not for showing off that you have just read a KAM book and can list all the models!

So, you have a plan. Add to this a few bucket loads of energy, a great deal of resolve, not a little patience, and finally that old stalwart of all successful business activities – a little piece of luck. But don't wait for fate to intervene. Figure 31.1 shows why time spent in the early days on analysis and planning will pay off in the long run, preventing you from wallowing in a morass of argument and painful rethinking.

Just as importantly good planning will allow your team to recognize good fortune when it smiles on you, know it for what it is, and turn it to your best advantage. So I don't just wish you good luck on your KAM journey, I wish you the best luck you can make for yourself.

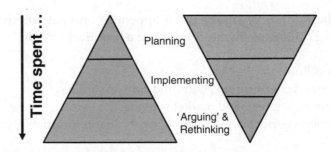

Figure 31.1   *Why time spent planning pays off in the long run*

32

Getting further help

Throughout this book, references have been made to seeking professional help and advice, from analysis of your business environment and customer attitudes to designing implementation programmes for KAM, including training.

The author of this book is a director of INSIGHT Marketing and People, an international training and consultancy firm that specializes in all aspects of KAM implementation and would be pleased to receive any enquiries for further help or advice on any of the issues raised.

Please contact:

INSIGHT Marketing and People Ltd
PO Box 997
Wexham Rd
Slough, UK
Tel: +44 (0)1753 877750
Fax: +44 (0)1753 877342
e-mail: Customer.Service@insight-MP.com
Web site: www.insight-MP.com

References and further reading

The following lists a short range of books that have been used as references in this work and will provide additional help and advice.

Cheverton, P (2000) *Key Marketing Skills*, Kogan Page, London

Cheverton, P (2001) *How Come You Can't Agree on Your Key Accounts? A ten step process to identification and selection*, Kogan Page, London

Cheverton, P and Smith, B (Forthcoming) *Key Account Management for Medical Markets*, Kogan Page, London

Cheverton, P, Stone, M, Hughes, T and Foss, B (Forthcoming) *Key Account Management for Financial Services*, Kogan Page, London

McDonald, M, Millman, T and Rogers, B (1996) *Key Account Management: Learning from supplier and customer perspectives*, Cranfield University School of Management

McDonald, M and Rogers, B (1998) *Key Account Management*, Butterworth Heinemann

Miller, R B, Heiman, S E and Teleja, T (1987) *Face to Face Selling*, Kogan Page, London

Miller, R B, Heiman, S E and Teleja, T (1988) *Strategic Selling*, Kogan Page, London

Millman, A F and Wilson, K J (1994) 'From key account selling to key account management', paper presented to the 10th annual conference of industrial marketing and purchasing (September), University of Groningen, Netherlands

Payne, A, Christopher, M, Clark, M and Peck, H (1995) _Relationship Marketing For Competitive Advantage_, Butterworth Heinemann

Porter, M (1980) _Competitive Strategy_, New York Free Press

Rogers, E (1962) _Diffusion of Innovations_, New York Free Press

Treacy, M and Weirsema, F (1995) _The Discipline of Market Leaders_, Harper Collins

Index